UN
LADY
LIKE

A HISTORY OF
LADIES
GAELIC
FOOTBALL

UN LADY LIKE

A HISTORY OF LADIES GAELIC FOOTBALL

HAYLEY KILGALLON

NEW ISLAND

UNLADYLIKE
First published in 2024 by
New Island Books
Glenshesk House
10 Richview Office Park
Clonskeagh
Dublin D14 V8C4
Republic of Ireland

www.newisland.ie

Print ISBN: 978-1-83594-003-7
eBook ISBN: 978-1-83594-004-4

At the time of print, all 2024 competitions had yet to conclude.

Cover images: front Dublin City Archives and the *Irish Press* Archive © University College Cork; back (clockwise from top left): Mary Power O'Shea; with thanks to Irish Newspaper Archive and the *Sunday Independent*; Sportsfile.

Book and cover design by Niall McCormack
Edited by Noel O'Regan
Indexed by Jane Rogers
Printed by L&C Printing Group, Poland, lcprinting.eu

The paper used in this book comes from the wood pulp of sustainably managed forests.

LGFA
PEIL na mBAN

Gratefully supported by the Ladies Gaelic Football Association

New Island Books is a member of Publishing Ireland.

10 9 8 7 6 5 4 3 2 1

	TIMELINE	vi
	INTRODUCTION	viii
CHAPTER 1	ON THE SIDELINES	xii
CHAPTER 2	NOVELTY ACT, 1960–1973	14
CHAPTER 3	NATIONAL ASSOCIATION, 1974	30
CHAPTER 4	THE EARLY YEARS, 1975–1980	46
CHAPTER 5	SEEKING RECOGNITION, 1974–1982	74
CHAPTER 6	MAKING STRIDES, 1980–1989	92
CHAPTER 7	GOING FOR GOALS, 1990–1999	116
CHAPTER 8	NEW MILLENNIUM, NEW GROUND, 2000–2009	136
CHAPTER 9	A MILESTONE DECADE, 2010–2019	164
CHAPTER 10	AN ERA FOR ALL, 2020–2024	182
CHAPTER 11	THE BEST IS YET TO COME	202
	ROLLS OF HONOUR	206
	SOURCES	228
	NOTES	234
	ACKNOWLEDGEMENTS	248
	INDEX	252

TIMELINE

1920   First recorded game of ladies Gaelic football takes place in St James's Park, Dublin

1960s   Ladies' football becomes a popular feature at local carnivals

1971   First inter-county ladies Gaelic football match takes place between Waterford and Tipperary

1973   Offaly play Kerry in July. In the absence of a national organising body, this match is dubbed the first ladies Gaelic football All-Ireland final

1974   Foundation of the LGFA

1976   Introduction of the Under–16 All-Ireland Championship and the Interprovincial Competition

1977   Introduction of the All-Ireland Club Championship

1979   Inaugural LGFA National League

1980   First All-Star Awards

Introduction of an Under–18 All-Ireland Championship

1982   The GAA officially recognises the LGFA

Kerry win the first of their nine All-Ireland titles in a row

1985   Inaugural Junior All-Ireland Championship

Inaugural Senior PPSA Competition

7-a-side All-Ireland Competition introduced

1986   The LGFA All-Ireland finals held in Croke Park for the first time

1987   First HEC O'Connor Cup Competition

1990   Introduction of an Under–14 All-Ireland Championship

1994   Inaugural Junior PPS A Competition

1997   Helen O'Rourke becomes the first CEO of the LGFA

1998   LGFA All-Ireland final televised live for the first time

Countdown clock introduced

2001   Partnership with TG4 begins

2004   First LGFA All-Star tour

2005   Cork win the first of their eleven All-Ireland titles

2006   Inaugural women's International Rules series between Ireland and Australia

2010   One Club Model introduced

2016   Partnership with Lidl begins

2017   First LGFA league game played in Croke Park

2019   Record-breaking attendance of 56,114 at the LGFA All-Ireland finals in Croke Park

2021   First LGFA league finals held in Croke Park

2022   Integration Steering Committee established

2024   50th anniversary of the founding of the LGFA

INTRODUCTION

Ladies Gaelic football matches (and they were advertised as ladies' matches rather than women's matches) first began to appear as early as the 1920s. However, the game lacked support, both socially and organisationally, and it was not until the 1960s that ladies Gaelic football began to take off. As shocking as it may seem to contemporary readers, it was at local carnivals that ladies Gaelic football burst onto the scene. Alongside the likes of tug-o-war competitions, children's races and fancy-dress parades, it was considered a novelty event.

A few years later, the Ladies Gaelic Football Association (LGFA) was founded in Hayes Hotel in Thurles, Co. Tipperary in 1974. The setting up of the LGFA, also known as Cumann Peil Gael na mBan, was significant as it meant that, for the first time ever, an association would actively manage and promote the playing of Gaelic football for women in Ireland.

The location of the inaugural meeting was significant, too – it was the same place the Gaelic Athletic Association (GAA) had met for the first time, ninety years earlier, in November 1884. The intention of the GAA when it was established had been the 'preservation and cultivation of national pastimes … for Irish*men* of all creeds and classes.'[1] It was hugely successful in doing this, turning Gaelic football and hurling into some of the most popular sports in Ireland by the early twentieth century.

However, at the founding meeting of the GAA there had been no discussion about facilitating Gaelic games for women. Perhaps this is not surprising, considering that the social norms of the time laid down that sport, generally speaking, was for men only. Women were assumed to have a naturally weaker disposition, which made them unsuitable for strenuous activities; furthermore, the idea of breathless women chasing after a football was deemed quite 'unladylike'. As a result, the traditional roles that women went on to assume within the GAA were those of kit-washer, sandwich-maker or supporter. These were important roles, of course, ones that meaningfully contributed to the running of the GAA. But it did also highlight how limited women's roles were within the association.

The idea of breathless women chasing after a football was deemed quite 'unladylike'.

Some people of the time likely argued that women already had enough of a Gaelic sporting outlet with camogie, a version of hurling adapted for females that was reported to have first been played in 1898 in Navan at an event commemorating the 1798 Rebellion. The setting up of the Camogie Association in 1904 certainly did fill a small gap in the sporting market for women who wanted to take part in Gaelic games.[2] Still, for a long time, the prospect of women playing Gaelic football was not entertained by the GAA, nor the Camogie Association. Despite this, they eventually managed to push ahead.

The emergence of women's Gaelic football as a competitive sport was part of the wider ascent of women's sports worldwide that began in the latter half of the twentieth century and coincided with the Second-Wave Feminist Movement (which began in the early 1960s and ran until the early 1980s). The movement's drive to attain equality between the genders highlighted the discrimination, disadvantage and under-representation that women experienced in Ireland under the law and in politics, in private and public life, and in society and culture. This led to a re-evaluation of the position of women in Irish society in general, with sport being one of the spheres seeing change.

It was not just in Gaelic football that Irish women broke new ground during and following this period, but also in soccer, rugby, athletics, swimming and boxing. Neither was it just on the field of play that women were afforded new opportunities, but also in sports administration and coaching. These efforts and achievements signalled that women were more than capable of practising sports and excelling at them. All of which reminds us that while the history of women's Gaelic football is a story about sporting achievement, it is also a story about challenging the status quo.

Perhaps the status quo in Irish sports writing needs to be challenged too. Until now, after all, no history had been written on women's Gaelic football and the LGFA. In fact, the historical position of women's sport has largely been ignored by Irish historiography. So, this book aims to record the history of women's Gaelic football and the LGFA over the last fifty years, documenting the key moments, developments, teams and figures that have contributed to the growth of women's Gaelic football and, in doing so, have helped change the position of women's sport, and women in society, in Ireland.

CHAPTER 1

ON THE SIDELINES

In August 1967, a farmer in Co. Cork wrote to the *Sunday Independent* to express his hope that the GAA would ban women from attending the upcoming All-Ireland finals taking place in Croke Park.[1] The GAA was a male-only organisation, he argued, and the presence of women in Croke Park would take up 'valuable space'. He went further, stating that 'the sight of a pleasure-bent woman up in the city for fun and enjoyment, instead of being satisfied with her lot at home' was, to him, both 'revolting' and 'unnatural'.[2]

The farmer was technically correct in saying that the GAA was a male-only organisation, as women could not become official members of the GAA. But while there was no official role for women, we know that women had a spirited interest in Gaelic games and were vital to the functioning of the GAA at a social level. Without the support women have given to the male members of their families – from cheering them on from the terraces, to preparing meals, washing jerseys, and encouraging their own children to get involved in Gaelic games – it is difficult to imagine that the wider day-to-day operation of the GAA would have been maintained, then or now.

It is likely, too, that the Cork farmer was not alone in his view that women had no place at a sporting event. After all, it was the prevailing mood of the time, exemplified by the 1937 Constitution of the Republic of Ireland, Bunreacht na hÉireann, which stipulated in Article 41.2 that a woman's place was in the home and without her presence there 'the common good cannot be achieved'.[3]

At the time the Cork farmer wrote his letter, the opportunities available to women inside the boundary of play on a Gaelic field were limited to camogie, a game that was weak in most parts of the island. However, it was not a lack of interest in sport that limited women's opportunities on the field of play but rather a complex web of social constructs.

Social attitudes have been a long-standing barrier to women's participation in sport. The sporting world and its structures that we know today took root in the mid- to late nineteenth century, when society, triggered by the Industrial Revolution, underwent a process of modernisation. As a result, sporting practices were transformed. Sport associations were established to codify games and organise national and international competitions; the general public (with more leisure time on their hands) began to flock to sporting events; the media began to cover more and more events with interest, and the process of tracking records began. However, there was a distinctive feature to these emerging developments – they were predominantly created for and controlled by white, upper- and middle-class men. Sport was seen to be a natural pastime for men, with the values and ideals underpinning it – strength, stamina, leadership, competitiveness – seen to epitomise and assert masculinity.[4]

Most sporting associations founded in Ireland in this period, such as the Irish Rugby Football Union (IRFU) (1879) and the GAA (1884), only served male playing interests. Women could not become participants in these associations and it is quite likely that the idea of women wanting to become members of these sporting codes would have been considered ridiculous at the time. After all, the acceptable qualities associated with being a woman included gentleness, modesty and passivity. These characteristics were reflected in the gender roles and stereotypes of the era and influenced social attitudes, medical beliefs and religious teaching, creating barriers to female participation in the 'physical' and 'masculine' world of sport.

The idea of a ladies Gaelic football match was therefore unacceptable. As was seen in the following incident. On 17 September 1920, a note from the Senior County Board of Dublin GAA appeared in the *Evening Herald*:

> The hon. sec. of the Dublin Senior Co. Board writes that the ladies' Gaelic football match announced to be played at St. James's Park on Sunday next has not been sanctioned – nor would it be sanctioned under any circumstances by the Senior County Board and he further states that any member of the GAA officiating or assisting will be suspended.[5]

As it reports, a ladies Gaelic football match was due to take place two days later, on 19 September, at St James's Park. The county board were anxious to state that this game was not being organised under the auspices of the GAA in Dublin and, more importantly, their view was that it was inconceivable that ladies Gaelic football would ever be authorised by Dublin GAA.

Despite making their disapproval clear and threatening their members with suspension if found to be involved in organising the fixture, the first women's Gaelic football match known to be played went ahead.

A photo printed in the *Freeman's Journal* captured some of the action: women representing Inchicore and Templeogue wore long skirts and chased after the ball while a sizeable crowd watched on.[6] Apart from the notice in the *Evening Herald* and the picture in the *Freeman's Journal*, little is known about the game. It is unclear who organised it or why. It is not known who the women participating

LADIES' FOOTBALL MATCH IN DUBLIN

The above is a snapshot taken at the ladies' football match which was played on Sunday at St. James's Park, Dolphin's Barn, between teams representing Templeogue and Inchicore. (Photo. Cashman, Dublin).

In September 1920 a ladies Gaelic football match took place between teams representing Templeogue and Inchicore in what is believed to be the first ladies Gaelic football game on record. With thanks to Irish Newspaper Archive and the *Freeman's Journal*.

in the match were and why they were motivated to play the match in opposition to the social beliefs of the time. No further mention of ladies Gaelic football appeared in the notes of the Dublin Senior County Board that year, which suggests that no member of Dublin GAA was suspended for assisting with the playing of the fixture.

A carnival was held at the same venue four years later where, once again, a ladies' football match was on the billing.[7] There is also evidence that a ladies Gaelic football league was run in a parish in Clare in 1926. The fact that these matches went ahead at all is interesting and suggests that there was interest in some quarters in women playing Gaelic football.

———————

While women had an active interest in sport, social beliefs restricted their participation in various activities throughout the early to mid-twentieth century.

Members of the ladies Gaelic football team from Cooraclare, Co. Clare who played Leitrim, a local townland, in a match in 1926. The match was organised by Tom Garry and refereed by his son, Fr Michael Garry (Joe Garry).

Many reasons were provided. It was argued that exercise would be too taxing for the female body and would take much-needed energy away from other activities. Young women were taught that playing strenuous sports could damage their reproductive system, make their bodies more masculine-looking, cause injuries and lead to exhaustion. For example, there was one persistent theory that if a woman was hit in the chest by a ball, causing bruising, it could lead to cancer.[8] At one time, cycling was also thought to be unsafe for women during this period due to the belief that sitting on a saddle for long periods could cause infertility.[9]

These medical myths prevailed for much of the twentieth century. An editorial in *The Irish Times* in 1928 criticised female participation in sport in Europe and stressed the supposed health risks, stating that women in France, Germany, Italy and 'even in England' were practising 'violent exercises' that required 'extreme exertion' in the form of running and rowing. They claimed that even for the 'most robust women; already, no doubt it had shortened many lives.'[10]

While women had an active interest in sport, social beliefs restricted their participation in various activities throughout the early to mid-twentieth century.

Then there was the so-called concern that sport would not protect a woman's modesty and would create an unwomanly body image. Dress was one way to 'protect' women's modesty, meaning long skirts were the norm in camogie, golf, hockey and tennis. Camogie skirts, though later shortened, at the time could not be more than eight inches off the ground.[11]

Much of this conservative thinking came from the fact that the newly independent Ireland was heavily influenced by the Roman Catholic Church. Politicians and the public looked to the Church for guidance on moral and social issues. In 1929, a Papal Encyclical by Pope Pius XI claimed that the 'physical and spiritual' differences between men and women 'complement each other in the family and in society and thus fit together into one whole'. The pope called for these differences to be respected in all aspects of society. Directly referring to women and exercise, he stated:

> [the rules of Christian prudence] must be observed also in physical training and gymnastic exercises, which special regard must be paid to Christian modesty in the case of girls, for whom it is most unsuitable to display themselves before the public gaze...[12]

This instruction would underpin an athletics controversy in 1934 that highlighted the influence of the Catholic Church, as well as how uncomfortable many sporting bodies in Ireland felt about women participating publicly in rigorous sports.

At the annual congress of the National Athletics and Cycling Association of Ireland (NACAI), a proposal was put forward by S. C. Bonner of Dublin that a women's championship be held in conjunction with the National Track and Field Championship, which, at that point, only featured events for men.

The idea was met with disapproval and caution by the likes of Dr Magnier of Cork, who labelled the suggestion 'immoral'. The GAA's General Secretary, Padraig O'Keefe, also advised that it was a sensitive issue. However, President of the NACAI, P. C. Moore, later berated the congress, saying they were the most backward association internationally with regards to women's athletics.[13] Moore was not wrong. To put it in context, women's athletics (five events) had been added to the Olympic programme in 1928, but no Irish woman competed in athletics events at that games or the games in 1932 – in fact, it would be 1956 before an Irish woman competed on the track at an Olympic Games.[14]

Following the congress, it was reported that the NACAI would hold a women's championship, though it was later disputed by Moore that such a decision had been made.[15] Nevertheless, two days later, letters by John Charles McQuaid, then President of Blackrock College and later Archbishop of Dublin, appeared in both *The Irish Times* and the *Irish Press*. He condemned the NACAI's supposed decision and threatened that Blackrock College would boycott any mixed athletics meet held by the NACAI 'no matter what attire they [women] may adopt.'[16] Mixed athletics, he argued, was a moral and social abuse, and he described the decision as 'un-Irish' and 'un-Catholic.'[17]

The issue forced the NACAI to hold a General Council meeting on 10 March, at which it was formally decided to suspend the decision of the congress on the issue for a period of one year.[18] In fact, it would be 1965 before the NACAI revisited the issue and adopted a motion to 'actively encourage ladies' athletics in Ireland.'[19]

In the meantime, the Catholic Church continued to discourage women from participating in popular sporting pastimes. A 1950 Pastoral Letter to the Diocese of Dublin noted the Church's 'grave disapproval' of the increase in the number of women participating in 'mixed public sports'.[20]

The only acceptable option for women in Ireland looking to practise a Gaelic sport during this period was, as previously noted, through the Camogie Association. Established in 1904, camogie was positioned as a feminised version of hurling – the hurl and sliotar were made lighter, the length of the pitch was shortened, teams were reduced to twelve a side, and the uniform was modest and ladylike with its white blouse, black stockings and gym frock that extended

below the knee.[21] As such, camogie was seen as an appropriate sport for women and a suitable alternative for Irish women to other games such as hockey.

The Camogie Association struggled in its early years to build strong foundations for both the game and the association. It even ceased operating in 1907 but was re-started in 1911 and re-organised again in the 1930s.[22] By 1935, there were 10,000 women playing camogie in twenty-eight counties.[23] Those running the Camogie Association were inexperienced and faced issues in getting access to pitches and raising funds to run the organisation. As well as that, 'lack of leisure time' was cited as an issue for players who had been forced to move on from the game when they married or became mothers or had other responsibilities at home.[24]

Still, the reason the Camogie Association struggled, and why women did not play Gaelic football, was without question ultimately linked to the aforementioned social beliefs.

However, in the 1960s and 1970s, Irish society began to challenge the traditional social beliefs that had restricted women's participation in sport and other areas of society. The Commission on the Status of Women was established by the Government of Ireland in 1970 and its report, presented to the government in 1972, laid bare the legal, social and cultural structures and beliefs that created inequalities for women. In relation to sport, the report noted that many sports clubs discriminated against women 'by not allowing them to become members or by refusing to participate fully in the club facilities'.[25] The commission made forty-nine recommendations on issues such as equal pay, sex discrimination, social welfare, education and family planning. Half of these recommendations were implemented by 1974.[26]

The responses received by the *Sunday Independent* following the publication of that Cork farmer's letter in 1967 about banning women from attending All-Ireland finals highlight the change in opinion that was occurring in Irish society. All the respondents disagreed wholeheartedly with the farmer's view.

Keep women out of Croke Park!

SIR—Now that the All-Ireland finals are at hand again, let's hope the G.A.A. will bar women from attending these games, taking up valuable space.

To me, there is nothing more revolting or unnatural than to see a pleasure-bent woman up in the city for fun and enjoyment, instead of being satisfied with her lot at home.

The G.A.A. is a man's organisation—for men only!
—CO. CORK FARMER.

A farmer from Co. Cork writes to the Sunday Independent *calling on the GAA to ban women from attending the upcoming All-Ireland finals in Croke Park as they will take up 'valuable space'. If the farmer was incredulous at the thought of women standing in the terraces of Croke Park, one wonders how he would have felt about women playing in the ground! With thanks to Irish Newspaper Archive and the* Sunday Independent.

The responses received by the Sunday Independent *after printing the farmer's letter. The letter elicited a strong response from readers and all the responses printed by the paper argued against the farmer's 'outdated' view. With thanks to Irish Newspaper Archive and the* Sunday Independent.

Should G.A.A. bar women?

★ Last Sunday's letter from a Cork farmer advocating that the G.A.A. should debar women from Croke Park has sparked off angry reaction from women readers. Here are some of their views:

Sir — The Cork farmer must not be a member of N.F.A. If he was he would be thankful to the ladies of Ireland, who helped in no small way to release his fellow farmers from jail.

What does he think they should do, stay at home and be satisfied with their lot? Come on. Meath ladies, and show the Cork farmer what you think is your lot on Sunday, Sept. 24.—CROSSAKIEL READER.

* * *

Sir — I was shocked to read the letter from the "Co. Cork Farmer". He should be shot. Women have just as much right to enter Croke Park as men.

The farmer stated that a woman should be satisfied with her lot at home. Does he think a woman needs no pleasure or enjoyment — that she should stay at home all the time, working and slaving for her husband, who is out enjoying himself every Sunday.

My advice to every woman in Ireland is to be first into Croke Park on the day of a big game — and enjoy themselves — CARLOW G.A.A. FAN.

Sir—So the G.A.A. is a man's organisation? Where does "Co. Cork Farmer" leave camogie?

Many G.A.A. wives spend all year at home while their husbands are out at local games, board meetings, etc., often sitting alone until perhaps 2 a.m. All-Ireland day is all the compensation they receive for a year of lonely nights and muddy togs to wash.

Believe me, after nearly 20 years of organising my life to suit the G.A.A., I know what I'm talking about. Good luck to those women who enjoy a match and can get a "Final" ticket. Myself — I'm just not interested any more — G.A.A. "WIDOW", Lurgan.

* * *

Sir — So we still have them with us — the mothers who rear selfish sons, in the belief that they are demigods because they happen to be born male. "Farmer From Cork" seems to be a specimen of the latter, reared by the former.

I don't recollect any Commandment that says Sunday is a day of rest for men only.

I have no interest myself in games, but more power to any woman who has. It is interesting to note that the farmer did not sign his name. I wonder what is he afraid of. A lynching party of outraged female neighbours?—M. BEAN UI STAFFORD, Ascal Mhuire Br. Ard, Gaillimh.

* * *

Sir — In reply to Co. Cork Farmer, I am horrified, as a visitor to your lovely country, to find this out-dated idea. No woman wants to be tied body and soul to a house. To get out and about broadens one's outlook and makes one a more contented and better companion at home. If the men can be pleasure-bent, why not the women — they work just as hard. Don't be so selfish! What about a little Christian charity. — PATRICIA COX, Park Hill Road, Wallington, Surrey.

* * *

Sir — The cheek of that farmer to suggest keeping women out of Croke Park. He must be either a jilted bachelor or a man with no respect for his wife — if he has one. Any decent man would be proud to bring his wife to a final at Croke Park after her year of toil, keeping house for him and rearing a family.

When a man finishes his day's work he can go to the local and chat with his friends. He should remember that women are human beings, not mechanical instruments; they need enjoyment and are keen followers of games. It is well we have not many men like him.

Could he tell us how long has the G.A.A. been for men only. If that were so, the crowds and gate receipts at Croke Park would be very small indeed.—ARDENT G.A.A. FOLLOWER, Co. Cork.

* * *

Sir — If Cork Farmer is married, God help his missus. Does he ever let her watch games on TV?

Roll on Sept. 24 when Cork play Meath in the final. I will be there, and thousands of other wives and hassles, to cheer on the Royal County. We in Meath turn out our players spick and span; we cheer them on, we organise functions for the clubs friends and we are entitled to go to Croke Park.

It takes more than Bingo to satisfy the Meath ladies. I know some of them capable of refereeing, don't mind going to see a match. Good luck, "Cork Farmer" and take the Cork ladies up to see the final. They will be dead long enough — MEATH ABU, Beauparc.

* * *

Sir — I am in Croke Park every Sunday with my husband who would not go without me. You women of Cork get out of your kitchen and get to Croke Park. Let this Cork "Yahoo" see it is 1967, not 1900. — (Mrs) MAURA CULLEN, 35 Thomas Street, Dublin 8.

* * *

Sir — Who does "Co. Cork Farmer" think he is? Why should women be kept from G.A.A. games? I think he should stay at home when his own county are not playing and leave plenty of accommodation for native Tipperary women like myself in the Hogan stand to see John Doyle collect his ninth All Ireland medal, which seemingly a Cork man is not capable of obtaining. — ANNE MORRISSEY, Barrowstown, Newbridge, Co. Kildare.

* * *

Sir — In this day and age when men are striving to obtain equal rights for women, it came as a shock when I read "keep women out of Croke Park" last Sunday. "Co. Cork Farmer" would wish all the women to be at home, but surely they are entitled to an odd day out, to the sport they hear so much about.—THOMAS P. McDERMOTTROE, 14 Thames Street, Belfast 12.

* * *

Sir — How dare "Co. Cork Farmer" say that he hopes women will be barred from attending G.A.A. games! His statement made my blood boil. We women pay just as much as men do to watch a game. Why prevent us?

To my mind this "Co. Cork Farmer" is a narrow-minded bachelor who doesn't like women for some reason or another — CATHERINE O'KEEFFE, Dublin.

* * *

Sir—Co. Cork Farmer, I am sure, is an old bachelor, jilted by some lucky girl. He is selfish and self-centred. Thank God, his equals are few.—UP TIPP, Co. Tipperary.

* * *

Sir—It is obvious from the letter written by "Co. Cork Farmer" that he is a misogynist. I was disgusted by his idiotic, selfish and narrow-minded attitude towards women.

Women are not second class citizens and have the authority to go to Croke Park at any time, at any all-Ireland, to have a pleasant and enjoyable time.—BROADMINDED, Cork.

* * *

Sir—I wish to express my horror at the Cork farmers' strange and selfish mentality.

Let the women be selfish just for a while and see how nicely our men will accept their lot at home.—KILKENNY CAT.

Two main arguments were put forward across the responses. First, the idea that a woman should be content 'with her lot at home' was disputed. Women are 'human beings, not mechanical instruments' who do not want to be 'tied body and soul to a house', it was noted.[27] The second point raised by multiple respondents was that women had every right to attend Gaelic games in Croke Park due to their involvement in the GAA. One woman argued that the GAA was a central part of the community and family life, and All-Ireland final day, she said, was the 'only compensation they [women/wives] receive for a year of lonely nights and muddy togs to wash'. After nearly twenty years of organising her life around the GAA, this 'GAA widow', as she called herself, wrote that she had lost interest but supported any women who wanted to attend the games. Another person highlighted how women had long been 'keen followers' with a genuine interest in the games. Another pointed out that if the GAA was for men only then match attendances and gate receipts would be smaller. References were also made to the push for equal rights to illustrate to the farmer that times were changing and his view was outdated.

While the farmer's views cannot be considered to be isolated ones, the responses to his letter demonstrate that women had long been involved in the GAA and that sport was becoming another area of society in which women's place was been reconsidered. It is no coincidence that, as the position of women in society began to change in the 1960s and 1970s, women's sport also began to prosper.

However, it should also be noted that, as Jennifer Hargreaves has stated, the growth of female sports in the twentieth century 'only became possible because they occurred in separate spheres from men. By being insular, sportswomen did not constitute a challenge in their relationship to men.'[28]

This was certainly the case for ladies Gaelic football. By creating their own space – wherever that space happened to be, even in carnivals – women were able to create opportunities for themselves to get involved in sport.

CHAPTER 2
NOVELTY ACT, 1960–1973

Ladies Gaelic football needed a space to grow – and it found it at carnivals and festivals across the island of Ireland in the 1960s. A key feature of the social scene in Ireland at the time, carnivals and festivals often functioned as fundraising events for local causes. Speaking to the GAA Oral History project in 2012, Marie McAleer, a founding member of the LGFA, recalled how women's Gaelic football was organised as a 'side event' at carnivals and that 'it was always a bit of fun' taking part.[1] However, newspaper archives reveal that these carnival games were not just a fundraising stunt or light entertainment; rather, they could be meaningful, competitive – and popular – matches that gave women an outlet to play Gaelic football.

Furthermore, newspaper archives revealed that festival matches had been organised as early as the 1940s. For example, in October 1945, the Lucan Pipe Band organised a GAA tournament and announced that a women's football match between Clondalkin and Leixlip would take place before a men's Gaelic football match featuring Saggart and Donaghmore.[2] In August 1949, *The Nationalist* newspaper in Tipperary advertised that a women's football match would be one of the attractions at the Kilsheelan Super Fete in aid of Power Charity Home and Kilsheelan Sportsfield Fund.[3] It is unclear from the notice alone what code of football the women would have played, but the paper reveals that 'there was very keen interest [...] in the novel Ladies' Football match which ended in a draw', 2–5 to 1–8.[4] A notice in the *Nationalist and Leinster Times* from June 1945 advertised an upcoming carnival in Athy, in which a women's football match would feature alongside other attractions such as a pram race, a children's fancy dress parade and golf putting.[5]

Once again, it is not clear what code of football the women played at the Athy festival, and this lack of clarity resurfaces in other newspaper notices, such as one that appeared in *The Nationalist* in June 1947, which only informed readers that the ladies' football match occurring at a carnival in aid of Cloneen National School would be seven-a-side.[6]

From the late 1950s into the 1960s, it appears that ladies Gaelic football was becoming a popular attraction at carnivals in Cork. Notices in the *Southern Star*, *The Cork Examiner* and *Evening Echo* map the spread of the game through the county at events in Ringaskiddy, Crosshaven, Carrigaline, and later in Fermoy, Bandon, Douglas, Roscarbery and Ballyvourney. At the same time, Gaelic football matches for women were being organised in other counties, such as Louth, Meath, Tipperary, Fermanagh and Offaly.

The popularity of the game was evidently increasing, and this was leading some to wonder – likely for the first time – whether things could be taken further. Reporting on a women's Gaelic football tournament being held in Offaly in September 1967, the *Offaly Independent* concluded that 'this tournament is no carnival catch penny [...] and if the idea catches on it may open up a whole new vista for the future.'[7] Four teams took part in this competition, organised by the Arden Pitch and Putt Club, and it was won by Tullamore Camogie Club, their 'positioning and combination' leading them to be 'deserving winners' over the other competitors: Sacred Heart School, Vocational School and Arden Pitch and Putt.[8]

The 'new venture' was labelled a successful 'experiment' and, ultimately, the success of this competition meant that the idea did catch on locally. Another women's Gaelic football competition was held in late 1967, this time expanding to eight teams.[9] The newly organised league featured seven teams from Offaly (Kinitty, Arden Pitch and Putt, Hairdressers, Cloonagh, Mountbolus, Marian Hostel and Vocational School), as well as Lorrha from Co. Tipperary.[10] The final was held in January 1968 and was described by the *Leinster Express* as 'a fitting climax to a highly successful league campaign for two evenly matched sides [serving] up splendid fare', with the Marian Hostel emerging victorious over Lorrha on a score-line of 2–3 to 1–2.[11]

Building on the success of the league, another seven-a-side competition was organised in the spring/summer of 1968 with ten teams from four counties (Offaly, Westmeath, Tipperary and Meath) slated to participate.[12] The final of the 'Midlands County League', the *Leinster Express* stated, was to be 'the feature event of the closing stages of the Carnival' taking place on Whit Monday.[13]

In Waterford, a tournament involving twenty teams was organised in the summer of 1970. Ahead of the final of the competition, the *Irish Press* noted that the tournament was played with ten players on each team and players were allowed to pick the ball up directly off the ground and throw it, but were not allowed to shoulder charge.[14] The paper also commented that many of the players togging out for the final were married and the captains of the two sides facing off for the championship were sisters.

Both single and married women played Gaelic football at the time, though it seemed that, for some reason, being a married woman was of added interest. Like when a note on the newly formed ladies' football team in the Pike-Killrossanty area in 1967 also commented on the relationship status of some of the players, stating (maybe with a tone of surprise) that some of woman 'are of the veteran married status'.[15]

Whether married or single, what is clear is that during this period teams and tournaments grew out of workplaces, existing sports clubs and organisations such as the Irish Countrywomen's Association (ICA) and Macra na Feirme. In Tipperary in 1969, a ladies' football competition was held that included teams from the local county council, Clonmel post office, and Showering's, a local cider manufacturer.[16] The inclusion of schools like the Vocational School in Offaly also points to a wide age profile of female Gaelic football players.

While the carnival games were generally organised as a fun activity, the recurrence and regularity with which games were organised suggested that women took Gaelic football seriously and were committed to playing games. Perhaps they were encouraged by local people involved in organising the games and tournaments. The desire to support a local fundraising initiative or community event may also have encouraged young girls and women to get involved. Still, it was clear that participation levels were rising.

These carnival games and festival tournaments were undoubtedly central to the progression of women's Gaelic football from a novelty act to a serious sport.

It is clear, too, that camogie players were drawn to Gaelic football. However, the Camogie Association appear to have been somewhat concerned, or to have even disapproved of, the growing popularity of ladies Gaelic football. It was noted by the *Southern Star* that members of the Coiste Camogie Vigilance Committee attended the football match between Clonakilty and Bandon that was organised as part of the West Cork Festival in July 1965.[17] Though the newspaper did not elaborate on the reasons for the Coiste Camogie Vigilance Committee's presence at the game, the *Southern Star* did remark that the game 'provided plenty of excitement' for the large crowd that gathered for it.[18] This suggests that there was considerable interest in women's Gaelic football in West Cork and it can perhaps be deduced that the Camogie Association – locally, at least – were concerned about the rising following of Gaelic football among women.

From the 1960s onwards ladies Gaelic football began to become a popular feature at local carnivals. Here, Ballycumber, Co. Offaly line out for a team photo ahead of a match against Clara in 1969 (Phyllis Price née Hackett).

This apparent concern was to be found elsewhere in the country. For example, in February 1967 in Co. Mayo, it was reported by the *Connaught Telegraph* that the Mayo Camogie County Board were unhappy with a Carmel Murray from Castlebar who had written to the Mayo Football County Board to propose that a women's Gaelic football team be set up in the county: 'they intend to inform her that her place is on a camogie team', the *Connaught Telegraph* revealed.[19] Murray's letter had also been reported on in both the *Mayo News*, which noted that it had been read to a 'surprised meeting', and the *Western People*, which called it an 'unusual request'.[20]

While the Mayo Football County Board's surprised reaction to Murray's letter highlights the still-novel nature of women playing Gaelic football in that era, the response of the Mayo Camogie County Board points to a growing uneasiness with women's Gaelic football. This uneasiness from within the Camogie Association may have been rooted in a fundamental disapproval of women playing football, or it could have been precipitated by a concern that Gaelic football might become more popular than camogie among women on the island of Ireland. After all, they had previously faced this problem.

A selection of photos from ladies Gaelic football matches and activities in the 1970s from a scrapbook belonging to Marie McAleer née Holland (a founding member of the LGFA).

Between 1934 and 1939 the Camogie Association had banned their members from playing 'foreign' games. This led to a number of issues at local and national level, particularly among members who played hockey as well as camogie. The removal of the ban in 1939 led to a split within the association. The separation ended after two years, thanks to the intervention of Padraig Ó Chaoimh, General Secretary of the GAA, and the ban was reinstated without issue.[21]

Camogie had not since faced any competition. Yet was it about to face a fresh competitor now – and from a domestic Gaelic sport, no less?

———————————

That women's Gaelic football matches were being played in various counties without the assistance of an overarching organising body is impressive. The game undoubtedly continued to flourish. And a growing game needed a standardised set of rules.

In March 1968 the *Meath Chronicle* published the rules of the game as played in Co. Meath at the time 'in view of the fact that ladies Gaelic football seems to be catching on rapidly in the county.'[22] The paper specified that each team should be made up of ten members – seven players and three substitutes – and games would be played over forty minutes in total on pitches sixty-eighty yards long and forty-fifty yards wide, using a size five football. It was noted that the game was to be played 'along the same lines as Gaelic football'. Five rules were highlighted by the paper:

(a) A player may pick the ball off the ground; (b) a player may run 5 yards with the ball without being penalised; (c) a player may use any method to get rid of the ball, i.e., kick, punch, or throw; (d) to score a player must either punch or kick the ball, goals and points scored as in Gaelic; (e) a player commits a foul by over-robust tackling, pushing, tripping, kicking, catching, holding, or jumping at a player; a free kick will be awarded for each foul, in all cases the referee's decision is final.[23]

It is difficult to say what might have constituted an 'over-robust' tackle, kick or catch, but the language used is interesting and implies that there were efforts made to modify Gaelic football so that it might be considered socially and physically 'suitable' for women to play. The *Meath Chronicle* also advised that 'each player must wear slacks. A player may wear shoes of her own choice but football boots are recommended.'[24] The direction that women should wear 'slacks' while playing football (and not shorts as the men would have worn) was undoubtedly another adjustment to ensure that the image of women playing Gaelic football was socially acceptable.

As rules began to be set down, and participation increased, the standard of the play appears to have risen quickly among the teams. A report in the *Southern Star* describes a final between Shamrocks and Carrigaline as a 'real thriller'.[25] The language that accompanied a picture published in the *Evening Echo* from the same year calls the match between the 'Knicks' and the 'Knacks' as a 'Crazy Ball Game'.[26] Reporting on games in the Midlands League in May 1968, the *Leinster Express* commended the 'level standard' of the 'close and exciting' games in the league.[27] Similarly, the *Waterford News and Star* described a match between Killrossanty and Ballyduff as 'a remarkably high standard' game in which the 'speed and excitement of the exchanges left spectators breathless'.[28]

Although the novelty tag was a feature that stuck to the game in this period, it is clear, too, that it was more than a novelty event, as noted by the *Drogheda Independent* in 1968, which, reporting on a match between Kells and Dulane, stated that the game 'demonstrated that these girls' football matches are being taken seriously and that it is certainly no parlour game. There was no draw back on either side and the game was thoroughly enjoyed by all.'[29] Entertaining football and genuine interest in the game was helping to drive the growing popularity of the game.

These carnival games and festival tournaments were undoubtedly central to the progression of women's Gaelic football from a novelty act to a serious sport. The influence of these games can also be measured by the expansion beyond local teams to inter-county fixtures.

It appears that Waterford and Tipperary were the first counties in Ireland to establish county boards, in 1971.[30] Following the success of their respective county championships, an inter-county match was arranged between the two sides in October 1971. Played at Ballypatrick, Co. Tipperary, the home side beat the Waterford outfit 2–1 to 0–3 in what can be assumed to be the first-ever inter-county women's Gaelic football match.[31] Tipperary followed up their victory over Waterford with another win, this time against Wexford, who they beat 2–12 to 0–6.[32]

At the end of November that year, Jim Kennedy, a key figure involved in women's Gaelic football in Tipperary, wrote to the *Evening Echo*, seeking to promote the game as 'it's beginning to catch on.'[33] Kennedy's letter set out the current situation, noting that there were twelve teams in Tipperary, around fifteen in Waterford, as well as teams in Cork, Kerry, Wexford and Mayo. The presence of women's Gaelic football teams in those counties, as well as in the midlands, as mentioned previously, indicate that Kennedy was right to say that the game was catching on.

He wrote to the *Evening Echo* again in February 1972, reassuring potential players, or perhaps parents, that in the forty-nine games played in Tipperary in 1971 not one player got injured.[34] Kennedy also mentioned that the game was played on a shorter pitch in comparison to the men's game and offered to 'furnish a copy of the rules of any club anxious to take part', suggesting that he anticipated that there would be further questions and that there remained concerns about the rules of the game and its suitability for women.

Still, he posed the obvious question: 'if we allow our ladies to take part in other forms of sport, why not Gaelic football?'

———————————————

The push to organise the game beyond individual county boundaries was off to a successful start, even if progress came at a relatively slow

The Offaly ladies' county team of 1973. As ladies Gaelic football became more popular, the game progressed beyond the carnival tournaments and efforts were made to establish county teams. Tipperary and Waterford were the first to set up county boards and they played the first inter-county ladies' football match in 1971, but other counties, such as Offaly, Cork, and Kerry soon followed suit (Phyllis Price née Hackett).

pace. Tipperary and Waterford played each other again in September 1972 and there were plans for Tipperary to play Wexford or Laois in their next game, though there is no record of a game having taken place between Tipperary and either county in the newspaper archives for 1972.[35]

Other counties also started to get involved in the action. In late 1973, a county selection from Kerry was invited to take on Cork at a festival in Banteer, Co. Cork.[36] The match was refereed by Cork footballer Denis Long and attracted a crowd of between 1,000 and 2,000 people. The spectators were treated to a close and exciting game that Kerry won marginally, 5–10 to 4–11, and in which Bridie Brosnan (Cork) and Mary Geaney (Kerry) starred.[37]

Efforts were also made in 1973 for the women of Offaly and Kerry to meet in a Gaelic football match. Writing to the editor of the *Westmeath Independent*, Seán Ó Dunagáin, President of the Offaly Association in Dublin, outlined the attempts made to organise a match between the two counties. Ó Dunagáin revealed that UCD GAA Club invited Kerry and Offaly to play between the semi-finals and final of the Carrolls seven-a-side football competition that was scheduled to be played at Belfield on 29 April. Due to the fixing of a replay of a league fixture between Derry and Kerry, however, the UCD-organised seven-a-side competition was subsequently called off, along with the women's football match. That is, until it emerged that Derry would not be fulfilling the replay fixture and it was decided on 27 April to proceed with the tournament in UCD. However, at this late stage, Ó Dunagáin said, 'there was no possibility of getting the ladies' game rearranged, with the result that the Offaly girls in particular, are slightly put out.'[38] Ó Dunagáin also (incorrectly) stated in his letter that the occasion would have been a 'historic one in G.A.A. affairs – it would have been the first inter-county ladies' game', and put a call out, challenging any county in Ireland to take on Offaly in a women's Gaelic football match.

Indeed, the women of Offaly and Kerry did ultimately get the opportunity to play against each other in 1973, thanks to the efforts of the Offaly Association in Dublin, who organised the fixture for July that year. In the absence of a national organising body, this match was billed as the first All-Ireland Gaelic football final for women and garnered media attention from national newspapers, such as the *Evening Herald* and the *Irish Press*.

In the run-up to the game, the *Evening Herald* commended the 'boundless' enthusiasm of the women whose 'dedication is most keen and the standard of their play is a marvel to those who thought that a leather ball and frail feminine fingers were incompatible.'[39] The article gives an insight into the popularity of the game in both counties and notes the important role the Offaly Association in Dublin and the Kerry Association in Dublin played in encouraging their members living in Dublin to take up the sport by organising training sessions for their members in the Phoenix Park and Fairview Park, respectively. The *Evening Herald* noted that there were eight women's Gaelic football teams in Offaly 'loosely associated with the local G.A.A.' while in Kerry the game was mostly organised in Tralee and the Gaeltacht area of the Dingle Peninsula, all without any official recognition from the GAA. The newspaper called on the GAA to organise a league or championship for the women's game, labelling it 'an urgent matter for the powers-that-be'.[40] The *Offaly Independent* also recognised the potential of

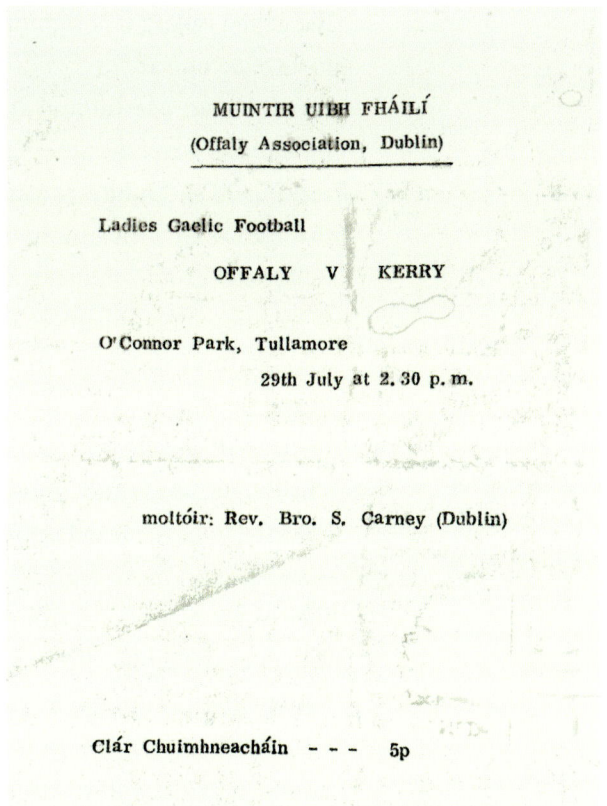

MUINTIR UIBH FHÁILÍ
(Offaly Association, Dublin)

Ladies Gaelic Football

OFFALY V KERRY

O'Connor Park, Tullamore
29th July at 2. 30 p. m.

moltóir: Rev. Bro. S. Carney (Dublin)

Clár Chuimhneacháin - - - 5p

Organised by the Offaly Association, Offaly and Kerry played at O'Connor Park in Tullamore on 29 July 1973, and in the absence of a national association it was styled as the first-ever All-Ireland ladies Gaelic football final (Phyllis Price née Hackett).

the game, calling it 'a significant breakthrough in the social sphere' in a GAA context.[41]

Brendan Martin and Ann Cooney of the Offaly Association in Dublin were the key figures involved in training the Offaly contingent in Dublin and organising this match, but it is notable that the Offaly GAA County Board supported the fixture, scheduling it between a football match and a hurling match that were played in O'Connor Park, Tullamore on 29 July.

'Perfume took over from embrocation as the prevailing odour in the dressing rooms,' stated the *Evening Press* in a vivid opening to its post-match report, which challenged the usual sights and smells associated with the Gaelic field.[42] Over 2,000 people were reported to have turned up at O'Connor Park for the match and the newspaper acknowledged the 'two dedicated teams' who proved that they had 'little to learn from their male counterparts' and admitted that many of those who had come to jeer at women playing Gaelic football left the ground in admiration.[43]

The game ended with Offaly emerging victorious and they were crowned unofficial All-Ireland champions. However, in the aftermath of the match between Offaly and Kerry, the women of Waterford took issue with the game being classified as the first inter-county women's Gaelic All-Ireland final, stating that they were 'more than annoyed' and 'would give a hell of a good run to the much vaunted Offaly team.'[44] A match was quickly arranged, Waterford being true to their word with a 'decisive' 5–8 to 1–7 win over Offaly.[45]

Clearly, there was an appetite among women in Ireland not only to play Gaelic football in their own locality but also on a national, inter-county stage. As noted by the *Evening Press* following the game between Offaly and Kerry, these female Gaelic footballers 'had succeeded in getting the message across that there is a future for this latest craze in the Irish sporting world'.[46]

In the fifty-three years between the first recorded ladies Gaelic football match that took place in St James's Park in Dublin to the first so-called All-Ireland ladies Gaelic football final in O'Connor Park in Tullamore, life on the island of Ireland had changed in many ways. Local carnivals advertising ladies Gaelic football as a novelty act had given women the opportunity to test their own abilities at the game and also the public's reaction to women playing the traditionally male-only game. The positive reception both on and off the field to the women's game had allowed for enduring boundaries to be broken and ladies Gaelic football to develop beyond a carnival act into a competitive sport for women and girls. The inter-county activity between 1971 and 1973 illustrated the enthusiasm for the game and a desire to emulate the activities of men's Gaelic football.

The next natural step was to set up a national association.

CIARRAÍ

1.
Julie Hickey
(Currow)

2.	3.	4.
Sinéad Ní Chairbhia (Gaeltacht)	Aingil Ní Luing (Gaeltacht)	Mary Lombard (Castleisland)
5.	6.	7.
Gobnait Nic Gearailt (Gaeltacht)	Monica Leahy (Causeway)	Máire Ní Chonchúir (Gaeltacht)

8.
Muiríde Ní Sheaghdha
(Gaeltacht)

9.
Kathleen O'Connor
(Currow)

10.	11.	12.
Máire Ní Sheaghdha (Gaeltacht)	Seosaimhín Ní Dhubháin (Gaeltacht)	Joan Shanahan (Currow)
13.	14.	15
Siobhán Ní Sheaghdha (Gaeltacht)	Eibhlín Ní Sheaghdha (Gaeltacht)	Mary Geaney (Castleisland)

Subs: Ann Leahy (Causeway), Eibhlín Ní Chinnéide (Gaeltacht), Treasa Ní Laoithe (Gaeltacht), Sinéad Ní Chonchúir (Gaeltacht), Nóirín Ní Sheaghdha (Gaeltacht).

UIBH FHÁILÍ

1
Geraldine Todd
(Ballycommon)

2.	3.	4.
Ann Molloy (Rahan)	Agnes O'Gorman (Kilcormac)	Kay Corrigan (Kinnitty)
5.	6.	7.
Ann Guinan (Rahan)	Phyllis Hackett (Ballycumber)	Frances McDc (Ballycommon

8
Fidelma Geraghty
(Ballycommon)

9
Catherine Hynes
(Clara)

10.	11	12
Mary Todd (Ballycommon)	Evelyn Malone (Ballycommon)	Mary Buckley (Kilcormac)
13.	14	15
Kathleen Buckley (Kilcormac)	Elizabeth O'Gorman (Kilcormac)	Mary Gunning (Rhode)

Subs: Kathleen Finnerty (Rahan), Catherine Conroy (Ball; Marion Hynes (Clara), Angela Cooney (Rahan), Phyllis Buckley (Kilcormac), Mary Nevin (Kilcorm

How the teams lined out in the ladies Gaelic football match between Offaly and Kerry in July 1973, which was won by Offaly (Phyllis Price née Hackett).

CHAPTER 3
NATIONAL ASSOCIATION, 1974

The game between Offaly and Kerry in 1973 was the catalyst to move ladies Gaelic football from novelty act to something more organised and nationally minded. It was clear by this point that there were consistent playing bases in enough counties to warrant the setting up of an inter-county championship. On top of that, the positive media attention given to the game in 1973 was an endorsement of ladies Gaelic football. There was a palpable sense that the game could establish itself across the country. What it needed was a national association. This next step occurred twelve months after the game in O'Connor Park, when the first meeting of the LGFA took place in Hayes Hotel in Thurles, Co. Tipperary.

As reported in the *Tipperary Star* and *The Nationalist*, an 'All-Ireland ladies Football Convention' would take place in Hayes Hotel on 5 July and all interested parties were invited to attend.[1] *The Nationalist* provided some more information on the planned meeting, noting that representatives from Tipperary, Waterford and Offaly had already agreed to attend the meeting in Hayes

Hotel, that it was the intention of the convention to organise an All-Ireland championship, and trips to London and the USA were in the pipeline for 1975.[2] These notices appeared in the papers on 6 July, the day after the planned meeting was due to take place – however the meeting did not take place on that date. Instead, it was adjourned to 18 July, at which point the convention did occur.

The first committee of the Ladies Gaelic Football Association was elected at the convention. Jim Kennedy, an instrumental figure in promoting ladies' football in Tipperary, took up the position of the first president of the association, holding the role until 1977. Marie Holland and Margaret Flanagan from Roscommon became vice-president and treasurer. The rest of the committee was made up of figures involved in ladies' football in Offaly: Mary Nevin was elected as secretary, assisted by Joe Feighery, and Brendan Martin was named assistant treasurer.

The draw for the first LGFA championship was also made at the meeting. Roscommon were drawn to play Laois, Galway against Offaly, Kerry versus Cork, and Tipperary were to take on Waterford. The games were scheduled to begin in August. The cup for the inaugural championship was donated by the new assistant treasurer, Brendan Martin.[3]

It was a start, but there was of course much more to do.

Developing a standardised charter of rules was one of the primary objectives of the newly founded LGFA. The Gaelic football played by women at carnivals and tournaments before the founding of the LGFA generally followed the rules for Gaelic football as set down by the GAA, albeit with some slight modifications, including the picking up of the ball directly off the ground and limited physical contact. However, the rules often differed from county to county. For example, in Tipperary the game was played with a size four football and allowed for two hops of the ball instead of the

Eight counties affiliated with the LGFA in 1974. Among them were Offaly and Galway, who met in the first round of the inaugural ladies' football All-Ireland championship (Phyllis Price née Hackett; original source unknown).

The victorious Offaly Lady footballers that defeated the Galway side in the 1st round of the All-Ireland Ladies' Football Competition at Kilcormac last Sunday by 5-5 to 1-3. Bottom picture shows the Galway team. Report in this issue.

Photo: Coller, [...]

traditional one hop and one solo and size five football, which were the rules as followed by those playing in Roscommon.[4]

A set of forty rules were agreed upon at the next meeting of the LGFA in Portlaoise. These rules for women's Gaelic football generally reflected the rules for men's Gaelic football, but with some of the same adjustments as before, including the use of a size four football, permitting the picking up of the ball directly off the ground, and with free kicks conceded by the defending team by playing the ball over the endline to be taken from the thirty-yard line as opposed to the fifty-yard line.[5]

As the LGFA set things in motion for their first championship, carnival games and tournaments continued. The annual Corofin

Carnival in Co. Galway held in August featured a ladies' football match between Galway and Offaly, with this game advertised as the 'All-Ireland Ladies Tournament final'. The *Evening Herald* noted that players on both sides were steeped in sport. Many of the Offaly players were related to players on the men's Senior football team while the Galway side featured Josie Kelly, holder of three All-Ireland camogie medals, and Nono McHugh, the captain of the Irish women's international soccer team.[6] The game was described as 'exciting and top-class' and saw Galway emerge victorious on a score-line of 3–3 to 2–2.[7]

The teams did not have to wait long to face each other again, the two sides facing off a week later in the first round of the inaugural All-Ireland Championship. The game drew a crowd of over 2,000 spectators, according to the *Westmeath Independent*, and saw a reversal of the result in Corofin.[8] While the local paper credited Offaly with a fourteen-point victory, the *Tipperary Star*, previewing the upcoming championship match between Tipperary and Waterford, gave the score as 3–5 to 1–3.[9] Next up for Offaly were Laois, who had been drawn against Roscommon in the first round but were awarded the win as Roscommon could not field a team.

'The general standard of sporting behaviour which prevailed during this game was such that many of our sporting males could and should try to emulate.'

On the other side of the championship, Tipperary beat neighbours Waterford 3–8 to 2–6 in their first outing and awaited the winners of Kerry versus Cork. A report in *The Kerryman* in August 1974 previewed the upcoming championship meeting between Kerry and Cork, due to take place in Fitzgerald Stadium in Killarney. The two sides had recently played each other at carnival tournaments and the paper noted that the 'wonderful fare served up in these matches has greatly whetted the appetite for the next meeting'.[10] Although a previous meeting between the sides had drawn a crowd of over 2,500 at a carnival game in Banteer earlier that year, those involved were 'very disappointed with the

The Offaly team of 1974. Offaly beat Galway and Laois to reach the All-Ireland final (Phyllis Price née Hackett).

attendance' at the All-Ireland championship game. The weather likely discouraged some people from attending, though it was noted that despite the 'continuous rain … [the players] served up some excellent fare'.[11] The game was a close encounter, with Kerry winning by three points (2–5 to 2–2).

In the run-up to the close of the championship, the LGFA held a meeting in Portlaoise where it was decided that representatives from the association would seek a meeting with Seán Ó Síocháin, Director General of the GAA, 'with a view to having the all-Ireland ladies' final played in Croke [Park]'.[12] A week later, Jim Kennedy, the Tipperary County Public Relations Officer (PRO) and President of the LGFA, explained in the Tipperary ladies' football notes printed in *The Nationalist* that Ó Síocháin was 'anxious' to see a ladies' football match 'before making a decision as to whether the ladies' final should be in Croke Park. The information we received is to the effect that if we had a good crowd and a fairly even match, he would be prepared to visit Kilsheelan on the 15th' for the All-Ireland semi-final between Tipperary and Kerry.[13]

Whether Ó Síocháin attended the game or not is unconfirmed but judging from the reports, the game exceeded Kennedy's hopes for it. The semi-final between Tipperary and Kerry was described as 'one of the finest exhibitions of the code' and finished 2–8 to 1–5 in favour of Tipperary, with *The Cork Examiner* noting that 'judging by the enthusiastic reaction ladies' football has come to stay.'[14] Meanwhile, in the other semi-final, Offaly had a 3–6 to 2–6 win over Laois.[15]

Mentors to the Offaly team in 1974: Brendan Martin (LGFA Assistant Treasurer and Offaly County Secretary), Phyllis Hackett (Offaly County Chairperson and player), Mick Talbot (team mentor) and Tom Kenny (team mentor) (Phyllis Price née Hackett).

All-Ireland 'first' for the women

By DAN COEN

IT had not the huge crowds, but yesterday's first Ladies' All-Ireland Football Final between Offaly and Tipperary (the winners by a single point) had all the enthusiasm and thrills of many an All-Ireland in Croke Park.

From the moment the ball was thrown in at Durrow, Co. Laois, by Derry referee, Paul O'Sullivan, the women got stuck in and by half time both teams were level with a goal and two points each.

Tipperary won the toss and elected to play uphill and that's exactly what they did. For though the pitch was in excellent condition, the incline would put the heart crossways in any trainer who might find his team trailing at the half-way stage and having to face it in the second half.

The play was fast and tough and, as referee O'Sullivan said: "not with out a good deal of expertise".

Tipperary were older, too, and maybe this combination helped them to become the first champions in a new branch of GAA which is hoping for full affiliation with the association's headquarters.

Towards the end of the first half, Tipp were in a comfortable lead of one goal and two points to nil and it seemed, despite the determined play of the Offaly women and the vocal support from the sidelines, that the match was over.

However, Mary Nevin, secretary of the All-Ireland Ladies GAA and a sub on the Offaly side, told me to keep an eye on her side because they never said die.

She was right. For within minutes of the restart, Offaly took the lead with a goal. Still, Tipp came back and with about eight minutes to go went ahead with a point from a free and that was that. Tipperary had won the first All-Ireland Ladies Football final 2-3 to 2-2.

The enthusiasm was there with

times for the devil, to do something about the flagging fortunes of either side.

It was a great day for women's football. And a nice "ladylike" touch was added after the match when the Offaly captain, Agnes O'Gorman, presented the cup to Tipperary captain, Kitty Ryan.

With a bit of luck, more than eight counties will take part in next year's championship, and the All-Ireland will be played at Croke Park.

The captain of the Tipperary team, Kitty Ryan, with her team after winning the All-Ireland Ladies' Football Final at Durrow.
Picture by John Rowley

Offaly fail to Tipperary

TIPPERARY .... 2-3 OFFALY 2-2

The final was fixed for 13 October and though efforts were made to get the final played in Croke Park, the venue was ultimately confirmed as Durrow in Co. Laois.[16] The *Irish Press* reported that the efforts to hold the All-Ireland final in Croke Park had been 'thwarted' by the replay of the All-Ireland camogie final.[17] However, it is likely that scepticism about ladies Gaelic football from GAA HQ was also a major factor in the decision.

Making light of the rejection, the *Irish Press* quoted Brendan Martin, assistant treasurer of the LGFA, as saying that Ó Síocháin

The All-Ireland final between Tipperary and Offaly made national headlines. Kitty Ryan triumphantly raises the Brendan Martin Cup as she is carried atop her teammates' shoulders (Via Phyllis Price née Hackett, the *Irish Press* Archive © University College Cork).

Player of the match Offaly's Phyllis Hackett gets a shot off despite the pressure put on by a defending Tipperary player during the All-Ireland final of 1974 (Phyllis Price née Hackett).

was 'very sympathetic to us. But we want to get ourselves established and make a success of ladies' football before we try to become affiliated to the Association.'[18]

There certainly were difficulties in getting a new sport and new association up and running. This was exposed by the Tipperary County Board, who admitted that they were 'in a bad way financially' and put out a public appeal to friends and supporters for donations to help 'defray the cost of training the team for the final'.[19] This appeal brought about possibly the first case of sponsorship for ladies Gaelic football, as jerseys for the final were sponsored by Barlow's Ltd, Clonmel.[20]

Despite the financial difficulties, there was a strong sense of anticipation in the Tipperary camp in the run-up to the final. It was noted in the county's football notes in *The Nationalist* that 'the Tipp girls have just completed their training programme and are as fit as fiddles and rarin' to go. We are in this final with a fifty-fifty chance, and win or lose we will be fighting for our lives.'[21]

Keen to drum up interest in the game, a pre-final conference was organised by the LGFA and held in Hayes Hotel in Thurles on

The All-Ireland-winning team of 1974, Tipperary, pose for a photo with the Brendan Martin Cup alongside their mentors, John Donovan and Jim Kennedy (Phyllis Price née Hackett; original source unknown).

The Tipperary team pictured with trainer and Chairman of the All-Ireland Council Mr. Sean Donovan and Mr. Jim Kennedy, Clonmel, after their victory in the first ever All-Ireland Ladies' Football final on Sunday. On the team— and among those included in the picture— were: M. Carroll, S. Clohessy, A. Croke, M. Sweeney, E. Hackett, P. Flynn, B. Looby, S. O'Gorman, E. Dudley, J. Keane, E. Carroll, L. Goery, K. Ryan (Capt.), M. Mc Grath, and M. Power.

Photo—A. Claffey.

9 October.[22] 'Make Way For That "Other" All-Ireland Final' was the headline in the *Irish Press* as they previewed the game.[23]

The final was described as a fast-paced game mixed with plenty of expertise and determination. Dan Coen of the *Irish Press* commented that it had 'all the enthusiasm and thrills of many an All-Ireland in Croke Park' and judged that 'it was a great day for women's football.'[24]

Tipperary commanded the lead coming up to half-time, having scored a goal and two points without reply. Offaly played their way back into the game and levelled the score, 1–2 apiece, before scoring an early goal in the second half to take the lead. The close nature of the match made for an exciting finish. With eight

Tipperary forwards Josie Keane, Lilian Gorey and Mary Power discuss tactics ahead of the throw-in of the All-Ireland final (Mary Power O'Shea).

THE TEAMS OF '74

OFFALY 1974 TEAM AS LINED OUT IN DURROW

1. Geradline Todd, Ballycommon
2. Ann Molloy, Rahan
3. Agnes Gorman (Capt), Kilcommon
4. Kay Corrigan, Kilcormac
5. Lucy Bryant, Offaly Association in Dublin
6. Phyllis Hackett, Ballycumber
7. Frances McDonald, Ballycommon
8. Catherine Hynes, Clara
9. Fidelma Geraghty, Ballycommon
10. Anne Malone, Ballycommon
11. Mary Boland, Ballycommon
12. Moll Buckley, Kilcormac
13. Catherine Conroy, Ballycommon
14. Mary Gunning, Ballycommon
15. Pauline Geraghry, Ballycommon
16. Kathleen Buckley, Kilcormac for Mary Gunning
17. Tona McDonald, Ballycommon for Frances McDonald
18. Mary Lowry, Ferbane for Catherine Conroy
19. Ursla Corrigan, Kilcormac
20. Deidre Geraghty, Ballycommon
21. Catherine Hanlon, Ballycommon
22. Mary Todd, Ballycommon
23. Rene Brennan, Ballycommon
24. Mary Nevin, Kilcormac

Manager: Brendan Martin
Trainers + Selectors: Joe Feery, Bro Sylvister Carney, Mick Talbot, R.I.P.

Offaly Scorers in Final: Kathleen Buckley (1-1), Moll Buckley (1-0), Catherine Hynes (0-1).

Phyllis Hackett awarded Player of the Match in '74 All-Ireland. In those days no trophy was presented. Geraldine Todd is sister of present Co. GAA Secretary Christy Todd. Mary Lowry sister of former Inter County GAA Players Brendan and Sean Lowry. Mary Gunning Sister of Jodie, former County Player. Special mention to Mick Talbot, R.I.P. who was instrumental in Ladies Football in the County and throughout.

TIPPERARY 1974 TEAM AS LINED OUT IN DURROW

1. Margaret Carroll, Ardfinnan
2. Sally Clohessy, Moycarkey
3. Ann Croke, Mullmahone
4. Majella Sweeney, Newcastle
5. Ena Hackett, Newcastle
6. Tina Flynn, Ardfinnan
7. Betty Looby, Golden
8. Susan O'Gorman, Ardfinnan
9. Eileen Dudley, Cashel
10. Lilian Gorey, St. Bridgets
11. Eleanor Carroll, Ardfinian
12. Josephine Keane, Mullinahone
13. Mary Power, Mullinahone
14. Kitty Ryan (Capt), Ardfinnan
15. Mary McGrath, Emly
16. Nora Moran, Newcastle
17. Mary Lonergan, Emly
18. Mary Burke, Emly
19. Alice Morris, Moycarkey/Borris
20. Cait O'Dwyer, Moycarkey/Borris
21. Ann Clohessy, Moycarkey/Borris
22. Marian Bryan, Moycarkey/Borris
23. Ann Bryan, Moycarkey/Borris
24. Noreen Blake, Golden
25. Katherine Keane, Mullinahone

Full Time Score: 2-03 - 2-02
Subs used in All Ireland Final: Nora Moran and Mary Lonergan

COUNTY BOARD IN '74
Chairman and 1st President of L.F.: Jim Kennedy
Secretary: Biddy Ryan
Selectors: John O'Donovan, Teddy Keane, Jim Strappe, Sean Gorey (R.I.P.)

Tipp Scorers in Final: Eleanor Carroll (1, 02), Mary McGrath (1, 0), Lilian Gorey (0-1).

Tipperary County Ladies team were presented with a set of jerseys for the final by Carrie Acheson MCC, TC, directors of Barlows Ltd. Clonmel and accepting the presentation was Tipp Capt, Kitty Ryan. Lilian Gorey was honoured by the sports awards GAA in '74 for her consistency with her club and county for L.F. All Tipp players were given instructions to be in Durrow for the game at heart one hour before kick off. A meal was organised by the great Mick Talbot of Offaly in the Castle Arms Hotel, Durrow and then it was back

55

Offaly captain Agnes Gorman presents the Brendan Martin Cup to Tipperary captain Kitty Ryan (Mary Power O'Shea).

minutes to go, Tipperary converted a free to take the lead once again – and the game finished with that solitary point between them, 2–3 to 2–2 in favour of Tipperary.[25]

The *Westmeath Independent* applauded the sporting nature of the women's final, stating:

> The general standard of sporting behaviour which prevailed during this game was such that many of our sporting males could and should try to emulate. It was noteworthy that the trophy was presented to the winning captain, Kitty Ryan, by the Offaly captain, Agnes O'Gorman, which in itself, was indicative of the spirit of the friendliness which existed.[26]

To celebrate the achievement, a reception was held in the Tipperary captain's home place of Ardfinnan, hosted by the Ardfinnan men's football committee and with the Brendan Martin Cup on display. The Tipperary men's County Board also extended their official congratulations to the team and referred a request for a grant from the women's County Board to their finance committee.[27] Tipperary

◄
The Offaly and Tipperary teams as they lined out in the All-Ireland final held in Durrow, Co. Laois in 1974 (Phyllis Price née Hackett).

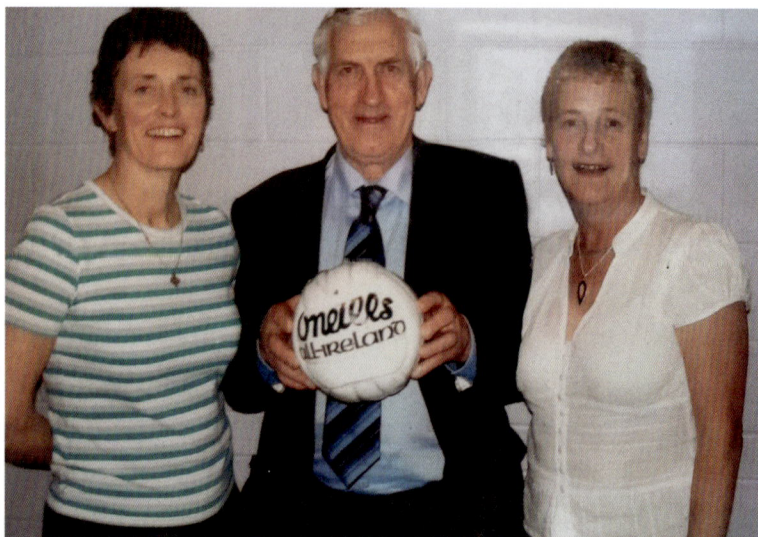

Twenty-five years on from the 1974 final, players Lilian Gorey (left) and Mary Power O'Shea (right) stand with John Donovan (centre – team mentor and founding member of the LGFA) and the match ball from the final (Mary Power O'Shea).

finished the year with a challenge match against beaten semi-finalists Laois and ensured that they finished the year unbeaten.[28]

If it was a successful year for the Tipperary ladies footballers, it was also a success for the LGFA as a whole. In the space of a few short months the fledgling governing body managed to organise and run a national championship without any hiccups. While small in numbers and short in duration, the championship was, nevertheless, a success.

CHAPTER 4
THE EARLY YEARS, 1975–1980

'All we need are more clubs around the country to get a firm grip of the game so come on girls! Step it out this summer – it's the best since camogie.'[1] This was the rallying cry of a 'Lady Footballer' from Tipperary writing to the *Irish Farmers Journal* in April 1975. With a national association now established for ladies Gaelic football, it was imperative that the LGFA build on the success of 1974 and grow the game across the country. The anonymous footballer from Tipperary also noted that the game was popular in her home county, as well as in Offaly, but that it was still very much in its early stages and more teams were needed to grow the game. She finished by encouraging women and girls to take up ladies' football 'to keep busy, fit and slim'.[2]

This call to participate was one of many, and they were being heard, as over the next few years the LGFA introduced more competitions at different ages and levels to cater to a growing membership. An inter-county All-Ireland Under–16 Championship and an inter-provincial competition were added in 1976, followed by an All-Ireland Club Championship in 1977, an inter-county

Tipperary not only had the distinction of winning the first LGFA final in 1974, but they were also the first county to win back-to-back titles when they beat Galway in the 1975 decider (Tipperary LGFA).

league in 1979, and an Under–18 Championship in 1980. Four new counties – Mayo, Kildare, Kilkenny and Cavan – joined the All-Ireland championship in 1975, while Armagh, Leitrim, Louth, Meath, Westmeath and Wexford also took part in competitions before the end of the decade.

Local and provincial newspapers illustrate the spread and growth of women's Gaelic football in the early years of the LGFA. In Mayo, a ladies' team was set up in Castlebar Mitchels in 1975 and support for the ladies' game within the county was given by Ray Prendergast and Dr Mick Loftus, both respected and influential personalities in the local and national Gaelic games community.[3] The Castlebar Mitchels club spearheaded the efforts to set up a county board that year.[4] The *Connacht Tribune* attended the Mayo Ladies County Board's dinner dance the following year and noted that 'although the organisation is but a young one in the county, there was much to celebrate.'[5] The chair of the county board, Rev. Gerry Gillespie, stated that while the association was still in its infancy and struggling somewhat, 'with the expected level of support he was confident they would progress.'[6] Meanwhile, in Laois, the *Nationalist and Leinster*

Times reported in January 1976 that there were eleven clubs in the county and that the county team and reigning Leinster champions were intent on achieving All-Ireland glory in 1976.[7]

The local newspapers also gave an insight into some of the women's motivations in taking up a new sport. Like the 'Lady Footballer' from Tipperary, Josephine Moylett from Mayo, who featured in the *Connaught Telegraph*, took up Gaelic football alongside two of her teenage daughters for their club, Islandeady, as an outlet to keep fit and make friends.[8]

It was observed too that playing Gaelic football would benefit not only women but also the wider Gaelic games community. When future LGFA President Tom Kenny addressed the Meath GAA County Board in 1976 regarding the possibility of establishing the women's game in the county, he was met with enthusiasm, with Chair of the Meath GAA Board Pat O'Neill remarking: 'If we can encourage our ladies to be involved then we are providing a breeding ground for the future.'[9]

As county boards were being formed in order to join with the LGFA to promote ladies Gaelic football, some counties, like Cork, were leading the way in showcasing the increasing popularity of the game. By 1976 there were reported to be an incredible twenty-seven clubs in Cork playing ladies Gaelic football.[10] The growth of the game within the county led the Cork Ladies County Board to set up an Under–16 inter-divisional championship alongside their adult Junior and Senior championships in 1977.[11] Ladies' football started to established itself in Westmeath where, following a meeting attended by nine clubs, it was decided to run a competition in the autumn of 1976.[12] A league was also organised in the winter of 1976 between Cavan, Armagh, Louth and Meath. Though it appears that this competition was not officially run by the LGFA, the fact that it was initiated highlights the appetite for competitions among ladies Gaelic football players.[13]

It was not just on the island of Ireland that there was interest from women in playing Gaelic football during this period. In 1975,

Ladies Gaelic football was played outside Ireland for the first time in June 1975 when Offaly travelled to London to play a seven-a-side exhibition match against a team made up of London-based players. Offaly's Lucy Bryant played with the Exiles, which left Offaly with just six players. Sisters Catherine and Marian Hynes from Clara in Co. Offaly, who played soccer with Chelsea at the time, played for London on the day.

Back row (L–R): Rosemary Sexton, A. Farrell, Attracta Egan.

Front row (L–R): Phyllis Hackett, Margaret Duggan, Maura Foy.

(Phyllis Price née Hackett)

a ladies' football match was held outside Ireland for the first time when members of the Offaly Association in Dublin visited London. The visit was organised by the Offaly Association in London and among the weekend activities was a seven-a-side ladies' football exhibition match. Seven players from the Offaly team that played in the 1974 All-Ireland final defeat to Tipperary travelled with the Offaly Association to London. Sourcing players for the match was a challenge for 'The Exiles'. One of the travelling Offaly players, Lucy Bryant, ended up having to tog out for the London-based team, which left the visitors with only six players. Also among the London players were Offaly-born sisters Catherine and Marian Hynes, both of whom played soccer with Chelsea at the time.[14] Two men, Charlie

Wren and Willie Molloy, played in goal due to the scarcity of players available for the match.[15] Spectators were treated to a high goal-scoring contest, with Offaly winning 7–3 to 6–1.[16]

The game was also spreading across the Atlantic, with *The Anglo-Celt* reporting that Cavan woman Kathleen Leddy, who arrived in New York in the summer of 1977, had set up a ladies' football team called the 'Annalees' in the city.[17]

Fr Cagney and Phyllis Hackett stand for a photo at a reception following the match between Offaly and the Offaly Association in London in June 1975 (Phyllis Price née Hackett).

Members of the Offaly Association stand for a photo in London in 1975 (Phyllis Price née Hackett).

The increasing popularity of the game led to a fresh examination of its rules and format. Coming into 1975, the Galway Ladies County Board sought for changes to be made to the championship. They labelled the structure of the organisation at national level as 'unsatisfactory' and proposed that the All-Ireland Championship be played on a league basis rather than knock-out.[18] A rulebook had been agreed upon ahead of the 1974 championship, but Galway also put a motion to the LGFA Central Council, suggesting that a committee be set up 'to review the rules and constitution of the organisation at national level' and, in addition, that the rules of the game as played in Galway be adopted.[19]

Galway's motion to have a committee set up to review the rules was passed and at a meeting of the LGFA Central Council a few weeks later, the rulebook was the sole item on the agenda. A document was drawn up and titled the 'Charter, Constitution & Rules of Ladies Gaelic Football Association', which included thirty-eight points relating to the aims and objectives and rules of the LGFA, and it was discussed at this meeting.[20]

It is unclear whether this draft document was passed as proposed or with amendments. However, further calls to review the rules in 1976 and 1977 suggests that there were still tweaks to make. In 1977, Lynda Colgan, the Chair of the Mayo Ladies County Board, publicly called for the rules to be revised and 'streamlined' in order to make the game more attractive for players and spectators. Colgan stated that the present rules were unsatisfactory due to the allowance of 'a great deal of hard physical contact' and should focus instead on 'the skill and speed of the game'.[21] Her statements echoed questions that Roscommon's Michael Naughton also raised in 1976. He wrote:

> [D]oes the Ladies Gaelic Football Association not consider that some changes are necessary in the playing rules to counter allegations from various quarters that the games as presently constituted for women bears too near a similarity to men's football?

> Strong doubts have been expressed by medical people, members of the GAA, parents etc. that the game if played strictly in accord (or even with slight modifications) with men's football, would be dangerous on medical grounds; too robust for participation by a great many girls and unattractive as a spectacle![22]

The decision was taken at a Central Council meeting in December 1976 to set up a committee to once again review the LGFA's rules. Each county board was contacted the following month and asked to get the views and suggestions of every club in their county 'as to how the existing Administrative and in particular the playing rules could be improved for the betterment of the game generally'.[23] Tom Dowd, Tom Kenny and Ultan Fitzpatrick were appointed to this committee, which was tasked with gathering this information, which they would then submit not just to the LGFA Central Council but also at an upcoming meeting with the GAA, 'who have already expressed reservation with some of the playing rules'.[24]

Rules around physicality was clearly an issue that the LGFA continued to grapple with, particularly in making ladies Gaelic football appealing as a new sport. Colgan and Naughton's calls had not gone unheard and at the National Congress in March 1977 the motion to disallow bodily contact was passed.[25]

In just a handful of years the LGFA had managed to cement itself as a recognised sporting organisation on the island of Ireland.

Given that the LGFA was a newly established organisation, it was only natural that adjustments would be made to the rulebook to adapt to circumstances and implement learnings. It also showed that the LGFA were open to hearing the views of both their membership and external bodies like the GAA.

Despite the business over the rules, things were going from strength to strength on the field. The association ran off six national championships in total across the 1975, 1976 and 1977 seasons at county and club levels, as well as introducing the inter-county and inter-provincial competition in 1976. Tipperary became back-

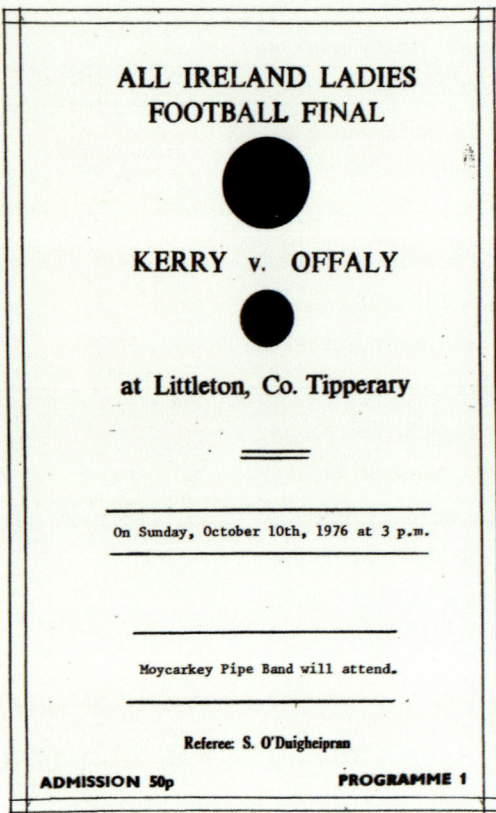

```
ALL IRELAND LADIES
FOOTBALL FINAL


KERRY v. OFFALY


at Littleton, Co. Tipperary


On Sunday, October 10th, 1976 at 3 p.m.



Moycarkey Pipe Band will attend.


Referee: S. O'Duigheipran

ADMISSION 50p                    PROGRAMME 1
```

▲
The programme from the 1976 All-Ireland final, which was played in Littleton, Co. Tipperary between Kerry and Offaly. (Phyllis Price née Hackett).

▶ (top)
Kerry's first All-Ireland winning team from 1976 (Marion Bowler née O'Doherty)

▶ (bottom)
Leinster champions Offaly were runners-up in the All-Ireland final of 1976 (Phyllis Price née Hackett).

to-back All-Ireland champions when they defeated Galway in the 1975 All-Ireland Senior championship. They would feature in three more finals before the end of the decade, losing to Roscommon and Offaly in 1978 and 1979, respectively, before winning their third and last Senior All-Ireland championship to date in 1980.

Kerry dethroned the reigning Munster and All-Ireland champions in 1976, beating them in the Munster final to secure their place in the All-Ireland semi-final against Ulster champions Cavan. Centre forward Mary Geaney (1–4) and corner forward Mai Lombard (2–1) scored the bulk of Kerry's 3–9 in the semi-final, in which they had six points to spare over Cavan. In the final, Kerry's captain Geaney starred once again and registered 3–2 of Kerry's 4–6 in the final against Offaly. The age-old adage of 'goals win matches' proved true in this case, as Kerry had ten points to spare over Offaly with a score-line of 4–6 to 1–5.

Geaney's natural footballing talents had been spotted when she scored 2–6 in Kerry's victory over Cork at a carnival game in Banteer in Co. Cork back in June 1974. After the game, the Kerry GAA PRO, Tim Linehan, remarked 'She would beat the majority of men playing football in Kerry today.'[26] Geaney went on to play in goals for the Irish women's hockey team and also won two All-Ireland camogie medals with Cork to go with her ladies Gaelic football All-Ireland medal from 1976.

As at Senior level, things continued to develop at underage level. In a curtain-raiser to the All-Ireland final in 1975, Tipperary

Kerry ~ ALL-IRELAND CHAMPIONS ~ 1976

An Kingdom Abu !

and Kilkenny each fielded an Under–16 team for a game that ended in a draw, six points apiece.[27] The following year, the Under–16 championship was officially introduced and Mayo had the honour of being the first county to win an underage LGFA title. Kilkenny were Mayo's opponents in the final and the *Mayo News* commented on the win, saying that 'playing fast, open football the Mayo girls dominated from the throw in and their tremendous 21 points victory set a very high standard for future teams taking part in the competition to live up to.'[28]

The game was undoubtedly growing; however, getting media coverage of women's Gaelic football proved a major challenge for the LGFA in the 1970s, particularly at national level. Television had arrived to many Irish households in the 1960s but print media and the radio remained popular forms of dissemination. Securing coverage was important to raise awareness about the game and to boost its status and it is clear that in areas where ladies Gaelic football was popular, local newspaper coverage was more forthcoming, even if the column inches on ladies Gaelic football were often provided by county board committee members.

Commentary on the standard of the play or the idea of women playing Gaelic football was a feature of many newspaper articles during this period. Many reporters were not afraid to admit that they held preconceived ideas about women playing Gaelic football, but that upon seeing a game their opinion often changed. Bill O'Donnell, writing under the pen name 'Divot' for *The Nationalist*, highlights the disdain that many in the media (and likely the general public) held for ladies' football before they had even watched a match:

> I went to Golden on Saturday evening last out of pure curiosity
> and prepared for an odd laugh. For Tipperary ladies were playing

a team of Cork counterparts in the Munster ladies football championship. I didn't laugh for there was nothing to laugh at. Out there on that well prepared pitch I saw fifteen Tipperary girls in the familiar blue and gold singlet give as fine a display of football as one could wish for. Indeed there were quite a few among them who could show some of our men folk quite a few of the arts of fetching and kicking. As for scoring. From play and placed balls these girls chalked up the magnificent total of 4 goals and 10 points and showed those Cork ladies, equally adept, 'courage and skill.' The column extends congratulations and best wishes for success in future games. Such was the interest displayed in this game that there must have been upwards of 600 spectators, very many of them of the fair sex, present.[29]

A fellow reporter at *The Nationalist* also praised the standard of play on display when they covered Tipperary's opening championship game in 1975 versus Waterford:

It's five years since I first saw a ladies football match and how the players have improved in the meantime, both in fielding and positional play. No longer do they chase the ball in bunches but rather do they now hold their places and make the ball do the work. I thought that the big Clonmel pitch would be too much for them, but it presented no problems as the girls swung the ball from end to end with hefty kicks.[30]

The *Connacht Sentinel* also praised the display put on by Galway and Mayo in the Connacht championship in 1975, stating: 'there was nothing of the gimmick about this game. It was both credible and creditable. It was earnest and hard-fought stuff and there was no lack of spirit among the players.'[31]

However, others continued to make their dissatisfaction known. A letter published in the *Irish Farmers Journal* in 1975 asked, 'What has happened to the petite, feminine female?' Concerned by the increased popularity of women's football and 'other boisterous sports taken up by the sex which is traditionally to be protected', this correspondent bemoaned what she considered the unfemininity of women's football.[32]

The *Meath Chronicle* published a letter received from Mrs Alice Farrelly in Athboy in response to similar comments that their columnist, Garrett Fox, made about women playing Gaelic football. Farrelly said:

> You're at it again, running down the ladies. What did they do to you? Some time ago I had a duel with you when you condemned camogie. Now that Meath G.A.A. are contemplating a ladies' football team you are not happy either. What do you want the girls to do? Spend their time in public houses or hanging around street corners? What kind of an 'Ould' crank are you? Let me tell you, a girl can kick a football or swing a caman as good as a man any time, and I think they have proved that so far. My proudest possession is a medal I won kicking football for the local I.C.A. when we beat the local convent girls in a friendly game in Athboy in 1973. So, come off it, Garrett, and be careful of Women's Lib.[33]

At the Annual Convention in 1976, delegates discussed the publicity afforded to ladies' football to date and resolved to make efforts to get greater publicity for the game as there was a feeling among some delegates that 'some reporters were making fun of the game and not giving it proper coverage.'[34]

Tom Rowley of the *Connaught Telegraph* – who had been elected as PRO of the LGFA at the convention in 1976 – prepared an information sheet on media practices and getting publicity for the LGFA. Rowley encouraged the association to develop strong relationships with local newspapers and reporters and to supply them with information and news. He also advised them to contact Jimmy McGee, the well-known sports broadcaster at RTÉ, to see if he would announce fixtures and results on his

```
KERRY TEAM  (Colour Green & White)                    OFFALY TEAM    (All Green)


                    (Sue Curtin)                                    (Geraldine Todd)


Noreen Thompson    Bernie Donoghue    Sue Moloney         Rose Dunican       Agnes Gorman        Patricia Glennon


Margaret Lawlor    Marie Murphy      Annette O'Connor     Ann Glennon       Phylis Hackett       Mary Carroll
                                                                             (Capt.)

        Del McLoughlin        Nora Donoghue                       Jo Glennon              Bernadette Dunne


Kathleen Brosnan    Mary Geary      Helen Slattery        Bridget Reynolds   Ann Molloy         Noreen Farnell
                    (Capt.)

Eileen Donoghue      Margaret Doherty · Mai Lombard       Evelyn Pyke        Mary Todd          Carmel Carroll




Subs.:    Anne Connell, Jackie Moriarty, Sheila Power,   Subs.:     Catherine Young, Catherine Hanlon,

          Melia Collins, Eileen O'Connor, Mary Ferris,              Margaret Prendergast, Madeline Flynn, Tara

          Mantilio McDonagh                                         McDonald, Mary Wyer, Francis Dolan.
```

Saturday radio show. Furthermore, he suggested that the LGFA make contact with camera operators in their local areas to get games recorded.[35]

Rowley also pointed out that it would be difficult to get national media coverage of women's Gaelic football. This could be seen in some counties, too, with the likes of Mick Fitzgerald, who held various coaching and administrative roles at county, provincial and national level with the LGFA, lamenting the lack of attention given by local media in Kerry to the women's team when they won their first All-Ireland title in 1976.[36] Still, Rowley ended by encouragingly stating: 'if there is enough publicity at local level in every County they will then realise the strength of the organisation of Ladies Football.'[37]

How the teams lined out in the 1976 All-Ireland final (Phyllis Price née Hackett).

The news that a nun was going to be lining out for Roscommon in the ladies Gaelic football final in November 1977 made national headlines (Via Marie McAleer née Holland, the *Irish Press* Archive © University College Cork).

The growing game was not without controversies, too. In the 1977 All-Ireland semi-final, Offaly beat Cavan 2–10 to 2–4, but Cavan lodged an objection to the LGFA, claiming that Offaly had fielded an ineligible player. There was much confusion regarding Cavan's objection and the All-Ireland final was postponed while the claim was investigated. Rumours that a man posing as a woman had played on the Offaly side were shut down as 'nonsense' by Phyllis Hackett, Offaly player and County Secretary. Offaly were insistent that all their players were correctly registered, including Alice Pendergast, who had a transfer to Offaly sanctioned by the LGFA. They were none the wiser as to the reason for the objection, with Hackett surmising that the situation was 'the most stupid set-up of all time'.[38]

Despite this, Offaly were disqualified from the competition for fielding an ineligible player and Cavan were awarded the place in the final. The Offaly ladies were 'despondent' and felt that 'somebody up there doesn't like them'. Furthermore, their trainer, Sean 'Whooper' Farrell, and Hackett, were both suspended for a year.[39] Incidentally, the LGFA National Congress had been due to be held in Tullamore in Co. Offaly the following February, but the host county were not officially informed about the congress and it was subsequently adjourned.[40]

In the other semi-final in 1977, Roscommon beat Kerry by a goal (2–3 to 1–3) to reach their first All-Ireland final. A 'master stroke of publicity' was also pulled off by Roscommon in the run-up to the 1977 All-Ireland final against Cavan, one which put women's Gaelic football on the front pages of the national media.[41]

The media attention was focused on Pauline Gibbons, one of the players on the Roscommon team who had recently joined the Augustinian Order of Nuns in Sussex. A key member of the Roscommon team, the Roscommon Ladies County Board wrote to her Mother Superior, asking permission for Sister Pauline to be granted special leave to in play the All-Ireland final.[42] Sister Pauline's Mother Superior (who also happened to be her aunt) duly obliged and joked in reply to Michael Naughton of the Roscommon board that 'we have told Sister Pauline that as well as keeping her eye on the ball to keep her eyes open for vocations, so do not blame me if you are minus many players by next All-Ireland Final.'[43]

According to Naughton, 'the media went to town' on the story of Sister Pauline lining out for the All-Ireland final and he maintains that the extensive coverage given to the story, in local and national newspapers, as well as on RTÉ, ensured that over 3,000 spectators turned out at Hyde Park, Roscommon for the final.[44] 'Big Match Prayers for Sister Pauline' was the headline that accompanied four photographs on the front page of the *Irish Press*. Despite the prayers said by the nuns at St George's Retreat in Sussex, Roscommon lost to Cavan on a score-line of 2–3 to 2–0, after which Sister Pauline returned to England to take up her vocation.[45]

Some of the 'making fun' of the game that delegates had worried about at the 1976 convention resurfaced in the aftermath of this game. Shocked that a nun was playing Gaelic football, a sports commentator with the *Southern Star* – writing under the pen-name 'Cois Laoi' – questioned if it was 'a joke or are we meant to take it seriously?' Acknowledging that he might be a 'male chauvinistic pig', the writer was outraged that a nun was partaking in this 'most-unladylike' activity and worried that convent schools might encourage such behaviour. His stance clearly stems from a patriarchal and religious outlook concerning gender roles. His disdain for 'unfeminine' women is obvious:

> In short, I don't like the idea of ladies' soccer or ladies' rugby or ladies' Gaelic football. By definition, no true lady would be seen dead or alive at such functions, but if there are tomboys or over-ebullient girls who like to participate in such activities, then the best of luck to them.[46]

Despite these negative comments, women were prepared to stand up for their right to practise sport and play football. In response to the article, the West Cork Ladies Football Board wrote to the editor of the *Southern Star* to defend women's Gaelic football and to clarify that the game was far from a joke. Similar to the letters received by the *Sunday Independent* a decade earlier in response to the letter from the Cork farmer, the women of West Cork once again noted the thankless jobs women had been doing in the GAA for years and their right to 'prove themselves worthy' of playing Ireland's national games.[47]

The 1978 Senior championship saw Cavan, Roscommon, Tipperary and Offaly take the silverware in their provinces to reach the All-Ireland semi-finals. Disappointed with losing both the Senior and Under–16 All-Ireland championship in 1977 to Cavan, Roscommon had the chance to settle the score when they travelled to Breffni Park in Cavan for the Senior All-Ireland semi-final. Ladies Gaelic football had only started up officially in Cavan in 1976 when the county board was founded, but the county had quickly established itself as a stronghold of ladies Gaelic football. The Mullahoran club won the first-ever All-Ireland club championship in 1977 and followed this up by reaching the final again in 1978. For the players on the Roscommon panel from the St Coman's club, there was added impetus to defeat Cavan as they had been Mullahoran's opponents in the 1977 club final. This score was duly settled, Roscommon coming away with a close 2–3 to 1–3 victory to march on to the final, where they beat Tipperary to win their first-

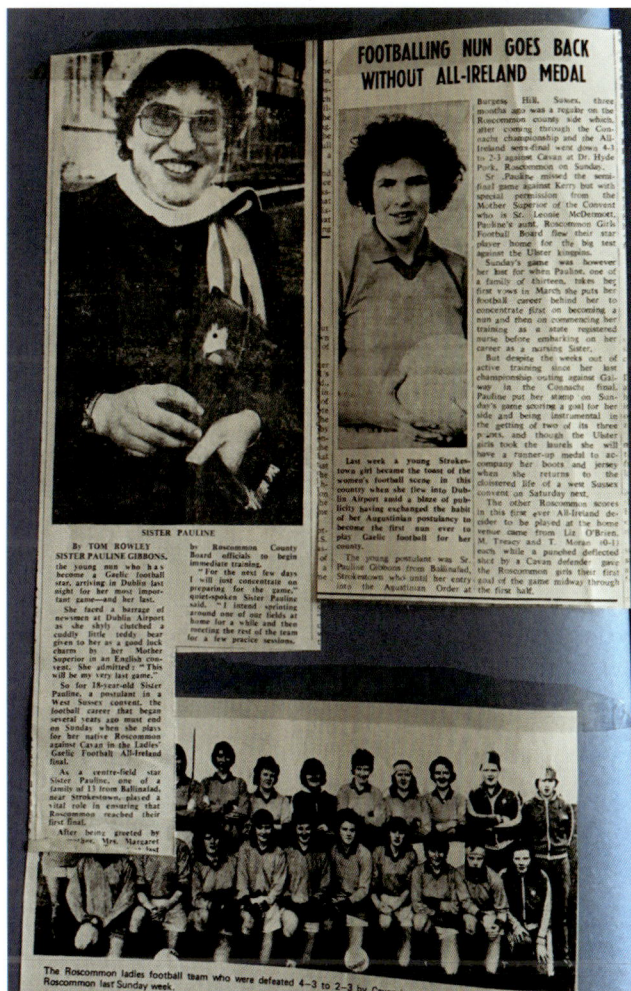

ever All-Ireland Championship, the first county from Connacht to do so.

A series of newspaper clippings about Sister Pauline's footballing exploits collected by Marie McAleer née Holland. (*Irish Independent* (left) and *Roscommon Herald* (right)).

Media attention was again unsatisfactory, causing Roscommon TD Terry Leyden to publicly condemn RTÉ for not televising the All-Ireland final, calling it 'discrimination against women'. Speaking to the Roscommon County Council, he advised them to send a 'resolution of protest' to RTÉ and implore them to televise the final in 1979, as well as the national Community Games finals. Leyden was supported by councillors Liam Naughton and Seamus

TELEPHONE BURGESS HILL 41527-8

Stations { Burgess Hill 2½ miles
{ Haywards Heath 3 miles

ST. GEORGE'S RETREAT,

P.O. BOX No. 1,

BURGESS HILL,

SUSSEX,

RH15 0SQ

I4th October, I977.

Michael Naughton Esq.,
Ladies Gaelic Football.
D..namult.
R..scommon.
Eire.

Received
20/10/77

Dea. Mr. Naughton,

Thank you for your letter of the 7th instant concerning Sister Pauline Gibbons. We are very pleased to allow Sister Pauline to play for Roscommon and arrangements have been made for her to go home on the 25th October. We wish you every luck with the game, all the Augustinian Sisters will be cheering your team on, we have told Sister Pauline that as well as keeping her eye on the ball to keep her eyes open for more vocations, so do not blame me if you are minus many players by next All Ireland Final.

Best wishes and good luck.

Yours sincerely,

Sister Mary Leonie

Reverend Mother

36, Lisnamult,

Roscommon,

Sun. 20.11.'77

The Mother Superior,
Augustian Order,
St. Georges Retreat,
Burgess Hill,
Sussex
England.

Dear Mother Superior,

With reference to Sister Pauline Gibbons. I have got
official confirmation that the All Ireland is on next Sunday 27th November, '77
at the Hyde Park, Roscommon at 1.30 pm. Our opponents are Cavan.
I would appreciate if Sister Pauline is allowed to play for Roscommon. Mrs.
Bridie Shiel was to ring you as confirmation of the game was delayed so that
before this letter arrives you will know the position.

Thanking you very much,

Yours sincerely,

Michael Naughton

MICHAEL NAUGHTON HON SEC.

◀

Letter from Sister Mary Leonie, Reverend Mother at St George's Retreat in Sussex, to Michael Naughton of the Roscommon LGFA County Board confirming that Sister Pauline had permission to travel back to Ireland to play for Roscommon in the All-Ireland final in 1978 (Marie McAleer née Holland).

Michael Naughton, Honorary Secretary of Roscommon LGFA, writes to Sister Mary Leonie with details of the upcoming All-Ireland final between Roscommon and Cavan. The final had been postponed after Cavan lodged an objection claiming that Offaly had fielded an ineligible player in their All-Ireland semi-final win over the Ulster county. The objection was upheld and Cavan were awarded a spot in the All-Ireland final (Marie McAleer née Holland).

Scott. Naughton called it 'deplorable' and suggested that if more prominent counties such as Cork or Dublin were playing in the final, RTÉ would have televised the game, while Scott added that the matter should be raised in the Dáil when RTÉ estimates were being debated.[48]

At the 1980 LGFA Annual Congress, the national media, including newspapers and RTÉ, were criticised for the lack of publicity they were giving the game.[49] Even the result of the All-Ireland final had not been reported by the national broadcaster.[50] Speaking to the *Evening Herald*, the Head of RTÉ's Sports Department, Fred Cogley, said that there wasn't enough national interest in ladies' football 'to warrant any fantastic response from us', while the Press Officer for the GAA, Pat Quigley, felt that the LGFA were not being persistent enough in seeking publicity.[51]

Senior All-Ireland honours were celebrated in Leinster in 1979 when Offaly became the fifth different county in six years (and the first from Leinster) to lift the Brendan Martin Cup when they beat Tipperary in a repeat of the 1974 final.

Again, this championship was not without controversy. Following Offaly's semi-final win over Galway, a complaint was lodged by Galway on the grounds that the Offaly team was not properly registered.[52] Despite lodging an objection, the final went ahead and the *Connacht Tribune* reported that Galway were 'furious' that their objection 'was not heard' by the LGFA.

Meanwhile, Tipperary added to their distinction of being the first All-Ireland champions by also being the inaugural winners of the LGFA National League in 1979. They were once again All-Ireland champions in 1980 when they beat Cavan in a very low-scoring game, 1–1 to 0–1. Keeping a link to Tipperary's first All-Ireland winning team, the 1974 All-Ireland-winning captain, Kitty Ryan-Savage, was part of the team's management in 1980, while

Lillian Gorey won her third All-Ireland medal, having featured in their previous two wins in 1974 and 1975. She was also rewarded with an All-Star at the inaugural ladies' All-Star Awards in 1980.[53]

By 1980 the LGFA boasted 2,300 members and thirteen counties were competing in the All-Ireland Championship.[54] The aforementioned first-ever All-Stars Awards in ladies' football were another sign of the game's development, featuring players from eight counties with Tipperary, Kerry and Offaly accounting for the highest representations.[55] The LGFA had fared well in establishing a competitive All-Ireland championship, expanding the number of competitions it offered at underage and adult level, and at county and club level, while also growing its membership base.

These wins were in spite of many challenges, as highlighted at a Donegal GAA County Board meeting in early 1979. A proposal was put to the board for the GAA to hold a ladies Gaelic football competition in the county. There was a mixed reaction to this proposal. One delegate argued that ladies Gaelic football would 'never get off the ground' in the county while the County Secretary suggested that if there was appetite for a competition it should fall on the women to organise it themselves. Another delegate expressed concern about getting referees for the games. The outcome appears to have been that 'if women want to start a competition the County Board will facilitate them as far as possible', according to one delegate.[56] Nevertheless, it demonstrates that support for the ladies' game was still not forthcoming from all quarters, a reality that was impacting the growth of the game.

Steps continued to be taken to combat this issue. The introduction of further underage competitions provided fresh opportunities for more girls and women to get involved in Gaelic football and demonstrated that the LGFA had a long-term vision for the game. After all, getting young girls involved in the game was essential if the game was going to have a future. The Roscommon County Board recognised this and set up a seven-a-side competition between local secondary schools in 1977. The board saw this as an 'urgent' matter, and noted that, although there might be some opposition to the competition, it was important to introduce young girls to the game as early as possible so that they could grasp the basic skills.[57]

There certainly was an appetite for these underage competitions. In 1974, the Roscommon Ladies County Board had received a letter from an 11-year-old girl in Boyle expressing her wish that someone would set up a team in her area.[58] In Cavan, 13-year-old Bernie Callaghan played in midfield on the All-Ireland-winning Senior and Under–16 county teams in 1977. Sensing an appetite for underage games, the Cavan County Board put plans in place to run an eleven-a-side competition in national schools in 1978 and also hoped that the game would feature in the Community Games programme.[59] Clearly, the sport was growing in popularity across all age groups and the LGFA needed to take advantage of this by running competitions at all levels.

Separate to the LGFA's competitions during this period, an inter-firms tournament was organised and took place in the Galway region in 1976. Among the workplaces represented were Digital (a computer manufacturing company), Ríomhaire Teo (an initiative of the industrial development agency Gaeltarra Éireann), University College Galway (UCG), Galway hospital, a veterinary practice, and CIÉ (the national rail company, today known as Irish Rail or Iarnród Éireann). The enthusiasm for the competition was high and it was expected that the women's competition would become a permanent fixture in the inter-firms calendar.[60] The competition was indeed held again in 1977 and featured teams from Quinnsworth, Vets, Gaeltarra Éireann, Digital, Northern Telecom, the Post Office and UCG.[61]

Despite the popularity of ladies' football, some counties did struggle in the early years to maintain interest. In Cork, translating interest from local level to inter-county football seems to have been an issue for the Cork LGFA County Board. Following their defeat to

Tipperary in the Munster Championship in 1979, one delegate at a county board meeting called the county side 'an utter disgrace'.[62] Recruiting players for the team and getting them to train appears to have been an issue, while it was also pointed out that some of the selectors on the team were not attending trials or training sessions.[63] Cavan faced a similar problem. It was noted at the County Convention in 1980 that they were finding it difficult to get players to turn up for training sessions and matches, though it was also noted that some players and clubs were dissatisfied with the county board.[64]

Women's Gaelic football faced distinct challenges in Northern Ireland in the early years of the LGFA. The political and military conflict of the Troubles created social and cultural challenges that made it difficult for women's Gaelic football to take off. There is evidence of women's Gaelic football being played at carnivals in Ulster in the late 1960s but only two counties from the province set up county boards in the 1970s and affiliated with the LGFA. Cavan founded their county board in February 1976 and celebrated much success in the subsequent years. The Armagh Ladies County Board was established under the guidance of Hugh Meehan in 1976, too, and were Cavan's only opposition in Ulster during the 1970s.

However, the Armagh Ladies County Board ceased operations in 1980. Armagh attributed the decline of women's Gaelic football in the county to a number of factors, including struggling to get new clubs involved and travel difficulties caused by the Troubles. An *Irish Press* report from 1974 highlights how Gaelic games were sometimes disrupted quite literally by the conflict, noting that a British Army helicopter landed on the pitch twice within minutes during a women's Gaelic football match between Crossmaglen and Culloville in Co. Armagh.[65]

Securing funding was also a challenge for the LGFA in the early years. Reviewing the activities of 1979, Michael Naughton, the Secretary of the Roscommon Ladies County Board, noted that 'our greatest difficulty is lack of funds' and concluded that 'this has an inhibiting effect on promotion and expansion' of the game in the county.[66] Women's Gaelic football in Roscommon lapsed in 1981, possibly due to the difficulties that Naughton mentioned in his Secretary's Report.

A letter received by the *Offaly Independent* in 1979 also raised the issue of finances. The correspondent claimed that the Offaly LGFA County Board had approached the Offaly GAA County Board for financial support, having reached the All-Ireland final. The reported request was turned down and the correspondent claimed it was because the secretary of the men's county board 'does not go along with the idea of women footballers' and wondered if he was a 'male chauvinist of the 18th century'.[67] The accuracy of the information in the letter could be questioned, however, as the correspondent also claimed that 'apparently all other counties recognise their women footballers – financially anyway', even though there is no evidence that ladies' football teams in the 1970s received any financial support from their male counterparts. The correspondent was correct in their assertion, though, when they noted that:

> Women today are doing a lot of things in sport, not open to them twenty years ago, and if they want to play football for recreation and to bring honour to their [counties] then they deserve all the recognition possible – financial and otherwise.[68]

Phyllis Hackett, Honorary Secretary of the Offaly LGFA County Board, subsequently set the story straight and asked the correspondent 'where on earth did she get her information', revealing that the ladies' board had never approached the GAA board for financial assistance.[69] In a follow-up letter, Hackett revealed that Mrs Maureen McLoughlin, the original letter writer, refused to reveal where she had sourced her information and clarified to readers that ladies' football was governed by a separate organisation to the GAA and had no need to 'beg', as they had been financially viable since the association was established in the county.[70]

What is undoubtedly true is that, despite some growing pains, in just a handful of years the LGFA had managed to cement itself as a recognised sporting organisation on the island of Ireland. Furthermore, the playing base of ladies Gaelic football increased in numbers, age ranges and geographical spread in this time. Organisational issues, such as defining the rules of the game and the laws of the association – so important in the development of the association – had been successfully set in stone. Growing ladies Gaelic football and the LGFA in these early years was a major success, particularly considering that the LGFA did not have the support of a more established sporting body or an international body.

Some issues endured, of course. The reaction to ladies Gaelic football from the media and the public was mixed. Generally it was well received but the game continued to face some backlash and scepticism. Then there was the matter of securing recognition from the GAA. Securing official recognition from the governing body and establishing a closer relationship was seen to be important in lending legitimacy to the game but, perhaps more significantly, to indicate that ladies Gaelic football was not just a passing phase.

This search for legitimacy, as they saw it, had faced many obstacles since the foundation of the LGFA.

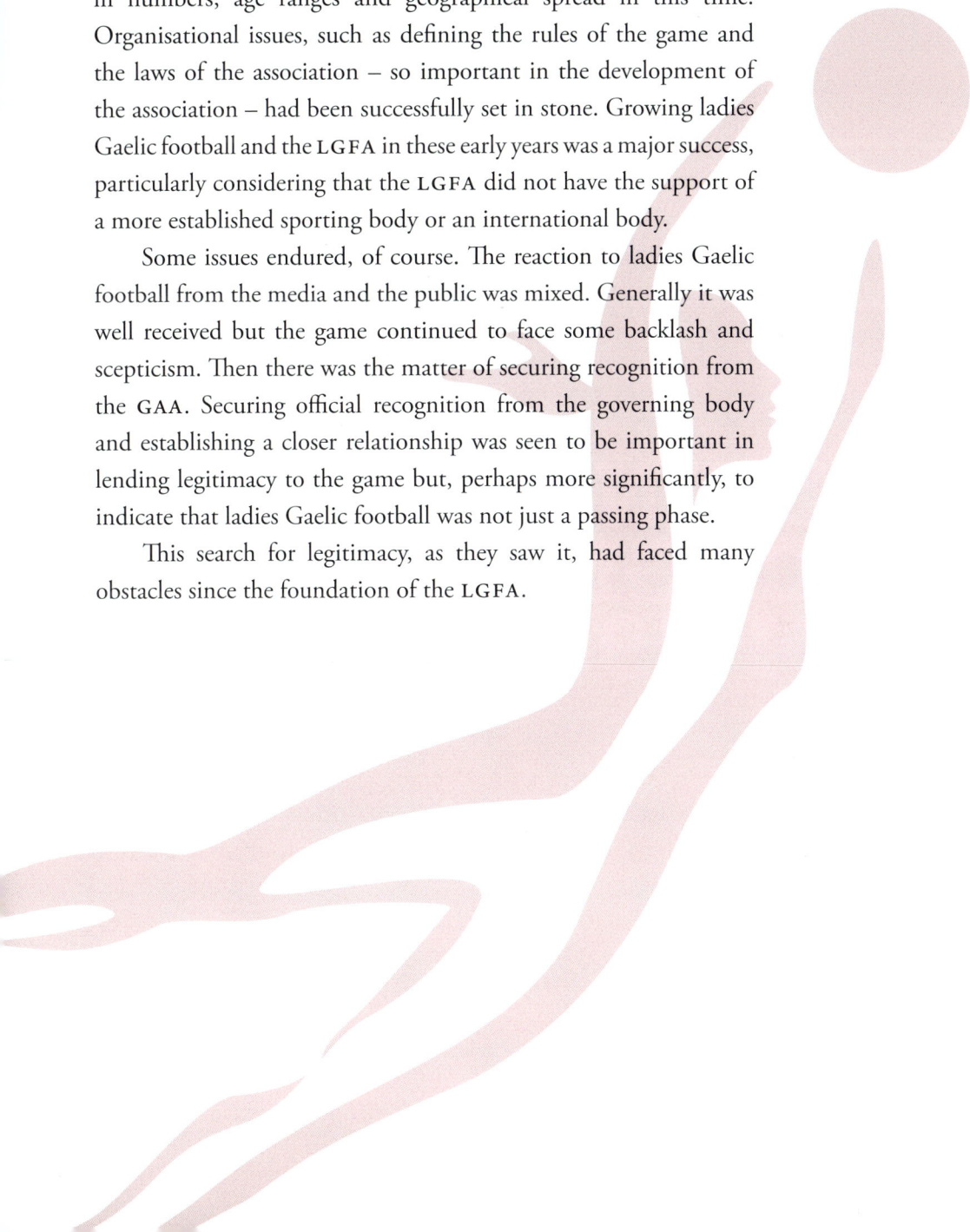

CUMANN LUTHCHLEAL GAE
MNA

— — ·· —

Membership Card

— — ·· —

CHAPTER 5

SEEKING RECOGNITION, 1974–1982

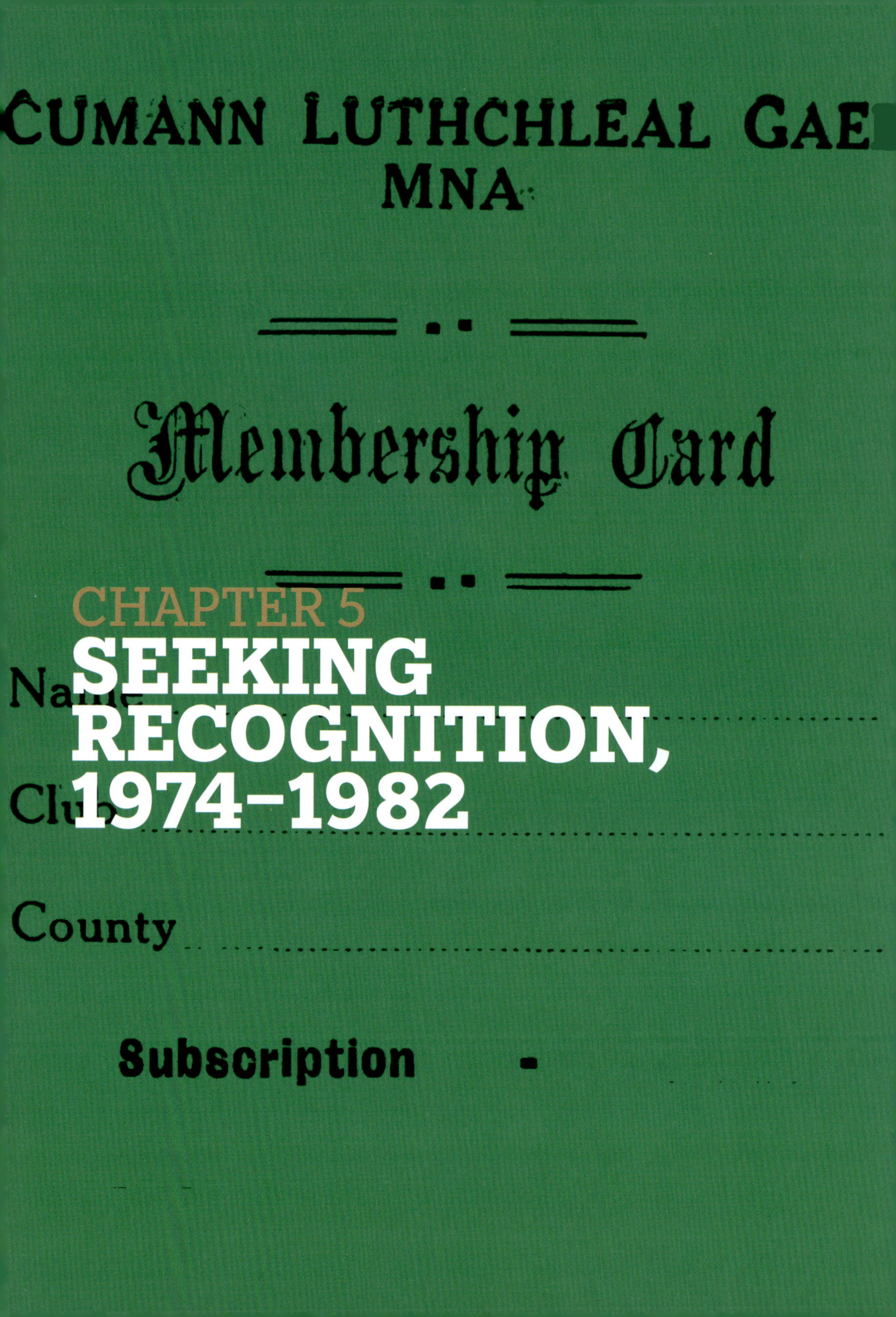

Name

Club

County

Subscription   -

From the outset the LGFA sought to establish a relationship with the GAA in order to get recognition for the women's game in the same way that camogie and the Camogie Association were acknowledged. The general consensus felt by LGFA members throughout the 1970s, however, was that the GAA 'didn't pass any heed' of the women's game when it was emerging, viewing it as no more than a fad that would fade away.[1]

As mentioned previously, the LGFA first tried to make contact with the GAA when it was established in 1974 to get recognition for the association and potentially get access to Croke Park for the first official All-Ireland final.[2] However, the GAA Central Council Minute Books from 1974 contain no reference to the newly formed LGFA or their request to play the final at GAA headquarter.

Before the end of 1974 there was a further call from a GAA club in Galway, Fr Griffins, for ladies' football to be affiliated to the GAA. The *Irish Press* called this a 'laudable idea' but suggested that it was a motion that should be considered by the Camogie Association rather than the GAA.[3] Chairman of the Galway County Board Sean

Purcell commented that the board 'has enough on its plate as it is' and did not believe that ladies' football was the correct way to get more women involved in the GAA, suggesting instead that involving women in the social side of the association might be a better policy, thereby reinforcing the belief that the GAA was an organisation that was only concerned with playing activities for men.[4] Sure enough, the proposal was not carried forward.

There is no mention of the LGFA again in the GAA Central Council Minute Books from 1975. The first official indication that the administrators of either the Camogie Association or the GAA were aware of the LGFA came in late 1975 when the Camogie Association sent representatives to a meeting of the GAA Connacht Council to outline the association's plans to re-organise the game in the province. The growing popularity of Gaelic football among women in the region was labelled a 'threat' to camogie at the meeting,

Central Council Officials

President: Tom Kenny, Belmount, Co. Offaly.
　　　　　　Phone: Ballinasloe 4139
Vice-Presidents: Provincial Chairpersons.
Sec.: Marie Holland, Ballintoiben, Castlerea,
Co. Roscommon Phone: Roscommon 0903/6232
Assistant Sec.: Veronica Sharkey, Co. Cavan.
Treasurer: Lynda Colgan, Co. Mayo
P.R.O.: Ultan Fitzpatrick, Sydanrath, Kells.
　　　　　　Co. Meath Phone: 338

Each player/official must hold a current membership card.
Membership fee divided into quarters:-
25 % to Club　　　　　25 % to County Committee
25 ,, to Prov. Councils　25 ,, to Central Council.
All returns i.e. 50% to be sent to the National Sec.
Marie Holland, Castlerea, Co. Roscommon

KELLS PRINTING WORKS

CUMANN LUTHCHLEAL GAEL MNA

Membership Card

Name *Phyllis Hackett*

Club

County

Subscription　　-

according to the *Tuam Herald*.[5] Tommy Lyons, Mayo Connacht Council delegate, noted that although many girls and women had recently turned to Gaelic football, he felt that 'the novelty will probably wear off', indicating again that the GAA did not consider ladies' football to be a game that had a long-term future.[6]

That said, this was clearly not a uniform opinion, as, at a meeting of the Mayo GAA County Board in December 1975, the board stated that they were 'very disposed towards anything that would help either the promotion of ladies' football or camogie' within the county.[7] At the same meeting, Fr Gerry Gillespie, President of the Mayo Ladies Board, called on the GAA to do more to encourage girls and women to get involved in Gaelic games in a playing capacity, and to recognise the role that women had long played within the association.

> The GAA is primarily catering for boys and men. This, for instance, is an all-male meeting. We should ask ourselves if we can do anything to provide for the young girls of the county. We have noticed that more young girls than boys are drinking today, merely because they have nothing better to do [...]For far too long girls

The membership card issued to LGFA members in the late 1970s (Phyllis Price née Hackett).

ALL IRELAND LADIES GAELIC FOOTBALL ASSOCIATION

Tel: 091/2141 (work)
     091/2842 (flat)

"St. Anthony's",
3 Eyre Street,
GALWAY.

<u>26th February, 1975</u>.

A Meeting of the All Ireland Ladies Gaelic Football Association Central Council will be held on Saturday, 8th March, 1975 in the Royal Hotel, Roscommon at 3.00 pm..

<u>AGENDA</u>

Discussion on Rules.

Enclosed is copy of proposed Rules.

Yours faithfully,

MARGARET COLLERAN.
Hon. Secretary.

A meeting of the LGFA Central Council was held in March 1975 with the rules of ladies Gaelic football the sole item on the agenda for discussion. A set of rules had been agreed for the 1974 championship but as the second annual championship rolled around there were calls to review the rules (Marie McAleer née Holland).

CHARTER, CONSTITUTION & RULES OF LADIES GAELIC FOOTBALL ASSOCIATION

1. The Name of the Association shall be the "Ladies Gaelic Football Association".

2. The membership and resources of the Association shall be utilized for the promotion of Ladies Gaelic Football.

3. The Association should co-operate with and actively assist other Organizations: the aims of which are the promotion of the Irish Language, Traditional Dancing, Music and Song and other aspects of Irish Culture.

4. The Association is a democratic Organization, structured on the following basis:-

   (i)   Members
   (ii) Clubs
   (iii) County Committees
   (iv) Provincial Councils, where feasible
   (v)   Central Council.

5. The game of Ladies Gaelic Football shall be played on a pitch not more than 140 yds. x 84 yds.. *Amend*

6. A Ladies Gaelic Football Team shall consist of fifteen players and will be allowed to have three substitutes.

7. A Team may commence a game with thirteen players, but shall forfeit the match unless the full complement has been attained by half-time.

8. A Team, not fulfilling a fixture, shall forfeit the match, unless three days notice of withdrawal has been furnished to the Central Council.

9. A Team, failing to field for a fixture, shall give three days notice to the Secretary of the opposing Team and also to the Secretary of the Central Council.

10. The match shall be refereed by a neutral Official, except in a case where agreement on a particular Official by both teams is reached.

11. The Referee shall be assisted by neutral Umpires and Linesmen.

12. If neutral Umpires are unavailable, each participating team must have a say in the selection of Umpires. If this is not acceptable, each team must have equal representation on the panel of Umpires.

The 'Charter, Constitution & Rules of Ladies Gaelic Football Association' was drafted for discussion at the March 1975 Central Council meeting. This document set out thirty-eight points regarding the aims of the LGFA and the playing of the game (Marie McAleer née Holland).

13. A Ladies Gaelic Football game shall last for a period of sixty minutes, with a ten minute interval. ✓

14. A Referee shall, if he deems it necessary, postpone a match. ✓

15. The Referee's decision in all matters relating to the actual game is final. ✓

16. A Referee must, within seven days of a fixture, furnish a full report of the match to the Secretary of the Central Council. ✓

17. If a Referee fails to furnish a match report within seven days, the Central Council has power to accept verbal report on that match from observers present. ✓

18. The game of Ladies Gaelic Football shall be played with a size 4 ball. ✓

19.. Where a size 4 ball is unobtainable, a size acceptable by both teams shall be used. ✓

20. The five-yard square will be in operation in all matches. ✓

21. A player shall be allowed to pick the ball cleanly off the ground. ✓

22. A forward obstructed within the square shall be deemed to have been fouled and a penalty kick shall be awarded to her team. Amend

23. A forward, within the square before the ball has been played there, shall be deemed to have committed a technical foul and a free out from the fourteen-yard line shall be awarded to the defending team. ✓

24. A player, who fouls an opposing player by tripping, kicking, pushing, elbowing, shouldering or pulling, shall be penalised and a free kick shall be awarded to the opposing team from the spot where the offence took place. ✓

25. A player, who persistently indulges in fouling, shall be warned by the Referee. If the fouling persists, the player's name shall be taken and the player shall be expelled from the field of play.

26. When the ball has been sent out of play over the sideline by a player, the opposing team shall receive a free kick from the spot in question. ✓

27. If a player deflects a ball over her own line, a free kick shall be awarded to the opposing team from the 30-yards range, at a parallel with the place where the ball went out of play. ✓

28. The goalkeeper shall not be charged or fouled in any way inside the parallelogram. ✓

Rules thirteen to twenty-eight proposed in the draft charter and constitution of the LGFA. Unlike men's Gaelic football where players have to put their toe under the ball to pick it up, rule twenty-one allowed the ball to be picked up directly off the ground. This rule was often in place for carnival games before the LGFA was founded and the rule still exists today (Marie McAleer née Holland).

29. A player shall be penalised for throwing the ball. ✓

30. A player is permitted to punch or palm the ball. ✓

31. The goalkeeper must wear a distinctive jersey. ✓

32. A player shall not take more than three paces when in possession of the ball. ✓

33. A player shall not make more than two consecutive hops with the ball. ✓

34. A player may make a toe-to-hand solo run for any distance. ✓

35. The ball must be punched, palmed or kicked into the goal mouth. ✓

36. A player, guilty of a late tackle, shall be penalized by having the free taken from the place where the ball landed. ✓

37. A player, mis-kicking a placed ball, may not play that ball again, unless it has been touched by another player. ✓

38. A player ordered off the field of play shall stand automatically suspended for fourteen days. ✓

Rules twenty-nine to thirty-eight up for discussion at the LGFA's Central Council meeting in 1975. There would be more calls in the future to review the rules of ladies Gaelic football as was to be expected for a developing sporting association (Marie McAleer née Holland).

have been doing the duty work in clubs, selling tickets, running buffets, etc. It is time something was now done in return for them.[8]

The lack of acknowledgment of the LGFA would appear to back up founding LGFA member Marie McAleer's estimation that the GAA thought that women's Gaelic football would not catch on.

Getting full recognition from the GAA, and getting the All-Ireland Ladies Football finals played in Croke Park, were objectives the LGFA felt 'very strongly about' in their early years.[9] This was once again demonstrated at the LGFA's Annual Convention in Roscommon in 1976 where it was decided to send a letter to the GAA Director General, Seán Ó Síocháin, seeking recognition.[10]

That year, talks between the two associations began to materialise. At a meeting on 9 April the first mention of the LGFA appears in the GAA Central Council Minute Books. At this meeting a decision was taken to 'give further consideration to the application for recognition by above Association [LGFA] and to defer the meeting which they sought with the officers'.[11]

Despite this apparent progress, it is clear that many within the GAA remained sceptical about the idea of women playing Gaelic football. At the GAA's National Congress in 1976, outgoing president Dr Donal Keenan gave an insight into the association's stance, as well as his personal viewpoint, in his speech:

> The closest cooperation exists between the Camogie Association and ourselves and this will continue in the future. Ladies' football has become a popular pastime recently and while we welcome their interest in any facet of our activities, as President, and also as a medical man, I suggest that camogie is a much more suitable game for our young women.[12]

Dr Keenan further expressed his fear that playing Gaelic football could cause serious injuries to women's breasts as a result of being struck by the ball. He advocated for sports bras to be

RULES

LADIES FOOTBALL IN IRELAND

1. The association shall be Cumann Luthchleas Gael Mna (The Ladies Gaelic Football Association).

2. The aims of the association shall be the preservation and promotion of Irelands National Games and pastimes in close co-operation with the main body C.L.C.G.

3. The association is a democratic organisation structured on the following basis:-

(a) Members (b) Clubs (c) County Committees

(d) Provincial Councils (e) Central Council

4. The membership and resources of this associaion shall be utilised for the promotion of Ladies Gaelic Football and Central Council shall appoint national organisers in each province.

5. Competitions shall be :-

(a) Senior Ladies over 14 yrs. 1st January, each year

(b)   under 16 yrs. after   ,,   ,, ,,

6. (a) A size four football to be used in all competitions.

(b) Players may pick up the ball in the usual manner or lift it of the ground with either or both hands

7. All deliberate body contact be eliminated but

(a) shading an opponent

(b) fielding the ball

(c) blocking the delivery of a ball by an opponent may still be continued as part of play and developed further to uplift the game

8. The attire shall be similar to that of the mens with the addition of a protective breast garment to be worn by all players

9. Referees shall be ladies but until sufficient members and standards are reached men from official panels may take charge of games.

10. The running of affairs in general shall be bound by the Official Guide C.L.C.G., except when covered by ''Rules for Ladies'' above.

On the back of the LGFA's membership card, the organisation and rules of the LGFA were set out. Ladies Gaelic football followed similar rules to men's Gaelic football with some differences including that the game was to be played with a size four football instead of a size five, players were allowed to pick up the ball directly off the ground, and deliberate body contact was disallowed (Phyllis Price née Hackett).

```
                                        36, Lisnamult,
                                        Roscommon,
                                        24th August, 1976.

The Secretary,
All-Ireland Ladies Gaelic Football
Council,
Ballintubber,
County Roscommon.

Dear Secretary,
                    On behalf of the Roscommon Ladies Gaelic
Football County Board may I ask if any progress has been made
in getting talks going between the G.A.A. and Ladies Gaelic
Football Association at top level?
                    Also does the Ladies Gaelic Football Association
not consider that some changes are necessary in the playing
rules to counter allegations from various quarters that the
game as presently constituted for women bears too near a
similarity to men's football?
                    Strong doubts have been expressed by medical
people, members of the G.A.A., parents etc. that the game if
played strictly in accord ( or even with slight modifications )
with men's football, would be dangerous on medical grounds; too
robust for participation by a great many girls and unattractive
as a spectacle!
                    Our County Board urges that contact be renewed
at once with the G.A.A. with regard to talks and that the Ladies
Gaelic Football Association consider as a matter of urgency the
setting up of a Comitte with a view to fresh appraisal of
existing playing rules.

                        Yours  sincerely,

                        Miceal O'Neactain, Runai
                        Roscommon Ladies Gaelic
                        Football County Board.
```

Michael Naughton, Secretary of the Roscommon Ladies County Board, wrote to the LGFA in the summer of 1976 seeking an update on the talks with the GAA and a 'fresh appraisal of the existing playing rules' as some people felt that the game was 'too robust' and 'unattractive as a spectacle!' See chapter 4 (Marie McAleer née Holland).

worn by female Gaelic footballers for protection and was relieved to hear when, in 1977, the LGFA arranged for a consignment of sports bras to be sent to playing members of the association.[13] Lynda Colgan, Vice-President of the LGFA, said:

We have been worried for some time about the danger of injury to our more tender areas the game could [cause]. It was Dr. Keenan who first came up with the idea of the padded bras and these, we are confident, will eliminate the main dangers of injury. The members of the Association are all for the bras. From what we are told they differ little from the ordinary type of bra, except that they are stronger and have special padding. As far as we know no girl so far has received any serious injury playing the game, apart from the odd bruise or cut.[14]

As previously stated, this was a prevailing medical myth, albeit one that would soon begin to be undermined. In a piece written by Geraldine Grennan about ladies Gaelic football for the *Evening Herald*, a spokesperson for the Irish Cancer Society stated that there was no evidence linking breast cancer to blows received to the chest area, calling it an old wives' tale.[15]

There were already voices of dissent to these views from within the LGFA. Dermot Shanahan, PRO of the Tipperary Ladies County Board, conveyed the board's disappointment at the sentiments expressed by Dr Keenan and voiced hope that the new GAA President, Con Murphy, would back ladies' football during his tenure.[16] Players in Kildare also took umbrage at Dr

Keenan's remarks and argued that Gaelic football for women was only dangerous if not refereed properly. 'Women are genuinely interested in the game but not for badly run carnival matches. Women in the game in Kildare are serious about it. It is a sport for them just as badminton, tennis, swimming is for other women,' said player Ruth D'Arcy.[17]

The month following the GAA's Annual Congress in 1976, the GAA agreed to meet with the LGFA for a 'general discussion'. It appears that the LGFA sought out this meeting in order to get recognition from the GAA, whereas the GAA set out in the minutes of a meeting on 8 May that their expectation for the meeting was that the LGFA 'might be influenced to make their game more acceptable and dignified and less dangerous for Irish girls'.[18]

Before the meeting, the GAA decided to first consult the Camogie Association to get their views on ladies Gaelic football. The President of the Camogie Association, Úna Uí Phuirséil, as well as the association's PRO and Secretary, attended the meeting with Con Murphy and Sean Ó Síocháin. The Camogie Association's Central Council Minute Books outline a summary of the discussion, which gives an interesting insight into the GAA's and Camogie Association's thinking at the time:

The GAA representatives sympathised with our views, accepted entirely that we would not be in a position

Keen to improve ladies Gaelic football, the LGFA wrote to all county secretaries in early 1977 asking for their input on the current rules of the game and the running of the association (Marie McAleer née Holland).

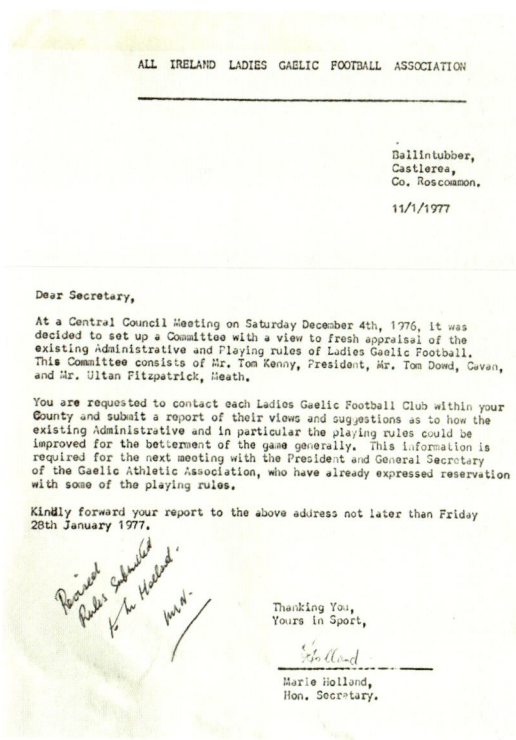

ALL IRELAND LADIES GAELIC FOOTBALL ASSOCIATION

Ballintubber,
Castlerea,
Co. Roscommon.

11/1/1977

Dear Secretary,

At a Central Council Meeting on Saturday December 4th, 1976, it was decided to set up a Committee with a view to fresh appraisal of the existing Administrative and Playing rules of Ladies Gaelic Football. This Committee consists of Mr. Tom Kenny, President, Mr. Tom Dowd, Cavan, and Mr. Ultan Fitzpatrick, Meath.

You are requested to contact each Ladies Gaelic Football Club within your County and submit a report of their views and suggestions as to how the existing Administrative and in particular the playing rules could be improved for the betterment of the game generally. This information is required for the next meeting with the President and General Secretary of the Gaelic Athletic Association, who have already expressed reservation with some of the playing rules.

Kindly forward your report to the above address not later than Friday 28th January 1977.

Thanking You,
Yours in Sport,

Marie Holland,
Hon. Secretary.

Following a request by the All Ireland Ladies Gaelic Football Assoc for a meeting, a delegation from the Association, met the President of the G.A.A, Mr. Con Murphy, the General Secretary, Mr. Sean O'Siochain and Dr. Donal Keenan, at Croke Park at 3. pm on Saturday 25th September.
Mr. Murphy welcoming the delegation and after hearing Mr. Thomas Kenny, President of the Ladies G.A.A. outline the aims, progress and activitie of the Association, expressed pleasure at the steady progress of the game in such a relatively short time. He hoped that there would be the most cordial and helpful relationship between the Ladies G.A.A. and the Camogie Association and expressed the hope that the rules of Ladies football , which are similiar in many respects to men's football, would be suitable modified , where necessary, to render the game as attract- ive and as safe as possible.
Mr. T. O'Sullivan (Kerry) assured the President that their was no conflict between Ladies Football and Camogie. In Kerry many girls were dual exponents of football and Camogie and compatibility was evident in every county in the Country where the two games were played.
Mr. T. Kenny added that this was his experience too and that co-existence was one of the aims of the Ladies G.A.A.
Mr. Thomas Dowd (Cavan) expressed the opinion that the playing of unofficial Ladies Football games at Festivals etc, more or less as fun games, without proper supervision, was damaging to the Association and gave a wrong impression of the game.
Dr. Donal Keenan spoke about the medical issues inherent in football as such issues might affect girls. He had nothing against the game. It was his opinion that a protective bra should be worn, just as female athletes competing in certain sports in the U.S.A. were obliged to wear protective gear. This protective bra would be light and in no way cumbersome. Mr. Sean O'Siochain added that he hoped some Irish Firm would manufacture this protective bra in the near future.
At the conclusion of the meeting the L.G.A.A. were happy with progress made and viewed it as a major step forward in recognition of the Assoc. The President of the G.A.A. Mr. Con Murphy has arranged a further meeting with the Ladies Football Assoc. for December.
The Delegation was comprised of a representative from each province.
Thomas Kenny , President (Leinster), Mr. Paul O'Sullivan (Munster) Mr. Thomas O'Dowd (Ulster) and Miss Lynda Colgan (Connacht).

Press release from All Ireland Ladies Football Central Council

A copy of the press release issued by the LGFA following a meeting with the GAA in Croke Park in September 1976 which expressed hope that a 'most cordial and helpful relationship' would develop between the LGFA, the GAA and the Camogie Association (Marie McAleer née Holland).

to organise it [the running of ladies Gaelic football] even if we wished to be associated with it, hoped that it would not have a detrimental effect on the progress of Camogie. Both gentlemen would prefer that Camogie rather than football would be promoted by the GAA County Boards + [and] members, + [and] while they would be extremely reluctant to give Ladies' Football official recognition as they felt it was an unsuitable game for girls, had one fear that total rejection by the GAA might result in the loss of these girls to GAA games.[19]

At a press conference in Dublin in August 1976, the LGFA outlined the two main objectives of the association. First, their ambition was to have all thirty-two counties affiliated to the LGFA and participating in the All-Ireland championship. Their second aim was 'to persuade the G.A.A. to recognise the game as [G]aelic sport, similar to camogie, and to take it under its wing.'[20] The urgency with which the LGFA wanted the GAA to recognise the association was spelt out clearly: 'However, the association is not willing to wait as long and go through the long and arduous battle camogie did before it was finally recognised by the G.A.A.'[21]

It appears that the LGFA was disheartened by the lack of support from the GAA and they looked to counter any possible arguments that this was a passing fad, highlighting that women and girls were playing Gaelic football out of genuine interest.

Ladies playing gaelic football may surprise many people. Yet if one looks at it seriously and realistically it was inevitable. For years wives and girl friends have been dedicated followers and morale support behind their men as they played their weekly games at club and even county level. Their interest in the game grew and [it was] only a matter of time before they decided to give vent for their interest by playing the game. Once a few ladies started the ball rolling, then there was no stopping it.

[...] Ladies football is played by an across-the-board selection of people, from secretaries, office workers, factory workers and schoolgirls to housewives. The game as played by ladies is based on skill and speed and contains only a fraction of the physical contact evident in men's gaelic football.

It has a bright future as more and more women become involved. It has the great advantage of needing few facilities, as virtually every town and village has a gaelic football pitch which the ladies can use. What was once a minority sport, played only in the back gardens by the wives and children of footballers, is now becoming really big.[22]

The LGFA was disheartened by the lack of support from the GAA and they looked to counter any possible arguments that this was a passing fad, highlighting that women and girls were playing Gaelic football out of genuine interest.

Following the eventual meeting between the LGFA and the GAA in 1976, the LGFA issued a press release. LGFA President Tom Kenny stated that delegates from the LGFA had met with the GAA at Croke Park on 25 September to outline the aims, progress and activities of the LGFA, and hoped that, moving forward, there would be a 'most cordial and helpful relationship' between the LGFA, the Camogie Association and the GAA. The LGFA stressed that there was little or no conflict between women's Gaelic football and camogie so far, and they were eager for both games to co-exist.[23]

Clearly the LGFA were looking to reassure the Camogie Association, as well as advocating for the idea that bringing the LGFA within the umbrella of the GAA would be a reputational benefit for the GAA as a whole.

Talks continued between the associations in the following years, with delegates from the LGFA and the GAA meeting a number of times between 1977 and 1979. During this period representatives from ladies' football also sought support from their respective male county boards to get recognition from the GAA.[24] The Tipperary men's County Board brought the motion to recognise ladies' football forward to the GAA Annual Convention in 1977, but it was withdrawn as the GAA were in discussions with the LGFA and were waiting on the association 'to conform with recommendations made'.[25]

In 1980, a motion calling for recognition of ladies' football was put to the GAA Annual Congress again, this time by Leitrim. The LGFA also noted their continued disappointment that the association and the game was still not recognised by the GAA at their Annual Congress in 1980.[26]

The following year a motion was put forward by Cavan.[27] The motion urged 'that the GAA should recognise Ladies Football and that a committee be set up at national level to establish how best this can be achieved'.

It was passed.

Former LGFA President Tom Dowd and Tipperary player Marian O'Shea sat on the committee alongside GAA officials.[28] Minutes from a meeting of the committee in February 1982 laid out three arguments against ladies' football: first, that the game was 'unladylike'; second, that there was a possibility that playing ladies' football could cause breast cancer (though it was noted that this was not proven); and, finally, that the game 'affects Camogie'. However, the minutes noted that there were no figures available to support this and that the Ard Rúnaí (General Secretary) of the Camogie Association 'preferred not to comment'.

On the other hand, six points were put forward in favour of ladies' football, including the large numbers already playing the game (approximately 4,000), the high standard of games, the association's well-established structures and 'keen interest' in working with the

GAA, that the game 'promotes better social climate in clubs', and the health benefits for women from being involved in physical exercise.

A further meeting took place in March on which some of the points above were discussed in more detail. The belief that the game was 'unladylike' and 'unbecoming' for girls was argued to be subjective and it was pointed out that this argument had been used against women taking part in other sports, such as athletics, in years gone by. The issue of insurance was also discussed, and the need to be sensitive to the Camogie Association was repeated, as ladies Gaelic football was seen to be in competition with it.

The meeting appears to have been in favour of ladies' football, overall, with further points in favour of the game added:

> [W]hen girls take part in Ladies Gaelic football they understand the rules of the game and because of that, they take a greater interest in watching the men playing Gaelic football. Secondly, they also are more skilled as spectators and have a better understanding of the game. Lastly, it was pointed out that it is better to have girls who wish to play football playing Gaelic Football rather than playing some other code.

Clearly, the GAA was coming around to ladies Gaelic football. The committee's report that was submitted to the GAA's Coiste Bainistíochta outlined that ladies Gaelic football was 'not going to disappear' and that the association should therefore develop a policy towards it, given that the association's early attitude – which was described as sceptical 'on the grounds of health and aesthetics' – no longer stood.

The committee also reported that they held a long discussion on the issue of recognition, after which it was agreed that 'it was not possible, in the normal sense of the Association, to recognise Ladies Gaelic Football, because this would have no meaning.' No further details are supplied on what a supposedly 'meaningful' recognition of the LGFA would require.

The committee's recommendation was that the GAA notify its county boards that they had 'no objection' to ladies Gaelic football and clubs should be asked to 'co-operate where possible' with the LGFA.

Later in 1982, a form of recognition did arrive – if with little ceremony. Mick Fitzgerald, the LGFA President at the time, recalls simply being handed a scroll in the Gresham Hotel in Dublin by GAA President Paddy Buggy. This said that the GAA recognised the LGFA.[29]

For all their apparent reluctance, however, it must be noted that prior to getting official support from the GAA Central Council, local GAA clubs and county boards did lend their support to women's Gaelic football through the provision of facilities, without which the game would have struggled to develop. For example, in September 1976 it was reported in *The Cork Examiner* that a 'Breakthrough for Ladies Football' had been made by fixing the upcoming Munster Final for the county grounds in Kerry: Fitzgerald Park in Killarney.[30] The game was fixed to take place before the Senior Kerry Club Final between Austin Stacks and Kenmare, which would have attracted a significant crowd. It also signalled that the Kerry men's County Board were willing to support the women's game. This was reciprocated in other counties, including Roscommon, who made Hyde Park available when possible.

Although the LGFA was (and remains) independent of the GAA, this cordial relationship – now enhanced by official recognition (whether meaningful or not) – had been central to the promotion and legitimisation of the sport.

CHAPTER 6
MAKING STRIDES, 1980–1989

As the LGFA approached a decade in existence, the game was building momentum. By the early 1980s, the LGFA were consistently running national inter-county championships at adult, Under–18 and Under–16 grades, as well as a national adult inter-county league, a national club championship and an inter-provincial tournament. In 1981 and 1982, there were enough counties taking part to warrant running a second division of the inter-county National League, which was introduced permanently from 1986. It was a time of cultural and social vitality in which the LGFA was firmly establishing itself as a legitimate sporting organisation, and the expansion of their competitions meant that more women and girls were playing Gaelic football.

The overall standing of the game was also on the rise, as pointed out by the *Nationalist and Leinster Times* in striking language:

> Not so long ago the sight of ladies trading tackles on a football field would have raised a thousand eyebrows. Times have changed. Now legions of lassies all over the country are mastering the arts of

Gaelic Football, for ages an exclusive male exercise. No longer are the fairer sex frowned upon as brazen hussies when [swapping] skirts for shorts and high heels for studs. Female football has developed into a more skilled activity enjoyed in many counties with Laois one of the leaders in the emerging code. Ladies' football was 'for the birds' as far as the guys were concerned but the gals are now drawing admiring glances, not for shape of figure but the way they adapted to the game.[1]

The standout on-field story from this decade was the ascent of a truly outstanding ladies Gaelic football team – Kerry. Kerry had announced themselves as an up-and-coming team when they won the National League in 1980. In 1981, they made it as far as the All-Ireland semi-final, losing to eventual winners Offaly by three points. This was the last championship match Kerry would lose until 1992.

The roll of honour speaks for itself: eleven National League titles in twelve years (1980–91), ten Munster Championships in a row (1981–90), and nine All-Ireland titles in nine years (1982–90). The sum of All-Ireland titles won in a row by the Kerry ladies is a feat not matched by an inter-county Gaelic football team, male or female, before or since. From 1982 to 1985 and from 1987 to 1990 Kerry won all the silverware available in a given year at Senior level. The county were also back-to-back Under–18 All-Ireland winners in 1980 and 1981.

Writing a piece for *The Kerryman* in 1984, then LGFA President and Kerry trainer, Mick Fitzgerald, praised the team:

The present team, having won the last two All-Irelands and four National Leagues in succession are, without doubt, the best team that I have seen since ladies' football started. They were undefeated from August, 1981, until Cork beat them in the first round of the National League in April this year. They are great girls to train, are very loyal and dedicated and deserve all the success that has come their way.[2]

Kerry captain Marion Bowler (née Doherty) is lifted onto her teammates' shoulders to raise the Brendan Martin Cup in 1982. Kerry defeated reigning All-Ireland champions Offaly in the decider, 1–8 to 1–2, and went on to win the next eight All-Ireland titles (Marion Bowler née Doherty).

Fitzgerald's appraisal was more than deserved. Their dedication and skill earned the county an incredible thirty titles at Senior inter-county level over a twelve-year period.

This was during a period, too, when ladies Gaelic football was expanding around the country and, with it, the number of counties competing and the number of games played. Kerry faced five different opponents in the nine All-Ireland finals they contested. Only one of these (Offaly) had reached an All-Ireland final and won it before. Wexford (1983, 1986, 1989), Leitrim (1984), Laois (1985, 1988, 1990) and Westmeath (1987) all made All-Ireland finals for the first time in the 1980s, a testament to the growth of ladies Gaelic football. It was just unfortunate that, as they were developing, they came up against one of the greatest ever ladies Gaelic football teams.

The Kerry football team was packed full of talent, evidenced by the amassing of a total of sixty-two All-Star Awards between 1980 and 1993. Among the awardees were sisters Eileen and Margaret Lawlor, who hold ten All-Stars and twenty All-Ireland titles between them, Kathleen Curran (née Kennedy; she won two All-Stars while playing for Dublin and a further five with Kerry), Marina Barry (six), Bridget Leen (five) and Dell White (four).

Kerry pose for a team photo before the throw-in to the 1989 All-Ireland final against Wexford. The Kingdom won their eighth All-Ireland title in a row, beating Wexford 1–14 to 1–5 (Mary Jo Curran).

The stand-out star, though, was Mary Jo Curran from Beaufort. Curran was awarded an incredible eleven All-Star Awards between 1980 and her retirement from inter-county football at the end of the 1993 season. This amazing number of individual accolades, coupled with her ten All-Ireland medals, makes for a strong argument that Curran is among the greatest ladies Gaelic footballers of all time.

Speaking to Sinéad Kissane of the *Irish Independent* in 2022, Mary Jo Curran recalled how only a small number of people celebrated their success, highlighting how ladies' football had yet to capture the popular imagination, both in Kerry and further afield. She added, 'We never thought about records. You'd just be looking at the next game. Like three-in-a-row and four-in-a-row, there was never a sense that we were creating history. The funny thing is, it [the lack of recognition] didn't bother us at the time and we didn't know any better.'[3]

Despite the small number of people who celebrated their achievements, it was clear that ladies' football was thriving in

Kerry. The strength and depth of ladies' football in the county was exemplified by the fact that Kerry was able to field both a Senior and a Junior team in 1987.[4] Success was clearly also bringing in a younger generation; the average age of the Kerry panel in 1987, when they won their sixth All-Ireland title in a row, was just twenty-two.[5]

It was clear that other counties were also on the rise. In 1986, Wexford qualified for four All-Ireland finals – Senior, Junior, Under–16 and Under–18.[6] Wexford and Laois were also able to field two teams at adult level.[7] Among the counties to affiliate to the LGFA for the first time in the 1980s were Longford, Limerick, Clare, Dublin, Carlow, London and Wicklow. In Munster, all six counties were affiliated to the LGFA by 1984, with Limerick and Clare having come on board in the early 1980s.

However, while affiliations were growing in Munster and Leinster, the other two provinces struggled somewhat during this period. Cavan and Roscommon, winners of the Brendan Martin Cup in 1977 and 1978 respectively, both experienced a drop-off in interest in the 1980s. The Roscommon County Board was disbanded around 1981, leaving just three counties competing in Connacht (until the board was re-grouped in 1985). Cavan, the only county in Ulster affiliated to the LGFA, disbanded its county board in 1984.

To lose two counties that had shown great potential and interest in the early years of the LGFA was disappointing. Still, considering that many counties reported diffic-

Kerry player Dell White celebrates winning another All-Ireland title with her daughter Melissa (Adrienne McLaughlin).

ulties in maintaining and growing ladies Gaelic football in the 1980s, it can be argued that it was a positive that more counties did not fold.

The Leitrim LGFA called an emergency meeting of the county board in March 1987 following the county team's narrow defeat to Wexford to 'discuss the future of ladies' football at senior level in the county'.[8] There was a feeling in the county that they were going backwards rather than forwards. Leitrim had established their county board in 1978 and within a few years were competing for silverware. They reached back-to-back finals in 1982 and 1983, while also losing the Under–18 All-Ireland finals in both years, winning the Division 2 National League title in 1982, and losing to All-Ireland champions Kerry in the Division 1 National League final in 1983. After that, results had worsened. The county team suffered a further league defeat in 1987 to Westmeath, and ahead of their clash with the reigning All-Ireland champions, Kerry, the local newspaper said that the Leitrim ladies faced a 'mammoth task' as 'good performances have been thin on the ground' recently, despite having made an All-Ireland final two years ago.[9] Indeed, despite the fact that Kerry could only field fourteen players, Leitrim lost heavily (1–14 to 0–1).[10]

Yet perhaps their emergency meeting was an inspired decision. By the following year, Leitrim had re-grouped and their hard work was rewarded when they won a first-ever All-Ireland title for the county, defeating London in the Junior decider. The effort and commitment put into rejuvenating Leitrim football was carried out by leaders both on and off the field of play, like Mary Quinn, who was the county's chairperson and team's left half-back. Her prevailing memory of that year's win was not necessarily the time and energy put into the football but rather the fundraising to run Leitrim LGFA. Her first thought after the final whistle in 1988 was, she said, 'where is the ball? Get it and put it back in the bag. Don't lose any of our stuff. Because, you know, you had to work so hard to get money, to get jerseys, to get balls.'[11]

The position of ladies' football in Longford also appeared to have weakened by 1987. At the AGM, it was noted that the small turnout for the meeting appeared to signify that 'interest in the game in Longford has rapidly decreased [...] Delegates from all clubs present seemed to agree that they have fewer members than in previous years.'[12] As a result of the reduced playing base in the county, it was decided at the AGM to run the County Senior League as a seven-a-side competition rather than a fifteen-a-side one.[13] The notes encouraged women to get involved and stated that an Under–16 competition would be organised later in the year to facilitate teenage girls to play the game, stating:

So for all you energetic girls out there this is the ideal opportunity for you to get involved in an entertaining sport which will keep you fit for the summer months! Remember, you don't have to be an expert to start – practice will make perfect![14]

Clare LGFA faced difficulties, too. At their annual convention in December 1987, proceedings had to be deferred to January 1988 due to the failure to fill a number of the administrative positions on the county board. It was noted that, although there were a number of clubs in the county and that the game had seen progress, 'the running of the affairs has been left to a few. If the game is to get stronger in the county then clubs will have to get people to fill these important positions.'[15]

The challenges were further highlighted by Laois footballer Connie Conway, who told the *Nationalist and Leinster Times* that, although ladies Gaelic football was no longer a novelty, it could be difficult to recruit players. Conway had initially played with Killeshin but the club folded due to lack of numbers in the area, with many young women moving away for employment. Conway cited a number of difficulties contributing to the slow expansion of the game, including lack of publicity, lack of women taking on coaching roles, administrative issues, a failure to introduce

GALWAY LADIES JUNIOR FOOTBALL TEAM 1985. ALL-IRELAND WINNERS 1985.

Back row left to right: Geraldine Geoghegan, Martha Mullarkey, Liz Lyons, Pauling McEvoy, Bernie Minton, Patricia Farragher, Mena Costello, Jeanette Hynes, Sally Carty, Eithne Bonner, Margaret Morris, Caroline Vaughan.
Front row left to right: Mary Daly, Marie Vaughan, Liz Hernon, Ann Morris (Player of the Match), Ann Marie Lynch, Sheila Flanagan, Kathleen Cronin, Una Burke, Nono McHugh, Margaret Coen, Mary Burke, Alma Quinn.

In 1985 the LGFA introduced the Junior All-Ireland championship and the honour of winning the first title went to Galway, pictured here. Galway beat Cork in the final on a score-line of 5–7 to 0–3 (Maura Conneally).

The All-Ireland Junior champions of 1985, Galway, reunite over thirty years later in 2016. The team were introduced to the crowd at half-time during the 2016 Division 1 match between Galway and Cork at Tuam Stadium and each player was presented with a commemorative medal to mark the occasion (Maura Conneally).

schoolgirls to ladies' football and the stubbornly persistent belief that playing football was an unladylike activity.[16] For an independent association with limited resources these were no doubt troubling issues.

Emigration in recession-hit 1980s Ireland, as people moved abroad in search of work, undoubtedly hampered the growth of ladies Gaelic football at home. However, it did open up new opportunities to take the game overseas. The London County Board was established in 1986. This was the first women's Gaelic football board to be established outside Ireland and they officially affiliated with the LGFA in 1988.

To support the new London LGFA, it was arranged for a group of players and coaches to travel from Ireland to London in 1988 to run a coaching course to bring the London board and players up to speed on the game. The course consisted of a refereeing course, a sports injuries seminar, a demonstration of the skills of the game, as well as an exhibition match between the travelling players and a London selection.[17] Though the Irish team defeated London easily, London were not disheartened and they entered a county team that year into the All-Ireland championships. In fact, the fast-rising strength of ladies Gaelic football in the English capital was evident in London reaching the All-Ireland Junior final in 1988, in which they were beaten by Leitrim.

Four new clubs were inaugurated in the English capital in 1989, symptomatic of the high numbers of Irish people now living in London. Teams were set up in other parts of Britain, too, including Lancashire in the north-west of England and Warwickshire in the west midlands, to facilitate those who had moved to cities such as Liverpool, Manchester, Blackpool and Birmingham. However, these areas outside the English capital struggled somewhat to sustain and grow ladies Gaelic football.

Another avenue the LGFA availed of to broaden its scope and get more women playing Gaelic football during this period was through higher education.

The interest was already there, seemingly as far back as the mid-1970s. A third-level competition appears to have taken place in late 1975 and into 1976. A report in the *Tuam Herald* recounted a match between Galway RTC (Regional Training Centre) and Athlone that featured county players from Galway and Offaly.[18] The following April, the *Connacht Tribune* reported that Galway RTC were victorious over Carlow RTC, winning 5–5 to 2–3 after extra-time, in the final of the so-called 'All-Ireland RTC competition'.[19]

Expanding ladies Gaelic football to new countries, counties and cohorts were essential milestones if the LGFA was to achieve significant growth and gain the sort of attention that the likes of the GAA and the state could not ignore.

Further third-level Gaelic football competitions for women were played in 1985 and 1986, showing the interest had endured. In November 1986, four delegates from a small number of third-level colleges – St Mary's Marino, Carysfort and Mary Immaculate Limerick (all teacher-training colleges) – met with members of the LGFA Central Council 'with a view of setting up a Board to run their own affairs under the umbrella' of the LGFA.[20]

They were successful with this, and from 1987 onwards third-level Gaelic football competitions were played under the auspices of the LGFA, involving colleges from Munster, Connacht and Leinster.

The growth of the game since that first third-level competition over a decade earlier was evident in the fact that seventeen colleges entered the competition run by the Munster Council in 1987. Not that it all went smoothly. Fixtures were unfulfilled, results were not recorded and registrations were not submitted. 'In fact every rule was broken', according to the minutes from a meeting in November 1988.[21] In the aftermath, the committee agreed that 'last year's competition was unsatisfactory and that the competition did not achieve what it set out to do – mainly to promote the playing of ladies Gaelic football in all the colleges'. They pledged that the following year's competition would be an improvement on the previous one.[22]

The Munster-based colleges were the most competitive teams in the late 1980s and the Munster Council appear to have been the key body involved in organising the third-level competition at this stage, rather than the LGFA Central Council.[23] In fact, the final of the competition, known as the O'Connor Cup, was contested by Munster-based institutions every year – until 1996, that is, when the University of Ulster Jordanstown broke through. By the end of the 1994/5 season the annual report noted that the number of colleges playing women's Gaelic football had increased from ten to twenty-eight and the number of competitions on offer from two to five in the past year alone.[24] Speculating on the reasons for the positive growth of the third-level competitions within ten years, it was noted:

> I feel the increase is also due to the fact that more girls who are now entering 3rd level have already been exposed to ladies' Gaelic football at secondary school and thus have an interest in continuing their sport. To date we would have had a large proportion of raw beginners. Obviously the hard work of those involved at school and under age level is now bearing fruit.[25]

Expanding ladies Gaelic football to new countries, counties and cohorts were essential milestones if the LGFA was to achieve significant growth and gain the sort of attention that the likes of the GAA and the state could not ignore. By the middle of the 1980s, it was clear that the efforts were beginning to pay off.

However, there was still some way to go in terms of getting recognition for the game and developing the LGFA as a sporting body. At the 1983 LGFA Annual Congress – following on from the GAA's official recognition of the LGFA the previous year – the Leitrim LGFA put forward a motion to hold the All-Ireland final

Adamstown-Cloughbawn show off the silverware they won in 1988, including the All-Ireland club title. The Wexford club beat Waterford's Ballymacarbry in the final, 2–6 to 1–4 (Kay McCabe).

at Croke Park. In support of the motion, the Leitrim delegate, Andy O'Rourke, called it a 'great privilege and honour to play at Croke Park' and a dream for women Gaelic footballers to play at the home of Gaelic games.[26] However, the motion was defeated on the grounds that ladies Gaelic football was not yet attracting enough national media attention or drawing attendances large enough to warrant playing the final in Croke Park.[27]

Saying that, things seemed to be going in the right direction. Going into its tenth year of operation, the standing of the LGFA and the place of ladies Gaelic football within Irish sport was laid out clearly at the LGFA's Annual Congress in Cavan in 1983. The association's membership had grown to 5,000 and the working balance of the organisation as of the start of 1983 was a reasonably healthy, if modest, £536. Local newspapers were also thanked for giving the game coverage, which was boosting the profile of the sport.[28] These factors were positive indicators of the growth of the LGFA.

Long-standing challenges still remained. National coverage in newspapers and on RTÉ radio and television remained difficult to obtain. This, along with a precarious financial position – despite the modestly healthy working balance from the previous year – was seen to be hurting the association in terms of growing the following of the game and its status. It turned out that though the LGFA entered 1983 with a surplus, LGFA President Mick Fitzgerald declared in his address at Annual Congress in 1984 that the association had finished the 1983 financial year with a negative balance of £670 and he criticised the government for failing to award the LGFA with a state grant. He surmised that the absence of annual state funding was restraining the progress of the sport and the association.[29] The LGFA had received a government grant in 1977 of £200 and again in 1978 but this time it had been reduced to just £100.[30] It did not receive government funding again until 1984, although this time it amounted to £500.[31] The association was still reliant on other forms of financial support and at the thirteenth annual congress of the LGFA a motion was passed to set up a committee to look into sponsorship opportunities.[32]

These issues were not new ones, of course; they were associated with the esteem in which the sport was held by the state, other sporting bodies, the media and the public. Raising the broader reputation of ladies Gaelic football was a key objective of the LGFA executive and doing this required a huge amount of effort off the pitch. Speaking to the *Evening Herald* after Kerry's sixth All-Ireland title in a row in 1987, Margaret Lawlor, Kerry player and treasurer of the Kerry LGFA County Board at the time, summed up the challenge the LGFA faced in establishing itself, as well as the ambition it held:

> We want to have our own identity. We have nothing to compare ourselves to, our mothers didn't play football. We want people to see that we can play football and come and watch us play like they do for any other sport.[33]

Organisationally, the LGFA was structured in a similar fashion to the GAA and the Camogie Association. A fully voluntary executive was elected each year with a president elected for a three-year term to lead the association. Speaking to the GAA Oral History Project in 2011, Mick Fitzgerald recalled the responsibilities the role of president held in the 1980s. These included chairing meetings, making decisions, attending functions and presenting medals. Fitzgerald epitomised the hard work and various roles that volunteers performed for the fledgling organisation. Not only did he serve as president from 1982 to 1985, he took on the role of national treasurer for over twenty years, as well as administrative roles at county and provincial level. His track record as Kerry manager during this period was equally impressive, of course, leading them to two Minor and seven Senior All-Ireland titles.

Wexford's Jackie Codd takes on Kerry's Phil Curran and Mary Lane during the 1989 All-Ireland final in Croke Park (Kay McCabe).

Following Fitzgerald's tenure as president, Pat Quill of Wexford took up the mantle for the first of his three terms (1985–8, 2009–12 and 2012–15). During Quill's first term, the LGFA first Official Guide was published. The guide was developed by Quill, Vice-President Peter Rice and Chair of the Wexford County Board, Kieran Dunne, to be a full constitution for the association and was ratified by central council in 1986. Mary Wheatley from Laois became the sixth president of the LGFA in 1988 and was the first woman to assume the role. Her election to the position was significant as it demonstrated that the LGFA was not just providing women with opportunities to get involved in Gaelic football in a playing capacity but was also allowing them to develop and showcase their administrative and leadership abilities.

Part of the president's role was also to try and broaden the reach of the game, to bring it to the public's attention. While national media coverage remained slow to come about, progress seemingly began to be made on this front in 1985 when RTÉ's *The Women's Programme* did a feature on ladies Gaelic football. They interviewed players, coaches and former president, Tom Dowd. A challenge match was organised between Kerry and Wexford in Stillorgan, so that highlights could be included in the programme.[34]

The significance of the match being filmed and broadcast was highlighted by *The Kerryman*: 'This is the first time that RTÉ had shown any favourable interest in ladies football. So, catch it while you can. You may not get a second chance.'[35]

This was a huge opportunity for the LGFA to spread awareness about the association. The players interviewed pushed back against the 'handy excuses' put forward by some people about the unsuitability of Gaelic football for women due to its 'ruggedness', while Dowd spoke about the differences between the ladies' game and the men's game in terms of its organisation, noting that there was 'practically no money' for the LGFA and the organisation was dependent on fundraising through the likes of raffles.[36]

Another chance to promote the game came ahead of the All-Ireland final in 1987 when the players from finalists Kerry and Westmeath appeared, togged out in their full kit, on *The Late Late Show* with Gay Byrne to promote the final.[37] In the short segment, Byrne asked about the physicality of the game, how seriously the players took their preparations, how they came to play Gaelic football, and whether the referee and umpires for the game would be male or female. Byrne's questions indicate how little was known among the general public about ladies Gaelic football coming into the late 1980s. Taking full advantage of the opportunity of featuring on prime-time television, the LGFA ensured that there was a ticket for everyone in the audience to the following day's final.[38]

As well as an improving public profile, the LGFA's relationship with the GAA and the Camogie Association also improved significantly in the 1980s – certainly compared to the scepticism and hesitation that had been evident in the relationships in the 1970s. The GAA extended their Public Liability Insurance in 1986 to cover the LGFA, a benefit that had already been extended to the Camogie Association.[39] At the Camogie Association Annual Congress in 1985, Wexford even put forward a motion for the closer cooperation between the Camogie Association and the LGFA so as to avoid fixture clashes.[40] This was deemed a 'good idea' by the *Evening Echo*,

KERRY WIN EIGHT IN A ROW

On a dry and sunny Sunday
In the month of October 89
The girls from Kerry came to Dublin
To play the girls of Wexford
And after an hour of splendid football
They had won eight in a row

Their captain came from Dingle
Her name is Kathleen Curran
And she is the goalie
Who gaurded her net like a panther
Leaping high and diving low
So that Kerry could win eight in a row

Bridgit Leen, Phil Curran and Tess Carroll
Formed the full back line
And when the Wexford forwards met them
They cleared their lines
And blocked the way to goal
So Kerry won eight in a row

Abbeyfeales Mary Lane was a colossus
Fetching and covering every ball
While Marian O'Doherty and Margaret Flaherty
Excelled at half back
Defending and attacking in turn
So Kerry could win eight in a row

Annette Walsh did Cordal proud
Holding the middle of the field
While Beaufort's Mary Jo
Soared as high as an eagle
Clearing her lines and setting up attacks
To win the player of the match
And Kerry win the eight in a row

A poem written by John E. Barrett, the Kerry LGFA PRO in the 1980s, to mark Kerry's incredible feat of winning an eighth All-Ireland title in a row. Kerry would go on to win another two All-Ireland titles in 1990 and 1993 making it nine All-Ireland titles in a row and ten in twelve years (Adrienne McLaughlin with permission from John E. Barrett and family).

Young Katie Liston led the attack
Scoring the opening point
While Eileen Lawlor scored the last
Marina Barry the girl from the rock
Broke Wexford's heart with a blistering shot
To help Kerry win eight in a row

Dell Whyte at full forward joined with
Ann Costolloe to trouble Wexfords defence
But it was at top of the right Margaret Lawlor
Or is it Slattery our scorer supreme
That sent over the points with left and right
Nine in all to win her ninth All-Ireland
And Kerry's eight in a row

Without the subs, Jackie, Elaine, Ann, Patrica,
Michelle, Mary Ellen, Siobhan, Fionnula and Sheila
Who trained every night
And turned up for every game
Kerry may not have won
Eight in a row

Galways Mick Fitzgearld as the Kerry Trainer
Strode around Croke Park
Knowing that his girls were as fit as could be
Their teamwork a joy to behold
He never feared Wexford would deny
Kerry win eight in a row

While Helen Dowling, Pat Lawlor and Tony O'Riordan
Are selectors for many a year
Young Florrie O'Sullivan of Glencar
Played his part in picking the team
That won Kerry's eight in a row

A tribute to a great team
By John E Barrett
P.R.O. Kerry Ladies Football
Board.

Barrett's poem pays tribute to the team of 1989 and the players and mentors who moulded Kerry into the dominant team of the 1980s (Adrienne McLaughlin with permission from John E. Barrett and family).

which noted that, although the standing of ladies Gaelic football was progressing, the delay in recognising ladies Gaelic football reflected wider social attitudes:

> Though some men are gradually copping on to the fact that football is equally entertaining whether played by women or men, there still seem to be plenty who'd rather see women cheering them on the sidelines than heading out onto the field themselves. This is evident from the length of time it took for the GAA to recognise ladies football as an official game.[41]

Much more clearly needed to be done in this regard. Lawlor, in the same interview with the *Evening Herald* quoted above, also stated that in order for the game to grow further, a full-time development officer based out of Croke Park was needed. However, she felt that this should be run under the auspices of the LGFA, not the GAA.

> We get support from the GAA in that we get the use of pitches. We do not have to go and buy pitches. There should be a ladies' football club in every parish run in conjunction with the men's clubs. We have our own organisation and there is nothing wrong with that. We do not want to be run by a men's committee.[42]

The fact that the LGFA did not own any pitches and was relying on the cooperation of the GAA at county board level for access to facilities was an issue. In fact, it was becoming a bigger one as ladies' football grew in standing. Although ladies' football was becoming more popular and an accepted game in local and national sporting arenas, it was still considered secondary to men's sport.

Take, for example, the prioritising of the 1984 All-Ireland final. This game was fixed for Portlaoise but subsequently had to be moved to a pitch seven miles outside the town to accommodate a men's championship game scheduled for the same time. Although the alternative pitch in Timahoe was in perfect condition, the facilities

were sub-standard. There was not enough room in the dressing room for all players to sit down, the showers were reported to be small and contained concrete blocks, there were no toilets, and no stand for spectators.[43] The *Kerryman* questioned why Croke Park was not made available to the LGFA:

> One wonders at the wisdom of playing an All-Ireland final at a venue like Timahoe before a few hundred spectators when the camogie final is accorded the honour and glory of Croke Park and an audience of over 4,000. Certainly, the standard of ladies' football compares favourably with top-class camogie and deserves a better setting on All-Ireland final day. Why not have a ladies day at Croke Park with both football and camogie?[44]

There was some progress the following year when the 1985 All-Ireland final was held in Páirc Uí Chaoimh. This was only the second time that the LGFA had had access to a county ground for the playing of the All-Ireland final, the previous instance being Hyde Park in Roscommon for the 1977 final.

The following year finally saw the LGFA reach a longed-for landmark – Croke Park was made available to the LGFA for the first time.[45] The *Irish Independent* described the holding of the LGFA Senior and Junior finals in Croke Park for the first time as 'a clear indication of the strides that the ladies' game' had made since the LGFA was set up in 1974.[46] Playing in Croke Park meant a lot to the players, as noted by Kerry player Margaret Lawlor, who said: 'Playing in Croke Park this year was probably the biggest thrill of all for all of us. Winning our fifth All-Ireland in a row was the icing on the cake.'[47]

There is no doubt that the LGFA had made great strides in fifteen years. Huge work was being done across the country to keep the LGFA running and to introduce new counties and new competitions. All of this meant that, by the end of the 1980s, there were eighteen counties affiliated to the LGFA. Kerry's supremacy also set a new standard for all ladies' footballers. The introduction of the All-Star Awards and the playing of the LGFA finals at Croke Park further enhanced the status of the game and went some way towards paying fair dues to the early generations of ladies Gaelic footballers.

Without doubt, the game had now lost its novelty tag.

CHAPTER 7

GOING FOR GOALS, 1990–1999

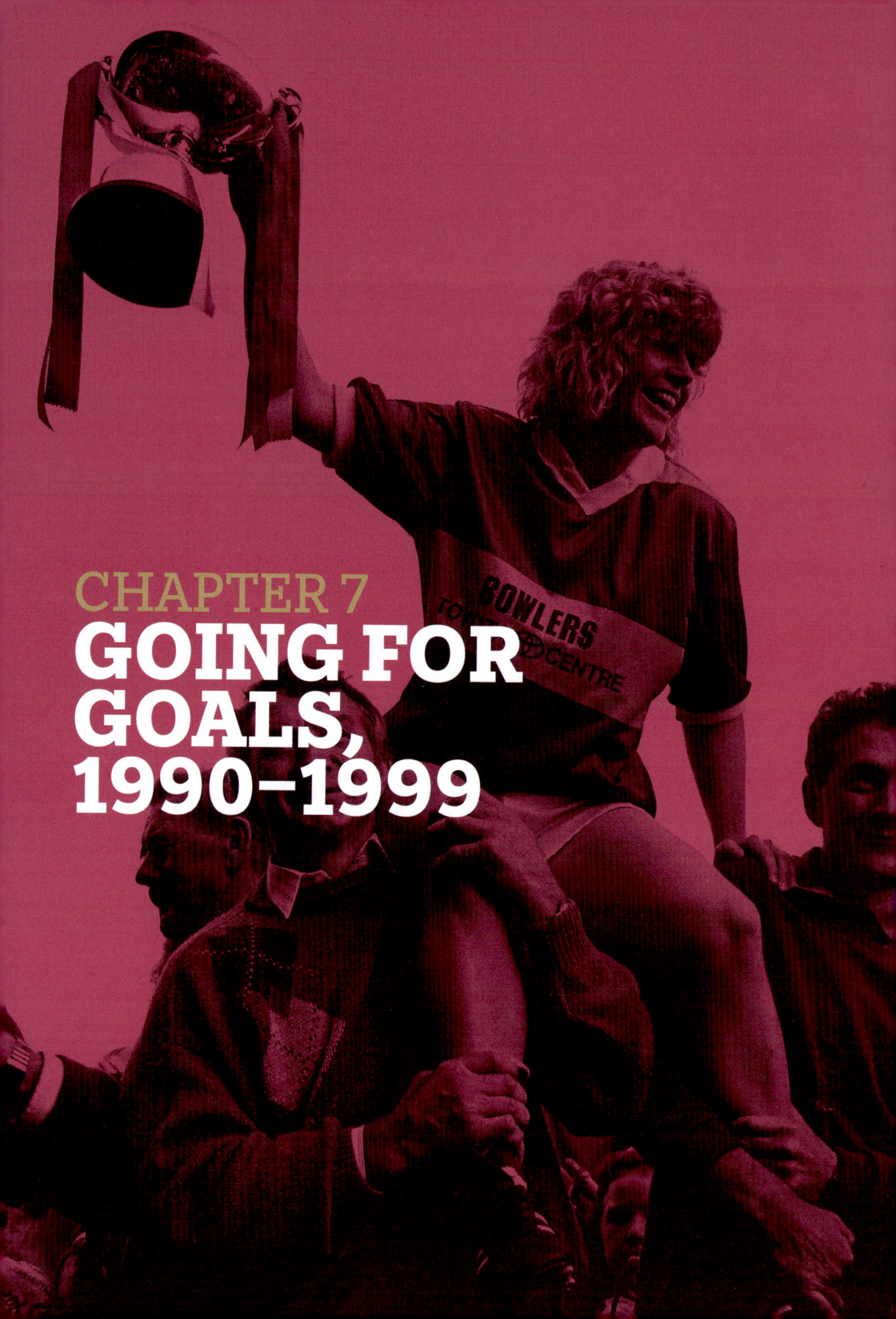

Ladies' Gaelic football grew gradually throughout the 1970s and 1980s, but it was in the 1990s that the game started to properly boom, spreading into even more counties. In Donegal, Monaghan, Tyrone, Sligo, Fermanagh, Down, Antrim and Derry ladies' football got going on an organised basis for the first time. County boards were also re-established in Limerick, Meath, Armagh, Kildare, Tipperary, Louth and Cavan.[1] Overall, sixteen counties affiliated to the LGFA in the 1990s, increasing significantly the number of counties running ladies Gaelic football activities at local level and taking part in national competitions.

The increased number of counties led to a restructuring of competitions. In 1996, a third division of the National League was introduced and in 1997 an Intermediate All-Ireland championship was inaugurated alongside the Senior and Junior competitions. This was done in order to both cater for the increase in inter-county teams and to account for the gap in playing levels among counties who were starting out against those that had been developing Gaelic football for longer.

The 1990s also saw change on the football field. Kerry's dominance of the All-Ireland championship came to an end in 1991 when they lost to Waterford in the Munster championship. It was Kerry's first loss in the championship since 1981 when they had lost to Offaly in that year's All-Ireland final. Following that loss, they failed to win either the National League or the All-Ireland championship in 1992, making it the first year since 1980 that their county team had failed to win either competition. While they did manage one last dance in 1993, winning the All-Ireland final, that loss to Waterford in 1991 came to be seen as the end of their era of dominance.

Waterford went on to win the championship outright in 1991, defeating Laois. This was Waterford's first appearance in an All-Ireland Senior championship final, having won the Junior All-Ireland in 1986. For Laois, this was their fourth appearance and fourth loss in the All-Ireland final since 1985. Laois would face further heartbreak in 1992 when they were again beaten by Waterford in the All-Ireland final and in 1993 when they were defeated by Kerry.

Laois and Kerry players take part in the pre-match parade before the ball is thrown-in for the 1993 All-Ireland final. In the background, the Cusack Stand can be seen partially demolished as work begins on the refurbishment of Croke Park (Marion Bowler née Doherty).

Waterford's rise to the top of the inter-county chain in the 1990s coincided with the success attained by its leading club, Ballymacarbry. Located near the Waterford-Tipperary border, Ballymacarbry ladies Gaelic football club's roots can be traced back to the late 1960s when the club was the driving force within the county in getting the game off the ground. This strong footballing tradition started to pay off when the club won their first Senior Club All-Ireland title in 1987. They went on to win ten titles in twelve years between 1987 and 1998.

This dominance transferred over to the inter-county game, too. The Waterford county team won five All-Ireland Senior titles, four Under–18 All-Ireland titles, and five Under–16 All-Ireland titles in the same time period. They also contested nine National League Division 1 finals between 1988 and 1999, winning the competition four times. Their success demonstrated the benefit of having the inter-county competitions run over a number of tiers in terms of aiding in the gradual development of a county team, given Waterford's rise from All-Ireland Junior winners in 1986 to

Kerry captain Eileen Dardis (née Lawlor) proudly displays the Brendan Martin Cup as she sits on the shoulders of former Kerry footballer Johnny Bunyan (left) and Willie Slattery (right), the husband of her sister Margaret. The Lawlor sisters won twenty All-Ireland titles and ten All-Star Awards between them while playing for Kerry (Sportsfile).

contesting Division 1 League Finals consecutively from 1988 to 1991 and winning their first Senior All-Ireland in 1991.

London, too, finally tasted All-Ireland success during this decade when they won the Junior title in 1993, having lost four finals in the previous five years. Monaghan also experienced success quite quickly. They won the Junior All-Ireland title in 1992, the Division 1 National League title in 1994, and narrowly lost the Senior All-Ireland final to Waterford that same year. However, this defeat spurred them on, setting them up to win back-to-back Senior All-Ireland titles in the mid-1990s. This was even more impressive considering that the Monaghan County Board had only formed in 1991.

Though Waterford came out on top in terms of the number of All-Ireland titles won in the 1990s, Laois, Monaghan and Mayo also captured the Brendan Martin Cup and played their part in developing and promoting ladies Gaelic football.

The 1990s also saw the development of a host of talented footballers. These included stars such as Áine Wall, winner of eight All-Star Awards between 1989 and 1998, as well as fifteen All-Ireland medals in the Ballymacarbry and Waterford colours, and many of

London celebrating winning the Junior All-Ireland title in 1993. Ladies' football took off in the English capital in 1986 and in 1988 London took part in the LGFA Junior Championship for the first time, losing to Leitrim in the final. They made the final again in 1990, 1991 and 1992 before finally taking home the trophy in 1993 (Maria Kelly).

her teammates, such as twins Geraldine and Martina O'Ryan, who between them picked up an incredible nine All-Star Awards and twenty-eight All-Ireland medals for club and county. Sue Ramsbottom of Laois, Mayo's Christina Heffernan and Jennifer Grennan of the break-through Monaghan team also established themselves as some of the greatest ladies Gaelic football players to ever play the game.

There were often only very fine margins between the top teams during this period. The 1996 and 1998 All-Ireland finals between Monaghan and Laois, and Waterford and Monaghan respectively, both required a replay to separate the sides. This exemplified the new-found competitiveness of the ladies Gaelic football championship, given that the only other time the LGFA Senior football final had needed a replay prior to this was in 1979 when Offaly won their first All-Ireland title. As well as being close-run games, the clashes at this time were often energetic and compelling. Lulu Carroll's injury-time goal for Laois to level the game against Monaghan in 1996 was described as a 'spectacular climax' to a thrilling game.[2] The close finals also put a spotlight on standards and skill in ladies Gaelic football, elevating the game to new heights.

The All-Ireland Senior final of 1997 was another closely contested match between Waterford and Monaghan. However, the final drew attention for another reason: a refereeing decision. Following the game, the referee was criticised for playing eleven minutes added time at the end of normal time. Waterford were ahead for a large period of added time but Monaghan fought their

Waterford and Ballymacarbry's Áine Wall goes for a score during the 1995 All-Ireland final against Monaghan. Wall won eight All-Star awards during her illustrious career, which also included five All-Ireland titles and ten All-Ireland club titles (Sportsfile).

The Ballymacarbry team that won the All-Ireland club championship in 1997. Ballymacarbry are the most decorated club in ladies Gaelic football history with ten All-Ireland titles to their name. In 1994 the All-Ireland club championship trophy was re-named the Dolores Tyrrell Cup in memory of the former Ballymacarbry player who captained the club to their first All-Ireland title in 1987 (Ballymacarbry LGFA).

way back and it was the Farney County that were ahead when the referee blew the final whistle on the seventy-first minute. The lengthy additional time was a massive talking point and there was understandable discontent in the Waterford camp – although, upon review, it was found that the referee had played thirty minutes of football in the second half.[3]

To ensure that a similar situation would not arise again, the LGFA introduced a striking new initiative: a countdown clock, which would be used for the 1998 All-Ireland finals. Announcing this, the LGFA stated that the LGFA believed that players were entitled to the full sixty minutes of football and that the countdown clock would be 'a fairer system not only for players, but also, spectators and referees'.[4] The referee would still control the amount of time played, signalling to two people on the sideline when the clock needed to be stopped in the case of an injury or other stoppage. The LGFA argued that, overall, this would give clarity to players and supporters on the amount of time remaining, with the end of each half being signalled by a hooter.

Costing approximately £500, the stop clock was a shrewd and innovative investment by the LGFA. Its primary aim was to ensure that players and fans were treated to exactly sixty minutes of football, but it has also added a buzz of excitement to the dying moments of a game, as evidenced in its first outing in 1998:

> An ear-splitting roar erupted from the large 16,421 crowd when, with the sides still level, the ball fell to Waterford's Martina O'Ryan and the clock showed just eight seconds remaining. In the event her shot went wide, the crowd counted down the seconds hysterically and invaded the pitch as the final hooter (eerily like a Fire Brigade siren) sounded on the subsequent kick-out.[5]

The 1998 championship was not only notable for the introduction of the countdown clock, but also for being the first time ladies Gaelic football was televised live. This was a major development for the LGFA. By the early 1990s, coverage of the ladies' game was noted to have improved in the national newspapers but securing television coverage had still been a major issue. Peter Rice, President of the LGFA, speaking at the annual congress in 1993 said, 'The finals were shown on *Sportsnight* on RTÉ, but the television coverage would not have been possible if this Association hadn't paid a large sum to

Waterford's Geraldine O'Ryan gets a shot off as Monaghan's Brenda McAnespie dives in during the 1997 All-Ireland final. The 1997 All-Ireland final between these two sides featured eleven minutes of added time. The amount of added time was a huge talking point after the game and though the referee was found to have played the correct amount of time, the incident led to the introduction of the countdown clock (Sportsfile).

have a camera made available to record the game for RTÉ.'[6] This was a financial burden for the LGFA, according to Rice, and he called on the national broadcaster to broadcast live radio commentary of the All-Ireland Senior final that year, and to include results of ladies Gaelic football games on television and radio bulletins.[7]

Increasing coverage at a national level continued to be a key focus for the LGFA. A major boost came when Bank of Ireland stepped in to sponsor the LGFA's championships in 1998, committing £1 million to print and TV advertising for women's and men's Gaelic games that year. At the announcement of the sponsorship it was revealed that an agreement to televise the LGFA's finals live on RTÉ for the first time had also been agreed.[8] The Bank of Ireland sponsorship and the television agreement represented a massive investment in ladies Gaelic football, one that went beyond the finances involved. After all, it is hard to put a price on the long-term value of having the backing of a major brand and the opportunity to broadcast the showcase match in the ladies Gaelic football calendar on national TV.

The 1990s saw lots of new counties affiliate to the LGFA for the first time, including Monaghan, who set up their county board in 1991. The following year the Farney County won All-Ireland honours for the first time when they beat London in the Junior final and they added a further six honours before the end of the decade, winning the Division 1 National League title four times and the Senior All-Ireland title twice (Sportsfile).

In that first televised final, viewers were treated to an exciting battle between Waterford and Monaghan. Such was the drama of the match, which ended in a draw, that Waterford manager Michael Ryan told the *Northern Standard* that he had heard from RTÉ's Jim Carney that when the television in a pub in Tralee was switched over from the ladies' game to Sky Sports for a soccer fixture between Liverpool and Chelsea 'there was absolute uproar in the place'. He added, 'I think that speaks for itself; everyone saw what a wonderful game ladies football can be.'[9]

The LGFA of the 1990s was clearly ambitious, building on the hard work of the previous decades. The introduction of the countdown clock on the back of a controversy demonstrated maturity and innovation from the association's leadership. Despite having been told in the past that the people of Ireland 'would be more interested in watching [tiddlywinks] on television than watch women play football', the LGFA were persistent and stood resolutely behind their belief that live coverage would be entertaining and worth the time and effort.[10]

In 1998 the LGFA introduced a countdown clock to ensure that there would be no further controversy regarding the playing of additional time as there had been in the previous year's final (Sportsfile).

The commitment to developing the LGFA was most noticeable, however, in the decision to appoint a Chief Executive Officer (CEO) to run the association for the first time in its history in 1997. Ladies Gaelic football was clearly growing at a speed beyond which volunteers alone could manage. So the LGFA decided to approach Helen O'Rourke and offer her the new role.

Helen O'Rourke, who had served as President of the LGFA from 1994 to 1997, accepted the offer and took a career break from her job as a primary school teacher to take up the full-time position

– a position she still holds today. Speaking to Cliona Foley at the time of her appointment, O'Rourke explained:

> We just felt the time was right, the game has gained great publicity and crowds in the past 10 years, people are realising that we have a very attractive product and we felt now was the time to expand.[11]

O'Rourke was the natural choice after her impressive tenure as president. However, speaking in 2013, she recalled how there had been mixed feelings about her capabilities before she was elected president. Some felt that O'Rourke was inexperienced and wouldn't be able to steer the association adequately as a result. Other people had been excited about the prospect of a young woman coming in to take on the role, of course, and saw that having O'Rourke as president would convey a positive image for the LGFA to put forward.[12] Clearly, the progressive thinking won out and O'Rourke proved any doubters wrong, to the point where she would now be the LGFA's first CEO.

The creation of this new role was a clear signal from the LGFA that they were serious about pursuing the potential of ladies Gaelic football to the best of their ability. The role was one that would oversee the general running of the LGFA – coordinating competitions and events, managing media and publicity, and approaching sponsors were some of the responsibilities.[13] O'Rourke described it as a 'general dogsbody' role in those early years, as she managed the day-to-day running of the LGFA alone.[14] O'Neills, the iconic Gaelic games sports brand, provided an office space in their shop in Walkinstown for O'Rourke, and so this was where she based the LGFA operation, catering to an LGFA membership that stood at over 70,000 at the time of her taking the role.[15]

Among the main priorities for the new CEO, employed initially as General Secretary on a five-year-term contract, was developing ladies Gaelic football in secondary schools and abroad.[16] School-age members made up just over forty per cent of all LGFA members in

1997.[17] Some efforts had already been made to develop this playing pool. A post-primary Senior All-Ireland championship had been played for the first time in 1985 and a corresponding competition at Junior level was introduced in 1994. The LGFA recognised that schools were effective channels through which to introduce young girls to Gaelic football and, in turn, feed into local clubs to grow the membership. By 1999 there were over 250 schools taking part in the Junior and Senior post-primary competitions, reflecting the growing interest of young girls and teenagers in playing Gaelic football.[18] To cater for the growth at post-primary level, the Junior and Senior schools' competitions were expanded to three divisions from 2003, with a cup to play for at 'A', 'B' and 'C' levels.

The aspiration to further promote ladies Gaelic football abroad was another sign of a modern and forward-thinking LGFA. The global growth of ladies Gaelic football that had already occurred in the 1990s was noteworthy. During this decade, the association expanded its affiliations to new territories, while overseas 'counties' such as London and New York held their own in the Junior All-Ireland championship.

That London reached the Junior All-Ireland final four years in a row in the early 1990s demonstrated the strength of ladies Gaelic football in the English capital. In 1992, they lost to Monaghan by just two points, the same Monaghan team that would go on to contest the next five Senior All-Ireland finals, winning the competition overall in 1996, thereby indicating that London were not too far off the level required for Senior football. This was

Programme for the 1993 All-Ireland finals, which featured Kerry and Laois in the Senior decider, and London and Donegal in the Junior final (Mary Jo Curran).

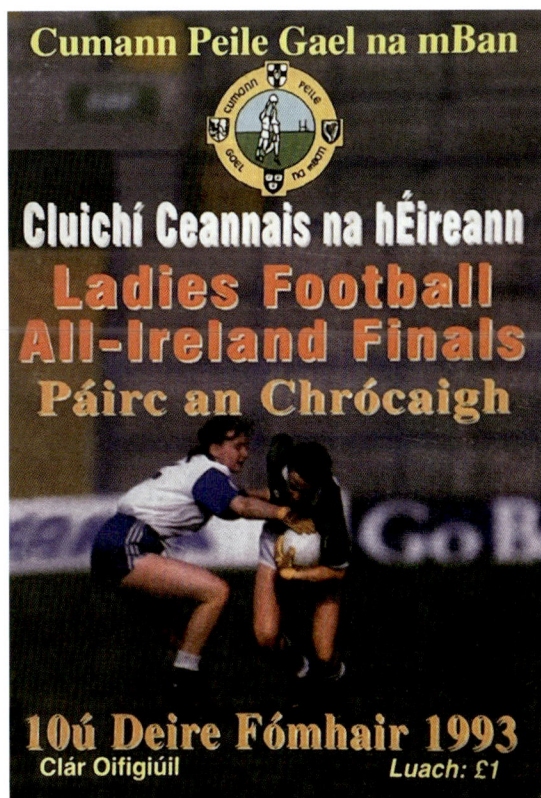

proved the following year when London claimed the All-Ireland Junior title in a comprehensive win over Donegal. London's Patricia Mimna (née O'Brien), originally from Co. Cavan, was the standout performer from the final and her performance helped to earn her a fourth All-Star Award.[19] Mimna won awards previously in 1981 and 1982 while representing Cavan before ultimately adding three more awards while playing for London.

However, the expansion of the game abroad was not universally going well. Outside the English capital it remained a struggle to sustain and grow ladies Gaelic football. In 1994, the All-Britain final was held in Lancashire by request of the Lancashire Ladies County Board to try and raise the profile of the game in the county.[20] Two years later, in 1996, Lancashire noted that they were struggling financially but were determined that this difficulty should not stop them from continuing playing and promoting ladies Gaelic football. They were honest in recognising, however, that 'without a sound financial policy we will falter. Therefore we are at present actively exploring different avenues in order to have a healthier balance for 1997.'[21] The Lancashire Ladies County Board report for 1998 conveyed disappointment that they, in collaboration with Warwickshire, could not manage to enter a 'Rest of Britain' side in the international competition that was held in September of that year in the run-in to the All-Ireland weekend. Lancashire congratulated London on winning the competition, defeating North America in the final in Parnell Park, and stated that it was a priority to enter a 'Rest of Britain' team in the next iteration of the competition in 2000. It was noted that the 'county is in dire need of new blood and competition in the area. To introduce [ladies Gaelic] football to the youth of Lancashire is our long term aim.'[22]

On the other side of the Atlantic, ladies Gaelic football was beginning to come to the fore in North America, as a high number of young people emigrated to North America in the late 1980s and into the early 1990s. In 1992, a team from Ontario in Canada visited Ireland to play a series of matches, and ladies Gaelic football featured at the national championships run by US GAA, the North American Championships (although an exhibition match had been previously played at the championships in Pittsburgh in 1987 between two clubs from Chicago – McBride's and Erin's Rovers).[23]

The first ladies Gaelic football championship played in North America was won by San Francisco Ladies, who defeated Erin's Rovers in San Francisco.[24] Between 1994 and 1997 clubs sprang up in the major American cities of Atlanta, Boston, Chicago, Cleveland, Detroit, Fort Lauderdale, Seattle and Washington DC, illustrating the spread of the Irish diaspora across the United States by the late twentieth century.

Rosie O'Reilly, winner of thirteen New York Ladies Gaelic football Championships with Cavan Ladies New York, recalled how nine clubs were formed initially in the city in the early 1990s, following the conclusion of a meeting in the Riverdale Steakhouse, owned by Terry Connaughton. He had seen ladies Gaelic football at the North American Championships and decided to try and get the game going in New York too. He put an ad in a newspaper, asking anyone interested in starting up a ladies Gaelic football team to attend the meeting. O'Reilly was among them.[25]

The LGFA of the 1990s was clearly ambitious, building on the hard work of the previous decades.

In September 1994, New York Ladies visited Ireland for a tour of the country. Upon arrival in Ireland the New York Ladies were treated to a welcome reception hosted by the LGFA Central Council before travelling West to play the Roscommon and Leitrim county teams in challenge matches before playing a final match on their return to Dublin against the Portobello club.[26] In total, a squad of twenty-five and six officials travelled to Ireland from New York, among them a former LGFA All-Ireland winner and two-time corner-back All-Star in Ann Kerr (née Maher) from Tipperary.[27]

A narrow one-point defeat to Roscommon kicked off the tour before New York accounted for Leitrim in the next match, 3–7 to 0–7.[28] The final match against Portobello was a replay of a challenge game played between the two sides on the other side of the Atlantic the year before. Finishing their tour on a high, New York beat Portobello 1–12 to 0–4 to claim victory in both the home and away legs of the challenge games.[29]

All their work paid dividends when, five years later, New York reached the All-Ireland Junior final, where Tyrone awaited them. There was just one point in it at the break in favour of New York, but Tyrone, competing in their third final since 1995, showed greater experience and star quality from the likes of Eilish Gormley – who finished the game with 3–6 of Tyrone's 3–12 – to win comfortably.[30]

Despite the disappointment of losing the All-Ireland Junior final, it was a major feat to get there. Ladies Gaelic football was up and running in a major way after starting less than ten years earlier in the city and having faced challenges in getting itself established. Interviewed as part of the GAA Oral History Project, Rosie O'Reilly recalls that when a ladies Gaelic football final had first been held in Gaelic Park in New York, the President of New York GAA at the time walked to a pub across the road instead of watching the game, returning only when the game was over, as he did not feel that ladies' football had a place in Gaelic Park. She said that others of this man's generation would have held the same view but that opinions had moved on since then and that they 'had come around to it'. The ladies' football final was now considered a great occasion in Gaelic Park, she added, one that drew a considerable crowd.

A further issue for New York and its clubs was – and continues to be – the recruitment of players. During periods of high emigration from Ireland, the overseas branches of the LGFA are bolstered by an influx of players; however, when trends reverse or circumstances change, the Gaelic games community abroad can face challenges in keeping activities running.

At the time of the interview, in 2009, O'Reilly said there were five ladies Gaelic football teams in New York and to keep teams going, she said, it was essential to get players coming from Ireland each year – whether those emigrating or just on temporary J1 visas – to bolster their playing base, as teams often lose players to

Sydney-based club
Central Coast in the
summer of 1994.
Ladies Gaelic football
started in Sydney
in 1991 and Central
Coast were one of
three teams to enter a
team in the New South
Wales championship
alongside Michael
Cusack's and Young
Ireland's (Pam
O'Mahony).

retirements or family commitments. In recent years, O'Reilly noted that a slowdown in emigration to New York meant that focus has had to be directed to getting native New Yorkers playing Gaelic football, though there is fierce competition with other sports in America in recruiting participants.

Summing up what Gaelic games means to her, O'Reilly said: 'The GAA is actually like a family. We treat it like a family here especially. We take people in and look after them and send them on their way. It's a way of life for us. I don't know how we would get through without the GAA. It's a meeting point, it's a social point, everything is all entwined into one. It's just a way of life.'[31]

Ladies Gaelic football made its way Down Under, too. It was officially added to the Australasian Championships, the annual inter-state competition run by the GAA-affiliated Gaelic Football and Hurling Association of Australasia for clubs in Australia and New Zealand, in 1995. The honour of claiming the inaugural title went to New South Wales, who overcame Auckland narrowly in the final, 2–7 to 2–6.[32] The final was described as 'a mighty game', which

saw Auckland stage a late comeback against New South Wales, creating great excitement.[33]

Ladies' football had actually started in Sydney in 1991. The minute book of the GAA in New South Wales in May 1991 noted: 'It was generally agreed that a ladies competition would be an attraction to our Sunday Programme and ladies should be encouraged to organise one.'[34] The association's next meeting two weeks later, was well-attended by women as efforts increased to get a ladies' championship organised. Three teams – Central Coast, Michael Cusack's and Young Ireland's – took part in the first New South Wales ladies Gaelic football championship. Michael Cusack's and Young Ireland's reached the final, which ended 4–7 to 4–3 in favour of Cusack's.[35] A fourth club, Clann na Gael, entered the ladies' championship in 1992. Since the early 1990s, the numbers playing ladies Gaelic football in Australasia have increased massively.[36]

Without doubt, the expansion of ladies Gaelic football in the 1990s can be described as phenomenal. As the LGFA celebrated its twenty-fifth anniversary, affiliations to the LGFA had almost doubled from eighteen counties in 1989 to thirty-three (including

London and New York) by the end of 1999. All counties in Ulster now had a county board and were affiliated to the LGFA, a huge upturn for the province, which at one point in the decade had not had an LGFA county board since the mid-1980s. The only county without a ladies Gaelic football board by this time was Kilkenny.

That the game was being played in major cities across the UK, USA, Australia and New Zealand was also promising, showing that Irish women were bringing the game with them wherever they settled. This growth was undoubtedly aligned, in part, with the arrival of the Celtic Tiger. With greater wealth and greater resources available in the country, the LGFA was able to employ someone to run the association full-time, and to compete for sponsorship. Furthermore, they were able to plan for the future growth of the game into the new millennium.

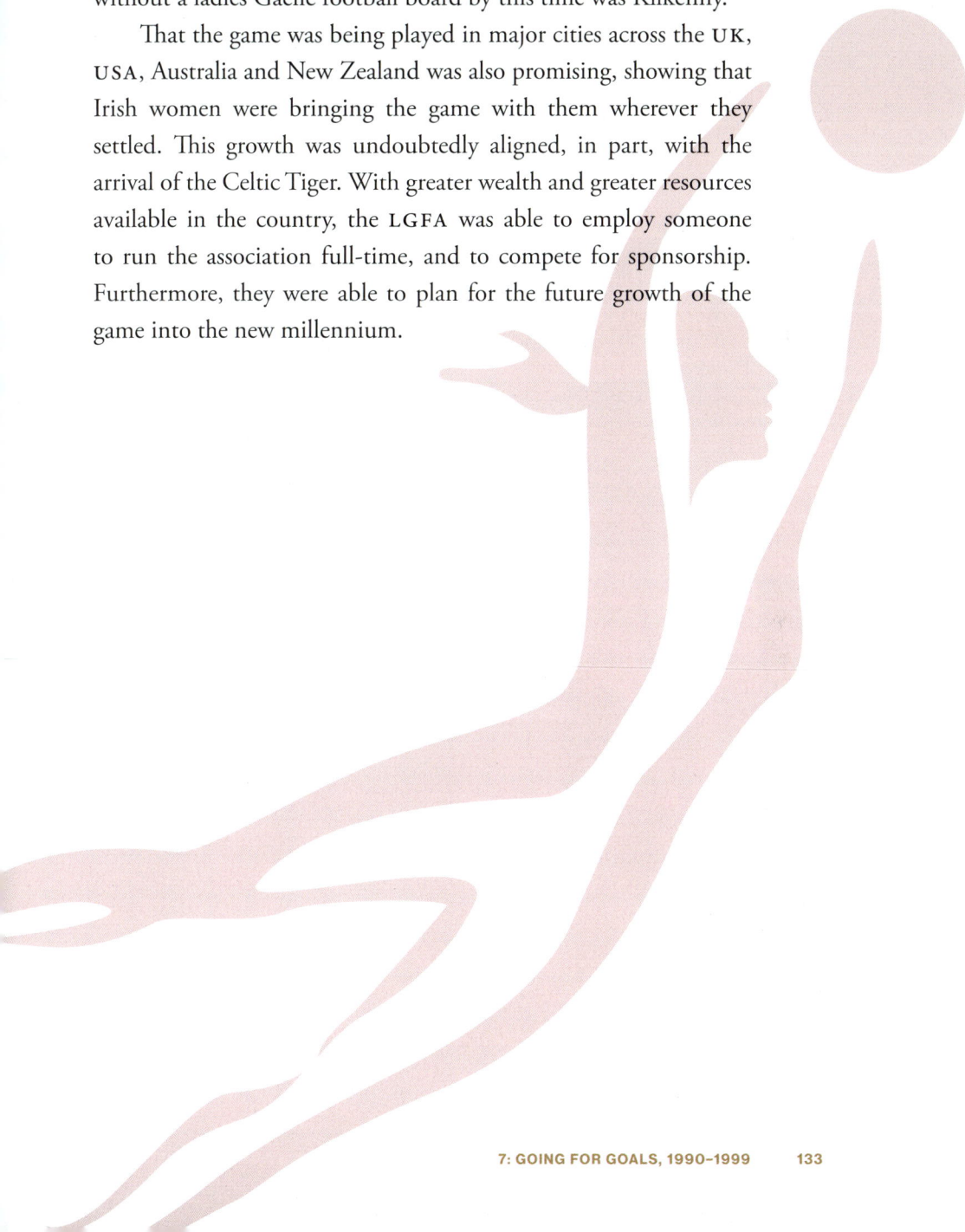

The Mayo team gather
in a huddle for a final
team talk before the
1999 All-Ireland final
against Waterford
(Sportsfile).

CHAPTER 8
NEW MILLENNIUM, NEW GROUND, 2000–2009

Speaking at the LGFA's annual congress in 2003 to commence her presidency, Geraldine Giles sized up how ladies Gaelic football had developed over the years:

Twenty years ago in my home town, when there was talks about setting up a ladies team, little did I think I would be standing here today addressing such a distinguished audience which, I am happy to say, includes one of the founder members of our club; many past and active Presidents of the Association and many of you as delegates that I have attended so may Congresses with over the years. If I had to be coaxed all those years ago to play football, it was with ease that I accepted the nomination for President Elect. [...] Cumann Peil na mBan has seen many changes since its foundation. Only last week on the Saturday evening sport programme on Radio 1 we were described as aggressive in development since our inception. Our profile has been growing steadily over the years and the advent of TV coverage has helped to put us on another plane. However time does not stand still and given the growth that we are constantly experiencing it's time for us to take ourselves onto the next level and I look forward to leading us into this new and exciting future.[1]

The LGFA was coming up on its thirtieth year. The youthfulness of the association was epitomised by the fact that many of those who had been involved in setting up ladies Gaelic football teams in their local areas, whether nearly thirty years ago or more recently, were in the room when Giles spoke. She was the eleventh president of the association, taking over from Walter Thompson of Dublin, who led the LGFA between 2000 and 2003. Much had changed, in society and in sport, since the LGFA was set up in the early 1970s. While the LGFA had managed to navigate these changes well, Giles was correct in her summation that it was time for the association to push boundaries and strive for even greater heights.

The new millennium was to be a fresh, exciting dawn for the LGFA. O'Rourke was growing into her role as CEO and the association's scope and potential was broadening. The standard of play by inter-county teams noticeably increased during this period, too, aided in part by the modernisation of coaching methods, provided through events such as the first-ever conference dedicated to coaching ladies Gaelic football. Held in DCU, it was called 'Unlocking the potential of Ladies Gaelic Football' and included sessions on coaching for fun, supporting high-performance athletes, overcoming the stigma of playing sport from a female perspective and injury prevention.[2]

The number of girls playing Gaelic football continued to grow quickly. Membership of the LGFA stood at approximately 78,000 in the year 2000. By the following year, it had increased by 6,000 to 84,000.[3] The overall outlook of the organisation was positive and contained energy and ambition.

Ladies Gaelic football was now an attractive package for players, for parents and for commercial partnerships. It was essential that the LGFA prepare themselves for these markets. Securing

LGFA CEO Helen O'Rourke and President Geraldine Giles at the launch of the association's three-year strategic plan in 2006 to steer the LGFA through its continuing growth (Sportsfile).

sponsorship remained a key priority. As O'Rourke noted when she became CEO, the LGFA wanted to capitalise on the attractive image and product that they had in ladies Gaelic football. Increased investment and backing would allow the LGFA to follow through on their ambitions. Bank of Ireland coming on board to sponsor the championship in 1998 had been the first major milestone partnership for the LGFA. This significance of this was twofold, according to O'Rourke. The financial backing was a key support but the fact that Bank of Ireland was already involved in sponsoring GAA competition added additional weight to the partnership and to the LGFA's image.[4]

Still, more backing was needed. A key partnership was formed three years later when the LGFA reached an agreement with TG4, the Irish language broadcaster, to enter into an initial three-year partnership to be the title sponsor of the LGFA championships. They also guaranteed to broadcast the All-Ireland finals, as well as a number of All-Ireland championship games live on the channel.[5] The new deal was launched in Galway by Taoiseach Bertie Ahern, who spoke highly of the work the two associations were doing in promoting Irish sport. For the head of TG4, Pól Ó Gallachóir, partnering with the LGFA fitted naturally with the station's '*súil eile*' motto, which promised viewers, literally, another perspective.[6]

Securing consistent media coverage, whether on television, radio or in print, had long been a challenge for the LGFA, as sports news was still seen as a predominantly male domain. However, TG4 saw the potential in ladies Gaelic football and subsequently filled a gap in the market. The move paid off. In 2003, the LGFA finals were watched by over 564,000 people on the channel, a record audience for a TG4 programme.[7]

The partnership with TG4 was game-changing, not just in terms of coverage, but also for participation numbers and further partnerships. Reflecting on the partnership twenty years on, O'Rourke said:

> TG4 was a major turning point in our whole development because all of a sudden parents saw that this was a great game and they wanted to get their daughters involved. In schools, they became more aware of it as well because of TG4 and it appealed to them because here was a game that you could get 15 girls playing. Before that, basketball was traditionally the biggest sport for girls in schools but there's only five girls on a basketball team. And once it started growing in schools, it was easier to set up underage competitions in every county then as well. TG4 were fairly young at the time and we grew together. Because we had television coverage, other sponsors wanted to get involved.[8]

Other brands did follow suit. The Japanese car brand Suzuki became the first-ever sponsor of the LGFA National Leagues in 2003. Speaking at the announcement of the deal, the General Manager of Suzuki Ireland, Niall O'Gorman, said the brand was drawn to the LGFA over other sporting organisations because of their professionalism but also because many of their customers were women and it seemed like a good idea to invest in women's sport.[9]

Happy with their relationship with the LGFA, they reiterated their support for ladies Gaelic football and re-committed to a three-year partnership in 2006, having previously renewed their sponsorship on an annual basis.[10]

Health insurer VHI also came on board in late 2006, in this instance as the sponsors of the LGFA All-Ireland Club Championship. The partnership included a series of workshops that took place in 2007 in LGFA clubs to provide guidance on health and lifestyle practices.[11] This coincided with the thirtieth anniversary of the All-Ireland club championship. Rounding off a decade of new partnerships under the stewardship of O'Rourke, Pat the Baker came on board as the sponsors of the post-primary competitions in 2007.

Mayo's Cora Staunton (right), alongside other Senior and Junior players and TG4's Pól Ó Gallachóir, watches Taoiseach Bertie Ahern kickstart the launch of TG4's sponsorship of the LGFA championships in 2001. The partnership between the LGFA and TG4 has continued to this day and has been transformational in terms of the coverage given to ladies Gaelic football (Sportsfile).

Securing sponsorship deals with well-known brands for the leading LGFA competitions was impressive, but it had also been essential to the continued running of the LGFA. After all, back at the end of 2000, the LGFA had reported that their income for the year was £371,267.08 and expenditure amounted to £363,105.41.[12] President Walter Thompson told the 2001 Congress in his address that the previous year had been somewhat 'static' due to lack of funds and that the cost of running the association was increasing year-on-year.[13] Indeed, the following year the LGFA's expenditure increased to £454,355.26, although their income increased too, with £454,392.33 brought in to cover the additional costs.[14] In euro today these figures sit around the €577,000 mark.[15]

The biggest portion of the LGFA's income came from registrations (£122,124.62), followed by gate receipts (£107,296.21). Sponsorship during that period made up around twenty per cent of the LGFA's income. Sponsorship from AIB covering 2000 and 2001 amounted to £32,000, while TG4's sponsorship for 2001 totalled

£60,000.[16] Costs jumped by almost €100,000 over the next twelve months with the expenditure for 2002 noted as €658,407.69.[17] By this point, income generated from grants and sponsorship was also on the rise, totalling over €172,000 for 2002.[18] Fundraising through other means, such as an annual golf classic, was also necessary during this period.

The association's precarious financial position during this period was made clear in 2001 when the GAA estimated that the security costs of hosting the LGFA finals at Croke Park would be in the region of £30,000, up nearly £10,000 on the previous year. The LGFA advised the GAA that these costs were beyond the LGFA's financial means and they would have to take their finals elsewhere as a result.

The prospect of the LGFA finals being moved out of Croke Park provoked outrage from the LGFA membership. The Monaghan County Secretary, Paul Swift, wrote to every county board to ask them to include the matter on the agenda of their next meeting and raised the possibility of pushing the LGFA executive to have a special Congress meeting to discuss the matter.[19] This call was reiterated in a similar letter addressed to Thompson, O'Rourke and all the county secretaries, which called for an Extraordinary General Meeting to rectify the issue and was signed by various representatives from across the country.[20]

In the end, the GAA made concessions on the security costs in order to keep the the finals at the home of Gaelic games.[21] However, in a letter to all county secretaries, O'Rourke made it clear that there was no guarantee the arrangement would be carried forward.[22] The GAA had suggested that the LGFA and the Camogie Association host their finals in Croke Park on the same day but this was rejected by both associations on the grounds that it could potentially create clashes for dual players, as well as the fact that the two associations had agreements with different sponsors and TV broadcasters.[23]

To ensure that the issue would not arise again, O'Rourke called on the LGFA membership to make themselves count among the attendance in Croke Park on All-Ireland final day:

Cumann Peile na mBan

Han Caherea i Co. Limerick

C.C. Mr. Walter Thompson President Cumann Peil Gael na mBan
C.C. Miss Helen ó Rourke National Secretary Cumann Peil Gael na mBan
C.C. All County Secretaries Cumann Peil Gael na mBan

16/07/2001.

A. Chara

Further to the Central Council Meeting of Wednesday May 30th 2001 where a decision was taken to remove the All Ireland Ladies football finals from Croke Park.

Delegates from all over the Country and abroad have now expressed regret at this decision.

We therefore request the holding of an extraordinary General Meeting to discuss the possibility of rescinding the decision and revert to holding our All Ireland finals in Croke Park this year.

We request you call a meeting in the next fourteen days from the above date and that you notify all County Secretaries immediately.

Maire Halvey Munster Secretary & St. Ailbes Ladies club Limerick.
Breda Martin Co. Offaly
Danny Brown Co. Clare
Graeme Marrenan Co. Clare.
Luis Ryan Ardfinnan Ladies Football Club.
Mary Keane Co. Clare
Michael Ryan Waterford Co. Banna
Eleanor Looby Waterford Co. Treasurer
SEAN O'BRIEN COORACLARE LADIES FOOTBALL
Nathalie Flinn o Mo o'Sullivan St. Ailbes Ladies Football Club.

Pat Looney Co. Sec Waterford.
Fr Terry O'Brien Rockban Cork.
Rose Phelan St. Ailbes Ladies Football Club
Michael ó Suilleabhain Ballyneary Cork.

When it appeared in 2001 that the LGFA would have to move their All-Ireland finals out of Croke Park due to the rising security costs associated with hosting the finals there was a strong reaction from the LGFA membership, and secretaries from counties across the country called on the LGFA management to reconsider (Fina Golden).

Unfortunately, though every effort has been made in recent years to increase the attendance at our finals, counties have not co-operated. At least 90% of county board officials and players are not supporting our finals. If we wish to continue playing our finals in Croke Park, this has to change and it is only counties that can change this situation. We need to get our attendances up to 30,000 on the day. Every county board has a part to play and a responsibility to our players and association to make sure that our finals remain in Croke Park. We saw the uproar and outrage the taking of our finals out of Croke Park caused earlier this year in every county. Counties were prepared to do anything to make sure that we got back to Croke Park, now let's see how serious we really are about playing in Croke Park!! All Ireland Final day is not about the 4 teams involved on the day. It is our showpiece for the year, it's about ladies football, our association, so let's start supporting it. If we don't support it ourselves, how can we seriously expect others to support us?[24]

O'Rourke's calls were heard and there was a record attendance of 20,207 at the 2001 finals.[25] This was an increase of over 5,000 on the finals in 2000.[26]

For most of the following decade, the attendance at finals averaged in the low 20,000s. The year 2003 was an outlier, with over 35,000 reported to have been in Croke Park at the LGFA finals.[27]

Mayo, in their fifth straight final, brought a large travelling support that was matched by the Dubs, who were in their first Senior LGFA final. On top of that, this was the last game in Croke Park before the revamping of the iconic Hill 16 as part of the general redevelopment of the GAA's national stadium, which added extra impetus for supporters to make their way to Croke Park.

Although turnout at the finals was fairly consistent throughout the 2000s, the LGFA was keen to see a bigger crowd at the games. In a letter to county boards ahead of the 2005 finals, O'Rourke noted that the association should be aiming to have 40,000 supporters in Croke Park on All-Ireland final day to continue justifying the playing of the finals in Croke Park.[28]

Cumann Peil Gael na mBan
(THE LADIES GAELIC FOOTBALL ASSOCIATION)
House of Sport, Long Mile Road, Dublin 12.
Phone: (01) 456 9113 (087) 258 5958 Fax: (01) 456 9114

Dear Secretary,

As you are aware our All Ireland final weekend commences on Saturday 29th September with our Club Sevens and our All Ireland Junior & Senior Finals will take place in Croke Park on Sunday 30th in Croke Park. Our Finals are back in Croke Park thanks to the concessions made by the GAA, which now makes it financially viable for us to host our finals there this year. This arrangement is for one year only and the GAA are encouraging Cumann Peil Gael na mBan and Cumann Camogaiocht na nGael to play their finals on the same day from 2002 onwards.

Unfortunately, though every effort has been made in recent years to increase the attendances at our finals, counties have not co-operated. At least 90% of county boards officials and players are not supporting our finals. If we wish to continue playing our finals in Croke Park, this has to change and it is only counties that can change this situation. We need to get our attendances up to 30,000 on the day. Every county board has a part to play and a responsibility to our players and association to make sure that our finals remain in Croke Park. We saw the uproar and outrage the taking of our finals out of Croke Park caused earlier this year in every county. Counties were prepared to do anything to make sure that we got back to Croke Park, now lets see how serious we really are about playing in Croke Park!!

All Ireland Final day is not about the 4 teams involved on the day. It is our showpiece for the year, it's about ladies football, our association, so lets start supporting it. If we don't support it ourselves, how can we seriously expect others to support us?

Is it too much to ask all counties to bring between 500 to 1000 people to our finals? Taking into consideration all club players, underage and adult, Primary & Secondary Schools, it is a realistic figure that most counties can reach if you are serious about staying in Croke Park for the future.
All Ireland tickets and Group tickets will be available from September 1st. Details will follow shortly.

Lets start taking our finals seriously. We are willing to travel anywhere to support the men's game, lets now start supporting our own. This is every county's responsibility.

Yours in sport,

Helen O'Rourke

General Secretary: Helen O'Rourke e-mail: info@ladiesgaelic.ie or visit us on www.ladiesgaelic.ie

The LGFA finals went ahead in Croke Park in 2001 thanks to a concession from the GAA on the security costs. CEO Helen O'Rourke urged the LGFA membership to support the association by attending the finals in Croke Park (Fina Golden).

The LGFA was growing, yet for a time in the early 2000s O'Rourke remained the only paid member of staff, managing all aspects of the association's day-to-day activities and longer-term planning. This was rectified in 2002 when an assistant was hired.

In the same year, the office of the LGFA moved from O'Neills on the Long Mile Road to the Cusack Stand in Croke Park.[29] This was shortly before Giles took up the position of president and she recalled how O'Rourke and the other member of staff were initially situated in the basement of Croke Park. The lower-level office did not reflect the association's ambitions, according to Giles, who said that it was clear that there was a strong vision for the LGFA being spearheaded by O'Rourke with support from the Sports Council.[30] They were determined to figure out the best ways to further grow the game.

As a result, a thorough strategic review began in 2002. This involved reviewing the policies, functions and performance of the organisation from top to bottom. As of early 2003, the committee tasked with the review had carried out interviews and surveys with staff, clubs and players across the regions, had met with the Irish Sports Council, and had assessed the LGFA's relationship with the GAA.[31]

By 2004 LGFA membership had grown again to 90,000. Provincial Administrator roles in Connacht and Leinster were advertised early that year on the back of this growth to provide administrative support to the respective provincial councils, as well as to liaise with a variety of stakeholders, including schools, clubs and the media. They were also tasked with sourcing sponsorship within the provinces for ladies Gaelic football.[32] Before the end of the year, a similar role for the Munster region was also advertised.

In early 2006, a three-year strategic plan was officially unveiled. The LGFA expected that their membership would rise close to the 150,000 mark within this period and among the areas the association had highlighted for development to deal with this growth were 'Coaching and Development', 'Competitions', 'Leadership and Management', and 'Commercial and Marketing'. Four full-time regional officers were to be appointed in the lifetime of the strategic plan and new initiatives were piloted to meet the needs of the membership, such as Gaelic4Girls, Gaelic4Teens and Gaelic4Mothers&Others. The purpose of these programmes was to introduce ladies Gaelic football to girls, teens and women in a fun, non-competitive environment.

At the launch of the strategy in 2006, President Geraldine Giles spoke purposefully:

Instead of basking in the glow of success we need to prepare for the demands of the future. Our game continues to experience massive growth and we have to prepare and be ready to sustain the growth. This is a very exciting time for our sport and the vibrancy and energy in Ladies' Football at present is reflected in the Strategic Plan.[33]

The growing interest in ladies Gaelic football in the 2000s was boosted by the arrival of new teams and new stars at inter-county level. Mayo were the first county to lift the Brendan Martin Cup in the new millennium. In a repeat of the 1999 final, Mayo beat Waterford to win back-to-back All-Ireland titles. Although Waterford kicked more scores on the day, Mayo – led by star forward Cora Staunton – put three goals past Waterford with Staunton contributing 2–2 of Mayo's final tally of 3–6 to win the game by a single point.

Mayo would go on to win two further All-Ireland titles in the early 2000s, with Staunton cementing herself as one of the greatest female Gaelic footballers ever during the following two decades. Marking Staunton was clearly a formidable task for any defender, as she often finished as the game's top scorer. Her overall record speaks for itself: she won four Senior All-Ireland titles and three Division 1 National League titles with Mayo, six Senior All-Ireland club titles with her club Carnacon, and was awarded eleven All-Star awards, which

Angela Casey, captain of the Laois Senior ladies' team jumps for joy with the Brendan Martin Cup. Laois lost seven Senior All-Ireland finals between 1985 and 1996. Their resilience was rewarded in 2001 when they overcame Mayo by one point to finally secure an elusive All-Ireland title (Sportsfile).

ties her with Kerry's Mary Jo Curran for the most All-Star awards ever won by a female Gaelic footballer.

Mayo also contested the 2001 All-Ireland final, seeking a third All-Ireland title on the trot. The game finished in dramatic fashion when Mayo were penalised for not kicking the ball out beyond the 20-metre line from a kick-out. Laois were awarded a free for Mayo's mishap and this was duly converted by Mary Kirwan, bringing her tally to 1–7 overall in the final, allowing Laois to emerge victorious by a single point. This was the ninth time Laois had contested an All-Ireland final since 1985, including one replay in 1996, and they had never before been able to bring home the Brendan Martin Cup. The win in 2001 was a due reward for many of the Laois players who had soldiered on after so many disappointments.

Mayo bounced back to lift the Brendan Martin Cup twice more in 2002 and 2003. However, their win in 2003 – their fourth in five years – was clouded in a controversy that rolled into 2004. In early 2003, Mayo had penned a deal with Azzurri, a Waterford-based sportswear manufacturer, to produce the Mayo LGFA county jerseys. The LGFA had their own agreement with O'Neill's, one that required that teams wore jerseys made and provided by O'Neill's for All-Ireland semi-finals and finals. To honour their agreement with Azzurri, which had been signed before the LGFA's deal with O'Neill's, Mayo covered up the O'Neill's logo on the jerseys supplied to them for the All-Ireland semi-final and wore their Azzurri-branded jerseys for the final. As a result, the LGFA Management Committee imposed a total fine of €22,000 on the Mayo LGFA County Board – €2,000 of this covered the Seniors' semi-final breach, as well as the failure of the county Minor team to wear the correct jerseys in the Minor All-Ireland final, while the remaining €20,000 was to cover the violation in the All-Ireland Senior final.[34]

Mayo refused to pay the fine and the row escalated. John Prenty of the Connacht GAA Council was approached to act as an independent arbitrator between the two sides. Prenty put forward nine recommendations. Mayo were agreeable to seven, seeking amendments on the two remaining matters – paying the fine, reduced to €2,200, to charity rather than the LGFA, and that they be given a special 'derogation' to maintain their deal with Azzurri.

The recommendations and amendments were discussed at a meeting of the Mayo County Board on Tuesday 6 April. As reported by the *Western People*, during that meeting Prenty was contacted by the Mayo Secretary, Mary Gallagher, to clarify if it would be 'viewed as a rejection of the initial proposals' if the Mayo County Board voted to accept the recommendations subject to their two proposed amendments. His opinion was that it would not be seen as an overall rejection and, so, the Mayo County Board voted unanimously to accept seven of the recommendations and proposed changes to the other two.

A fax was sent to the mediator and Central Council the following afternoon, which stated: 'the meeting had no issue with seven of your recommendations, but it was felt that two issues needed to be further explored via the mediation process, and it was agreed that these should be explored expeditiously.' Prenty replied, 'as the negotiations are now at a critical stage, I require a final answer from you as to whether or not the recommendations as presented are acceptable or not.'

A second letter was drafted by Gallagher, detailing precisely the decision taken at the meeting, and this was read over the phone to Prenty, who felt it would be acceptable. However, after consulting the Mayo chairman, P. J. Loftus, Gallagher was told not to send the letter, based on legal advice the board had received. Prenty relayed the events to Central Council and declared that this, therefore, amounted to a rejection of all recommendations and a breakdown of the mediation. Based on this, the Central Council voted to remove Mayo from all LGFA activities.[35]

Helen O'Rourke said that every avenue had been 'exhausted' in the efforts to resolve the disagreement and that the decision to give Mayo the boot from footballing activities was not taken lightly.[36] However, O'Rourke also noted that if Mayo supplied 'new evidence' they could appeal the matter.

A 'heated' emergency meeting of the Mayo board was held that Friday to discuss the situation. The feeling among the delegates was that the 'full and proper representation' of the board's vote that Tuesday had not been communicated to the mediator or Central Council and, on that basis, the Mayo board appealed the decision and clarified their position on the recommendations. The appeal was ultimately upheld and Mayo were reinstated.[37]

Reflecting on the incident some years later, then-president Geraldine Giles said the incident 'blew up in our [the LGFA] faces'. She had expected that there would be pushback at the meeting at which the €22,000 fine was proposed, either from the Mayo County Board or from another county. There was not, however, and instead the Mayo County Board went directly to the press over the issue. With hindsight, Giles said she wouldn't have imposed such a large fine and would have primed someone to make an objection on the floor to get a discussion going before the situation could escalate as it did.[38]

The mid-2000s saw the arrival of a new dominant team on the LGFA Senior inter-county stage: the women of the Rebel County were next to become the Queens of Gaelic football.

The negative attention that the incident garnered was unfortunate and took away somewhat from the on-the-field activity. The adult inter-county scene was going from strength to strength. All thirty-two counties took part in the 2003 National League, with six counties also fielding a second team.[39] Galway won their first and only Senior All-Ireland title to date in 2004, bringing the number of counties that had won the Brendan Martin Cup to eleven. The rules of the game were modernising, too. In 2001, the motion to introduce the yellow and red card system for fouling, as used by the GAA, was passed at congress.[40] In 2004, the rule was modified and a ten-minute 'sin bin' was introduced for yellow card offences to deter fouling.[41]

The mid-2000s also saw the arrival of a new dominant team onto the LGFA Senior inter-county stage, one that would bring ladies Gaelic football to new heights. Following on from the success

of Kerry in the 1980s, and the ascent of Waterford, Monaghan and Mayo in the 1990s and early 2000s, the women from the Rebel County were next to become the Queens of Gaelic football.

Although Cork had been one of the eight counties to take part in the inaugural All-Ireland championship in 1974, the county's roll of honour was short prior to this point. Kerry and Waterford had won every Senior Munster championship since 1974; that is, until Cork beat Kerry to win the title in 2004. Their arrival at the top of the Senior ranks was preceded by a Junior All-Ireland title in 1995, an Intermediate All-Ireland title in 1998, and Division 2 National League titles in 1988, 1992 and 2003. Cork would go on to win five Senior All-Ireland titles in a row between 2005 and 2009, as well as four Division 1 National League titles. This was bolstered by success at underage level, as Cork won three Under–21, four Under–18, five Under–16, and six Under–14 All-Ireland titles in the decade. Cork also featured prominently in the Club All-Ireland Championship. Donoughmore reached the final on four occasions

and twice secured the Dolores Tyrrell Cup (2001 and 2003). Inch Rovers also reached back-to-back finals in 2007 and 2008 but lost on both occasions to Carnacon. During this period the likes of Briege Corkery, Bríd Stack, Geraldine O'Flynn, Angela Walsh, Juliet Murphy, Rena Buckley and Valerie Mulcahy became household names. The footballing talents and never-say-die attitude of the team drew admiration from all over.

At the helm, orchestrating it all, was Éamonn Ryan. Affectionately known as 'the Master', Ryan transformed the fortunes of the Cork ladies' football team while in charge from 2004 to 2015. In Mary White's brilliant book *Relentless*, the story of the rise of the Cork ladies' team, it's clear to see that Ryan was an astute coach who chased excellence. He was also a coach who put his players at the centre of his coaching ethos, as he remarked to White – 'it's all about them, and then it's all about technique.'[42]

Things were also developing underneath the highest level of the inter-county game during this period. Between 1997 and 2000, and again in 2005, an Intermediate championship in the form of a Senior B competition had been held, but in 2007 it was officially introduced as part of a reconstitution of the championship.

The introduction of a third grade allowed for a levelling of the playing field. Among the first five counties to win the Junior All-Ireland title after the grades were reconstituted were Sligo, Kilkenny and Antrim. None of these counties had previously won an adult All-Ireland title before and only Sligo had contested a final previously (they lost the 2005 Junior final to Armagh before winning the title in 2006).

The cup bestowed upon the champions of the new Intermediate championship was named after Mary Quinn, the mother of the talented Quinn sisters who played for Leitrim, to honour her involvement in ladies' football. Fittingly, Leitrim were the first county to lift the Mary Quinn Memorial Cup when they defeated Wexford, 0–17 to 1–10, in the 2007 All-Ireland Intermediate final. In fact, Mary Quinn's daughter and granddaughter were part of the team that day in what was described as a 'hugely special' day for the Quinn family.[43]

Apart from Quinn, the LGFA has honoured others by putting their names to sought-after silverware. Offaly's Mick Talbot was involved in ladies Gaelic football from the beginning in 1974 and his name is now bestowed upon the inter-provincial cup. The All-Ireland Club championship trophy was named the Dolores Tyrrell Cup in 1994 following the death of the former Ballymacarbry and Waterford player who had captained Ballymacarbry when they won their first All-Ireland club title in 1987. Then there is Aisling McGing, a young Mayo player who was on her way to watch the Mayo ladies in a championship match in MacHale Park in 2003 when she died in a tragic car accident. Her death shocked the ladies Gaelic football community both in Mayo and further afield. In 2007, the LGFA named the Under–21 championship cup the Aisling McGing Cup in memory of the talented young player.

Another sign of the LGFA's development came in 2004 when the first All-Star Tour took place, the All-Star selection from 2003 travelling to New York to take on a Rest of Ireland selection in Gaelic Park. Traditionally, the All-Star team played the All-Ireland Senior champions at the end of the season but here existed an opportunity to reward players while connecting with the growing international base of ladies Gaelic footballers.

Sligo players Joanne O'Connell, Siobhan O'Sullivan, Fiona Maye, Ruth Goodwin, Valerie O'Beirne, Niamh Mannion, Karen Maloney and Caroline Currid stand behind supporters' banners as they show off some silverware (Fina Golden/Patricia McCaffrey).

The sign held by the players reads:

Valerie — *Caroline...Fast & Furious* — *SLiGO LADiES MAD for it... the Ball that is!!!! — Shake it Ruthie Baby! — A quality PRIDE — Super Mannion*

The previous November, the guest of honour at the first-ever LGFA All-Stars banquet, President of Ireland Mary McAleese, acknowledged the significance of awards themselves, but also spoke of the event in the context of a widening Irish sporting scene:

> These awards I believe, with great passion, are hugely important, because they give due and proper recognition to the enormous contribution made to Gaelic games from women of every corner of this island. Tonight the spotlight widens as it should, well beyond the image, so often of men and boys who gather to discuss our National games, in the wider spotlight we see clearly the true picture of sporting life in Ireland. In that picture we see the role of women gathering what we can describe, as a huge, huge momentum. Is there any other game in Ireland with the potential that this game has? I doubt it.[44]

The All-Star game acted as a curtain-raiser to the Connacht Championship match between New York and Mayo.[45] O'Rourke said that the game would serve a dual purpose: to boost the profile of ladies Gaelic football in the Big Apple, and to reward the commitment and skill of the inter-county players.[46]

Seven players from the reigning All-Ireland champions Mayo travelled to New York for that inaugural All-Star Tour and featured across the two teams, while runners-up Dublin supplied five players. Players from Kerry, Waterford, Galway, Monaghan, Roscommon, Donegal, Tyrone, Laois and Kildare also featured and the subs for both teams were supplied by teams based in New York.[47]

The tour was a success and the next one was pencilled in for two years later. This time the contingent were to fly to Singapore to connect with the growing Gaelic games community in Asia.

As of 2006, around 5,000 of the LGFA's 100,000-strong membership were playing ladies Gaelic football outside Ireland.[48] Over 700 members were registered in the USA and the New York

County Board had even established a Gaelic4Girls programme to encourage the development of the game at underage level.[49] There were thirty teams in Australia and new clubs were being set up in Hong Kong, Beijing, Dubai and Singapore, signalling how the reach of the Irish population was expanding.[50]

The European contingent was smaller, however, coming in at around 150 registered players.[51] Ladies Gaelic football had started to emerge on the continent around the summer of 1999, when Brussels were the first to set up a ladies' team, soon spreading to the likes of Luxembourg, Holland, France and Spain.[52]

Other avenues for growth and development were also considered during this time. While in Singapore in 2006, the LGFA met with officials from the Australian Football League (AFL) to explore the possibility of holding the first-ever women's International Rules test series in Ireland later in the year for women Gaelic footballers and Australian footballers.[53] It was proposed on the back of the men's series that had taken place on-and-off since 1984 and was due to come to Ireland later in 2006.

The discussions were successful. The tests were scheduled to take place under lights in late October and early November and would be shown live on TG4. The game would differ slightly from the men's version of the game, with differences in rules including fewer steps being allowed and a mark only allowed to be called inside both 45m lines.[54] Former Armagh captain – and current President of the GAA – Jarlath Burns was chosen to manage the squad.[55]

The fixtures took place in Breffni Park and Parnell Park.[56] Ireland easily won the first test by 115 points, 6–26–16 (130) to 1–2–3 (15).[57] In their second test at Parnell Park, Ireland's score was wiped from the board in the third quarter when Ireland fielded an extra player following a sin-bin. TG4 presenter Micheál Ó Domhnaill approached the referee live on air to have the decision explained, such was the confusion. Reduced to zero, Ireland still managed to win the test, 3–5–6 (39) to 0–4–6 (18). Ireland's superiority was clear but perhaps this was to be expected, given that, at the time, there were only 19,000 women playing Aussie Rules in Australia – a figure that paled in comparison to the health of ladies Gaelic football in Ireland.[58]

———————

Despite the undoubted progress, there was a long way to go in terms of establishing equality between male and female athletes. After all, the reality was that ladies Gaelic football continued to play catch-up on the GAA's ninety-year head start. Yet steps were made throughout the decade to bridge this gap.

In early 2000, a national forum on women in Gaelic games had been held in the Burlington Hotel in Dublin. Sponsored by Bank of Ireland, this forum was the first of its kind and was attended by over 300 delegates from the LGFA, the Camogie Association and the GAA.[59] The chair of the working group, Liz Howard, gave an insight into the forum's work:

> I see the Forum for women in Gaelic games as an exciting and important new development. However, it is only a starting point, the follow-on from the Forum is vital if women are to increase their active role in all areas of the GAA. Society is changing quickly, young women today rightly expect true equality. The GAA must remove the barriers to allow women to enter into all roles within the Association, such as coaching, refereeing and management. If attitudes are positive that is possible. The greater participation of women in the games will ultimately strengthen the Association.[60]

The national forum was an example of the expanding working relationship between the LGFA and the GAA. The LGFA was establishing itself more prominently in the Irish sporting landscape and was seen as an association with great potential. Speaking to Vincent Hogan in 2001, O'Rourke reflected on the ground made by the LGFA in this regard. She recalled how, when she was PRO in the early 1990s, 'it was a constant fight to get anywhere. We certainly

seemed to be fighting the GAA constantly.' She did also concede that they still were fighting the GAA in many ways.[61] However, the power of the LGFA had strengthened over the years and this was reflected in the concession the GAA had made in 2001 to ensure that the LGFA finals were not taken out of Croke Park. The image of ladies Gaelic football, as well as the relationship between the two associations, had developed to the extent that the GAA was prepared to remove the cost barrier to ensure that the LGFA finals continued to be held at Croke Park.

A review carried out by the same working group who had organised the forum made a number of recommendations in 2002, including the formal integration of the women's games into the GAA structure, increasing the profile of female inter-county

An outstretched Brianne Leahy of Kildare and Ireland blocks an effort from Meg Hutchins of Australia. While in Singapore for the 2006 All-Stars tour, the LGFA reached a deal with officials from the Australian Football League to stage a women's International Rules series in Ireland later that year. Ireland overpowered the Australians in both tests to win the series (Sportsfile).

players, the inclusion of women in the GAA's decision-making structures, and auditing the suitability and availability of facilities for female sports.[62]

A further development came when efforts were made to formalise the relationship between the three associations. This occurred in 2003 when a pilot integration scheme was trialled in eight counties. The press release issued at the time stated that the scheme's aim was to 'highlight the various challenges which integration poses and provide solutions ahead of closer liaisons between the three Associations in a national context'.[63]

Then president-elect of the LGFA, Geraldine Giles, said of the scheme:

> This is an important step forward. The project on the ground at present will provide us with a more structured approach to the future discussions and the final integration where we maintain our autonomy, but have the support of an Association that has greater resources at its disposal.[64]

On the back of the pilot, the report prepared by the Integration Task Force recommended that, overall, the three associations should retain their autonomy, but that they should come together as one at club level, and develop closer working relationships at county, provincial and national levels.[65]

Logistically, there was obviously much to work out between the associations. However, both socially and culturally, there would also have to be changes. After all, while the GAA have been very accommodating and encouraging of women's Gaelic games in recent years, this had not always been the case. As a result, establishing understanding and trust between the associations would be essential to moving forward towards a more equal working relationship.

This was highlighted during an incident in 2005 when comments by GAA President Sean Kelly caused controversy. Efforts were made in 2005 to play the All-Ireland quarter-final between Dublin and Tyrone before the quarter-final replay between the same two sides in the men's football championship.[66] The discussions were ultimately successful; however, things turned sour when LGFA CEO O'Rourke took issue with Kelly's comments in the match programme. He suggested that a 'Queen of Fashion' competition should take place in Croke Park, which would involve the best-dressed women marching around the Croke Park pitch behind the Artane Boys Band with the winner being presented with a prize such as 'a day at the races, or a day in the bog, two tickets for the All Ireland etc.'[67]

O'Rourke saw this as a condescending insult that equated women to 'prize heifers'. Kelly felt that his comments were not derogatory towards female GAA fans and said that he was merely complimenting the large number of women who were attending inter-county matches.[68] O'Rourke made the counter-point that women were not coming to Croke Park to use it as a runway and felt that Kelly's comments 'undermined the interest women have in the sport'.[69]

The report on the fallout from this controversy that appeared in the *Irish Independent* was accompanied by a picture of Miss Ireland, Aoife Coogan, modelling a Dublin GAA jersey, wearing nothing but the jersey and a pair of high heels. One wonders why the national newspaper could not find a photo of one of the many female fans in Croke Park, or indeed a photo of the action from the LGFA quarter-final between Dublin and Tyrone, to highlight women's interest in Gaelic games.

Speaking in 2010, Giles felt that there wouldn't be full integration of the LGFA with the GAA because of a lack of resources. This, she felt, would make it impossible to integrate completely at a national level. Instead, she believed that the way forward would involve a closer alliance between the two associations, but with the LGFA retaining autonomy. The relationship between the two had evolved, in her eyes, to one which was 'not just an accommodation' but a 'working relationship'. Giles spoke highly of Liam Mulvihill, the Director General of the GAA from 1979 to 2008, for changing mindsets regarding ladies Gaelic football, and credited his successor, Paraic Duffy (2008–18), for working to evolve the relationship since then.[70]

In comparison, she described the relationship between the LGFA and the Camogie Association as mixed and dependent on circumstances in each county. At a national level, she described it as 'hit and miss' and more of an 'accommodation', suggesting that there remained an element of rivalry between the two bodies, the Camogie Association perhaps viewing the rise of ladies' football in recent years as being to the 'detriment of camogie' in some areas. However, Giles did also state that this was something they should work on to improve.

Overall, the 2000s was a period defined by growth and strategic planning. Increased funding allowed the LGFA to expand their number of employees and, as a result, design and deliver more impactful initiatives for players, officials and volunteers. Its partnership with TG4 in particular was proving to be a resounding success, and with the increased visibility, the LGFA was attracting interest from other brands and organisations who wanted to invest in women's sport. At a playing level, the changes made by the LGFA to the inter-county competition structures went some way to levelling the playing field and helped to inspire a new generation of female Gaelic footballers.

It was clear to see that the LGFA were no longer the little sister of the GAA and the Camogie Association. Now in its mid-thirties, the LGFA was asserting its autonomy and exploring exciting new opportunities, all of which was helping it to cement itself as the fastest-growing female sport in the country.

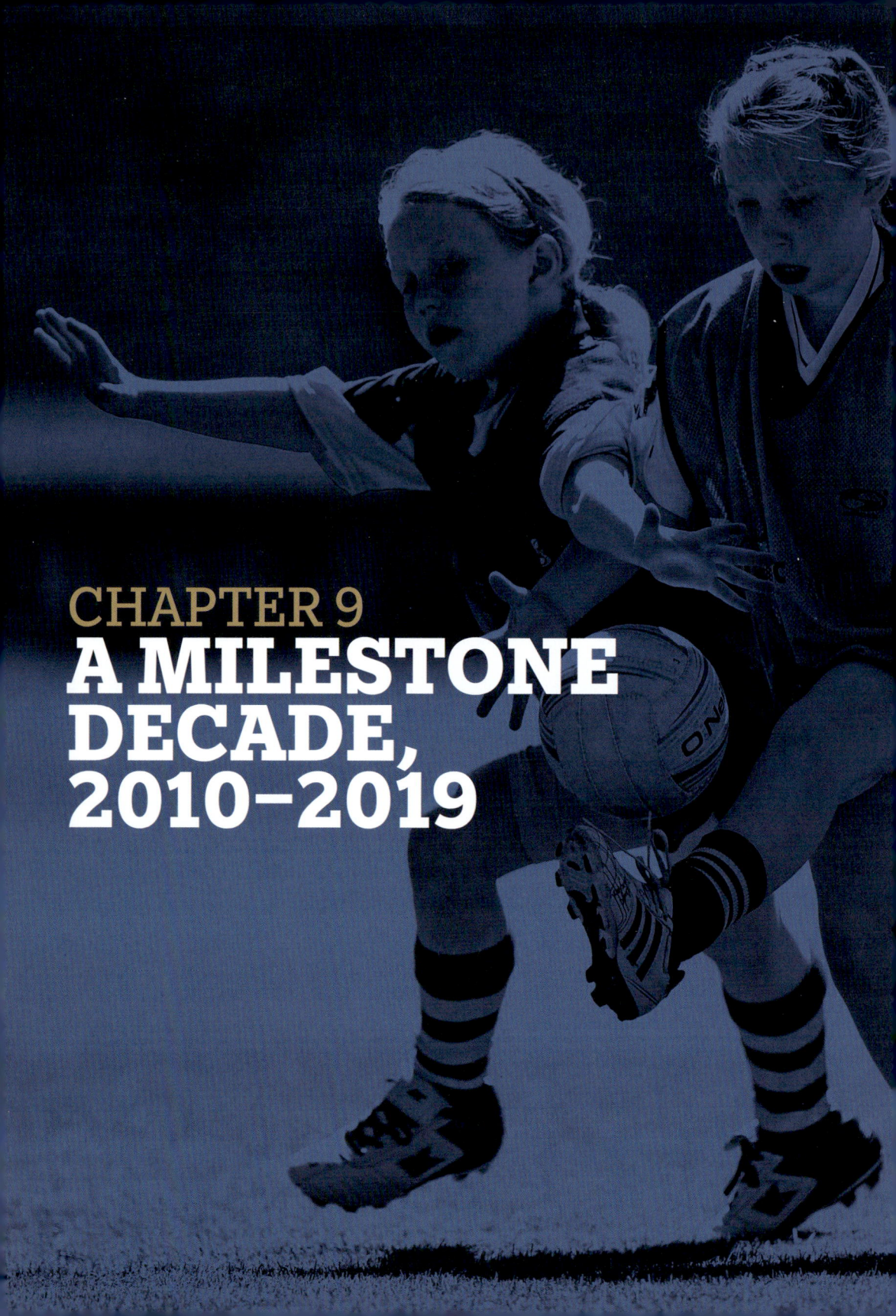

CHAPTER 9
A MILESTONE DECADE, 2010–2019

The 2000s were a remarkable decade of growth and modernisation for ladies Gaelic football. By 2011, the LGFA was the largest female sporting organisation in Ireland with over 142,000 members.[1] The key question stepping further into the next decade was: could the LGFA sustain this growth?

Steps were being taken to ensure that it did. One such step was a new strategic plan for the period 2011–16, setting out the LGFA's vision to be 'The Sport for Females, The Game for Fun, The Place for Community.'[2] In numbers, the LGFA's goals were clear for the end of this period – 200,000 members, 40,000 spectators in Croke Park on All-Ireland final day and €600,000 raised in sponsorship.[3]

The new decade also saw new All-Ireland winners. With five All-Ireland titles won in a row between 2005 and 2009, it appeared – albeit briefly – that Cork's dominance would not continue into the 2010s when they failed to reach the 2010 All-Ireland final. The Rebelettes had succeeded in retaining their Division 1 National League title earlier in the year, beating Galway on a score of 2–10 to 1–9, but they crashed out of the All-Ireland series at the quarter-final

Tyrone put a stop to Cork's quest for six All-Ireland titles in a row when they dumped the Rebelettes out of the competition at the quarter-final stage in 2010. Tyrone and Dublin, both vying for a first-ever Senior All-Ireland title, faced each other in the final with Dublin taking the victory, 3–16 to 0–9 (Sportsfile).

stage when they were comprehensively beaten by Tyrone, 3–11 to 0–13. Tyrone backed up their win over the reigning All-Ireland champions by reaching their first-ever Senior All-Ireland final thanks to a one-point win over Kerry in the semi-final replay. In the other semi-final, Dublin had two points to spare over Laois. Subsequently Dublin, in their fourth final in eight years, had too much strength for Tyrone and won their first-ever All-Ireland title on a score-line of 3–16 to 0–9, with Sinéad Aherne starring on the day with a tally of 2–7.

There were also new winners in the Intermediate and Junior grades. Donegal won their first Intermediate title, having won the Junior grade in 2003, while Limerick, contesting their second Junior final in a row, overcame Louth to take home the West County Hotel Cup. The success of the regrading of the championship can be seen in the fact that in the ten years between 2010 and 2019, nine different counties won the Intermediate title and eight counties were victorious in the Junior grade.

For counties where ladies Gaelic football was still a small or emerging sport, competing at Junior or Intermediate grade provided teams with achievable routes to All-Ireland success and helped encourage the growth of the game within their respective counties. Donegal were an example of the benefits of this pathway. Having won the Intermediate title in 2010, they received promotion to the Senior ranks the following year and have kept their Senior status since.

The Junior grade saw the likes of New York and Scotland compete in All-Ireland finals in 2011 and 2014 (New York) and 2015

(Scotland). New York and Wicklow could not be separated in the 2011 Junior final at the first time of asking. The New York County Board had to appeal to the LGFA for financial assistance to return to Ireland to play the replay.[4] This was the team's third trip to Ireland that year to compete in the Junior Championship and it was estimated to have cost in the region of €25,000 for New York to travel each time.[5] This was New York's first foray since 2001 in the All-Ireland championships and their success was a sign of the growing strength of ladies Gaelic football in the Big Apple. Fortunately, the LGFA were able to support New York, reportedly granting them €10,000 towards their travelling expenses.[6] Unfortunately, it was not a case of third time lucky for New York on their third trip to Ireland, as they came up short in the replay, losing 2–11 to 0–8.

Although the three divisions for the championships were intended to ensure that counties of similar ability and standard were competing against one other, it was not always easy for teams to bridge the gulf. Speaking about the gap between teams in the adult championships in 2011, LGFA President Pat Quill said:

> This is the thing with women's sports, it seems to go in stages and some of those counties who are struggling now could well bounce back next year. [...] Sometimes it can be down to structures, sometimes it can be down to the fact that girls are gone to college or Leaving Cert or some who have emigrated and if you have two or three key players missing in any team their colleagues can become demoralised.[7]

Gulfs in standards were still evident, like when Cork and Kerry shipped big wins over Clare and Tipperary respectively in the Senior Munster championship. In other provinces, Monaghan had big wins over Down and Armagh, while Mayo beat Sligo by twenty-eight points.[8] Kilkenny also struggled and, after a terrible league campaign in 2019, they withdrew from that year's Junior championship.[9]

Cork soon returned to dominant ways at Senior level in 2011, defeating the reigning All-Ireland champions Dublin at the quarter-final stage after a tense and close encounter by a single point, 2–14 to 3–10. It marked the beginning of a thrilling rivalry between the two counties that would repeat on various occasions over the rest of the decade. Cork beat Laois easily in the semi-final and Monaghan came out of the other semi-final against Kerry to set up an interesting encounter between two counties who had established themselves as supremos of ladies Gaelic football. Cork were victorious again.

They followed up their return to the top of ladies Gaelic football with another All-Ireland win in 2012, this time against Munster rivals Kerry in the decider. Although Cork had nine points to spare over Kerry that day, Kerry got the better of Cork when the sides met in the 2013 Munster championship, beating the Lee-siders in the group series and again in the provincial final by one point, 1–16 to 1–15, which put a stop to Cork's campaign to win a tenth Munster title in a row.

Down but not out of the All-Ireland championship, this was such a disappointment to Cork that five-time All-Star Juliet Murphy was persuaded to come out of retirement in an attempt to boost the county's efforts to retain their All-Ireland crown.[10]

Following the group stages, Cork were drawn to play Dublin in the quarter-final in a repeat of the 2011 knock-out stages. This was Murphy's first game back and, according to reporter Mary White, she was 'the main woman, dictating play in the second half' as Cork pulled off an incredible comeback.[11] Nine points behind with twenty minutes remaining on the clock, Cork scored 1–10 without reply to beat Dublin by four points, 1–19 to 2–12, and set up their third contest that year against Kerry in the semi-final. In that game, Valerie Mulcahy scored 2–3 of Cork's 2–9 versus Kerry's 0–11 to get them into another All-Ireland final versus Monaghan.

A tough battle ensued, Cork ultimately gaining a slim one-point victory over the Ulster team, ensuring that the Brendan Martin Cup returned to the Lee-siders for the eighth time since its first trip to the Munster county in 2005. Murphy scored two points in the final and was rewarded for her inspirational comeback with her sixth All-Star at the end of the season, after which she once again retired.

In 2014, Cork and Dublin were fated to meet again, this time in an All-Ireland Senior final. Cork beat Mayo and Armagh in the knockout stages, while Dublin saw off challenges from Kerry and Galway. Just two points had separated the sides in the Division 1 National League final earlier in the year and on that result and their experience, Cork went into the final as favourites.

However, Dublin were the stronger team in the opening half, leading 1–7 to 0–4 at half-time. Ten points down with fifteen minutes remaining, Cork needed another remarkable comeback to snatch victory from Dublin's clutches and win their ninth All-Ireland title. Goals from Rhona Ní Bhuacalla and Eimear Scally helped to bring Cork level with seven minutes left. Geraldine O'Flynn followed up scores from Siobhan Woods of Dublin and Ciara O'Sullivan of Cork to put Cork ahead at the final whistle. Heartbreak for Dublin, elation for Cork. The comeback was one of the greatest that manager Éamonn Ryan had ever seen in Croke Park.[12] So impressive was the way in which Cork won the 2014 All-Ireland final, demonstrating skill and determination, that Cork were named the RTÉ Sports Team of the Year by the public.

In a replay of the 2014 decider, Cork faced Dublin again in the 2015 final, winning an incredible tenth All-Ireland title in eleven years. There was controversy following the 2015 All-Ireland decider, however, as a point scored by Dublin's Carla Rowe that was waved wide by the umpire was later shown by TV replays to have been a score. HawkEye technology was not in place for this game. The LGFA had decided that as the technology was not available for all games in the championship, it would not be utilised in the final.[13] Dublin manager Gregory McGonigle suggested that they might seek a replay because of the error but a decision was made by the Dublin County Board not to proceed with this request.

Cork celebrate winning their tenth All-Ireland title in eleven years in 2015. Manager Éamonn Ryan stepped down at the end of this season but the group went on to win one more All-Ireland title and three more Division 1 titles before the end of the decade (Sportsfile).

This was not the first time an incident like this had occurred. The 2006 All-Ireland semi-final between Galway and Armagh ended in similar controversy when a point scored by Galway, confirmed by video evidence post-match, was waved wide by an umpire. Moments later, as the Galway players remonstrated with the referee, Armagh went down the field, and won and scored a free to win the game. Galway launched an appeal and Armagh a counter-appeal to the LGFA Central Council, who ultimately upheld the result given on the day.[14] Galway manager P. J. Fahy stepped down in protest at the LGFA's refusal to call a replay, calling the decision a 'joke.'[15]

In light of this oversight in 2015, the LGFA moved to implement changes for the 2016 season, amending Rule 518 of the LGFA official rulebook to allow for referees to be assisted in determining scores through the use of video technology during all televised games.[16]

At the end of that 2015 season, Cork Manager Éamonn Ryan stepped down in order to take up a position with the county's men footballing team in 2016.[17] Ryan's stewardship of the Cork team was an iconic period in the history of ladies Gaelic football and there's no doubt that the impact of Ryan's coaching philosophy and style extended beyond the county boundaries of Cork.

Despite the loss of Ryan, Cork retained their All-Ireland title in 2016, beating Dublin again in a close game to claim a sixth title in a row and an incredible eleventh All-Ireland title in twelve years, putting the county level with Kerry for the most number of All-Ireland Senior title wins. Overall, between 2000 and 2019 Cork teams took home an incredible fifty-nine All-Ireland titles – eleven at Senior level, twelve league titles, five at Under–21, nine at Under–18, seven at Under–16, ten at Under–14, and five club All-Ireland titles.

A new team were on the rise, however. A huge crowd of over 46,000 – surpassing the LGFA's hoped-for attendance from their latest strategic plan – were in Croke Park in 2017 to witness the beginning of a new takeover at the top of ladies Gaelic football by Dublin, as they had a commanding win over Mayo in the All-Ireland final, 4–11 to 0–11.

The attendance was up again in 2018 when Dublin beat Cork (3–11 to 1–12), this time to 50,141. That record was surpassed in 2019 when 56,114 people passed through the turnstiles. The record attendance in 2019 was particularly impressive, considering that it was a very wet and dull day that impacted the footballing spectacle. Dublin won this low-scoring affair, 2–3 to 0–4, against Galway.

All of this showed that ladies Gaelic football was entertaining, of course, and its finals were a great day out, but it also made clear that there was a movement brewing around women's sport. One that was bringing it ever more into the public eye.

One such example of the general public's increased interest in ladies' football came in January 2016 when the launch of a new product, 'The Ladyball', drew a strong public reaction. A pink Gaelic football embossed with the slogan 'Play like a lady,' the football was described as being 'soft-touch for a woman's grip, eazi-play for a woman's ability, and fashion-driven for a woman's style.'[18]

Dublin and Cork parade around Croke Park in front of a crowd of over 50,000 at the 2018 All-Ireland finals. This attendance was almost 30,000 more people than had attended the first All-Ireland final of the 2010s (Sportsfile).

A record attendance of 56,114 for the LGFA finals was set in 2019. Since 2012, when fewer than 16,998 travelled to Croke Park, the crowd for the finals had increased year-on-year up to the 2019 finals (Sportsfile).

Social media erupted in disbelief in January 2016 when advertisements began to appear for a new Gaelic football called the 'Ladyball', which was supposedly designed especially for females. The product and the advertising campaign around it turned out to be a marketing con to stir up conversation about women's sport ahead of the announcement of Lidl's partnership with the LGFA (Lidl).

Social media and the airwaves erupted with incredulity, refuting the idea that a football marketed at girls and women in the stereotypical pink colour would encourage female participation in sport. However, it turned out that the product was a con. The real intention of the ad was to provoke a discussion around women's sport ahead of the announcement of an official partnership between supermarket chain Lidl and the LGFA.[19]

The partnership between the LGFA and Lidl was a landmark one. Lidl committed to a three-year deal and to invest €1.5million in the LGFA in the first year, making it the biggest partnership announcement in women's sport in the past decade.[20]

An injection into the advertising of ladies Gaelic football was also part of the partnership with #SeriousSupport the adopted slogan. Television and print advertisements on a scale that the LGFA would not have been able to afford before helped to increase the visibility of the game yet again. The ads presented the toughness and thrills of ladies Gaelic football and picked up where 'The Ladyball' had started in getting people talking about ladies Gaelic football and, most importantly, giving recognition to the players' efforts. Other efforts such as the 20x20 campaign, which was launched in 2018 and aimed to create a cultural shift in the perception of women's sport in Ireland, also bolstered the public image of ladies Gaelic football.

While these were high points for ladies' football, controversies and conflicts clouded some of the progress made by ladies Gaelic football during this period. Often, they required the LGFA management to get involved to find solutions.

The decade started with one such controversy when the Mayo Senior team was withdrawn by the Mayo County Board from the 2010 Senior championship following the resignation of team manager Pat Costello, who felt that his position was undermined by certain players.[21] LGFA President Pat Quill and CEO Helen O'Rourke intervened in an attempt to find a resolution to the disagreement, meeting with both the county board and the players on a number of occasions. However, the county board upheld their decision to withdraw the Senior team from competitions. The LGFA noted that this was 'extremely disappointing' and 'wholly unsatisfactory'.[22]

Aishling Sheridan (Cavan), Karen McDermott (Westmeath), Áine Haberlin (Laois) and Lorraine O'Shea (Tipperary) jump for joy at the announcement of Lidl's sponsorship deal with the LGFA in 2016. An initial three-year deal was penned worth €1.5 million but the partnership has continued to the present day (Sportsfile).

The saga rolled on for several months. Mayo did not take part in the Connacht Championship but did enter the All-Ireland series at the qualifier stage thanks to an appeal by three Mayo clubs (Castlebar, Carnacon and Knockmore) to the LGFA's Central Council to have the county team reinstated to the championship. With less than three weeks to prepare for a knock-out game against Kerry, Fr Michael Murphy agreed to take charge of the team.[23] The Mayo players acquitted themselves admirably, losing by just one point, 0–12 to 1–8, bringing to a close a short but tumultuous season for the Mayo ladies.

The LGFA conducted a review into the issue and concluded that the issue arising with the Senior county team was that a faction of experienced senior players 'constantly tried to exercise control over the team', which led to poor relations between players and management. The LGFA also stated that the 'situation was exacerbated by the poor procedures adopted by the County Board in the appointment of managers'.[24]

The LGFA set out ten recommendations to rebuild relations, which included that a Senior county manager be appointed by the county board with the support of the LGFA Central Council, and also suggested the appointment of a liaison officer to ensure communication was open between players, management and the county board.[25]

A committee was established and, in January 2011, Jason Taniane, who had previously managed Kilkerrin-Clonberne to win the LGFA Intermediate club All-Ireland title in 1999 and Leitrim to win the Intermediate All-Ireland title in 2007, was appointed as the new Mayo ladies' team manager.[26]

The instability continued, however, as Taniane stepped down at the end of the 2011 season. Fr Murphy took the reins once again, this time with joint manager Jimmy Corbett for the 2012 season, before passing the baton to Peter Clarke in 2013. Clarke managed the team for two consecutive seasons, bringing to an end a cycle of one-term (or less) managements that had started in 2005.

The LGFA was required to step in to deal with county affairs again in 2014, this time in Tipperary, when a number of players expressed concerns about the quality of training sessions under the management of John Leahy. Five players were dropped and a further fourteen players left the county panel following a breakdown in relations with the county management and the county board.[27] In response, the LGFA instructed a mediator to help to resolve the situation.[28]

The 2018 season was overshadowed by conflict within Mayo LGFA. In July, eight members of the squad, all from the Carnacon club, left the panel, citing player welfare concerns. Captain Sarah Tierney also departed the panel due to a breakdown in the relationship with the manager and unhappiness with manager Peter Leahy's communication style.[29] In total, twelve players left the Mayo panel, with the Mayo County Board backing Peter Leahy throughout.

The partnership between the LGFA and Lidl was a landmark one, the biggest partnership announcement in women's sport in the past decade.

In August, a vote at a meeting of the Mayo LGFA County Board was passed to throw Carnacon out of all competitions under Rule 288, which allows for expulsion on the basis of bringing the association into disrepute. This was appealed by the club at provincial level and they were reinstated.[30] The Carnacon players were subsequently hit with a four-week suspension by the Mayo LGFA County Board and a €500 fine was placed on the Carnacon club.[31] The LGFA National Appeal Committee dropped the ban from four weeks to two but this was counter-appealed by the Mayo LGFA County Board on the grounds that it was too lenient.[32]

The dispute rolled on for much of the summer, with a series of statements of denial and rebuttal from numerous parties, all of which impacted the reigning All-Ireland club champions' preparation for and playing of the club championship. Despite this, Carnacon won the Mayo Senior Championship and progressed to the Connacht Senior Club Championship final, where they were beaten by Galway's Kilkerrin-Clonberne.

Earlier in 2018, issues had also arisen in Leitrim. With some difficulty, a county board had been formed but failure to find a manager for the county's Senior team meant that Leitrim could not field a team and were therefore at risk of being suspended from LGFA activities at all levels for a twelve-month period. However, a dispensation was agreed with the LGFA that allowed football to continue within the county but disallowed Leitrim clubs from progressing into the provincial championships.[33]

Arguably, considering how the LGFA had grown so quickly, and how Gaelic games was modernising and had become professional in all but name, it was perhaps inevitable that more disputes and issues would arise.

———

When the Women's Gaelic Players Association (WGPA) was launched in 2015 – a move that signalled a closer alliance between inter-county ladies' football and camogie players – its chair Aoife Lane was asked why the WGPA was separate from the men's GPA, which had been founded in 1999. Her response was clear: 'we have totally different issues, we are starting from a very different place. We have to work a whole lot harder to promote our games. Men were already up there, on a different level [when the GPA started].'[34]

This statement was backed up by the results of a survey of nearly 600 female inter-county players (football and camogie) conducted by the WGPA. The findings revealed how playing at the highest level was costing them physically, financially and emotionally. For example, only seven per cent received expenses for travelling to training, only one-third had access to hot showers after training on a regular basis, sixty-three per cent were out of pocket from their inter-county commitments and eighty per cent of players felt 'overwhelmed at times' by the pressure of their inter-county commitments.

The LGFA had done stellar work in modernising the association and raising the profile of ladies Gaelic football; however, their

Erin Kelly from Down attempts to dispossess Saoirse O'Keefe from Waterford at the Gaelic4Girls National Blitz Day in Croke Park in 2014. The Gaelic4Girls initiative introduces girls to Gaelic football in a fun, non-competitive environment (Sportsfile).

resources were still in a different league in comparison to the GAA's. Closing this gap would be a key issue going into the 2020s.

Still, this was undoubtedly a decade of milestones for ladies Gaelic football. Membership was inching closer to the goal of 200,000 set at the start of the decade, with 188,000 registered as of 2018; the target of an audience of 40,000 in Croke Park on All-Ireland Final day had been met in 2017 and exceeded in 2018 and 2019, and Lidl invested over €3.5million in the LGFA over three years from 2016, helping to bring much more visibility to the sport. Their commitment in 2019 to a further three-year deal worth another €3million promised big things leading into the next decade.

The One Club Model, a single administrative structure for clubs under which to organise all Gaelic games, had been agreed between the LGFA, the GAA and the Camogie Association in 2010, and a draft memorandum of understanding was signed by the associations

University of Limerick (UL) players celebrate winning the O'Connor Cup final in 2014. UL are the most successful university in the ladies' higher education flagship competition with twelve titles won under the UL name, and a further one under Thomond College (Sportsfile).

in 2018 that was seen as a breakthrough for the organisations in terms of establishing a shared vision. It also meant that from 2019 onwards the women's organisations would sit on the GAA's Ard Comhairle (its governing body, made up of representatives from all counties, overseas sectors, schools and other bodies under the GAA umbrella) and Coiste Bainistíochta, which is a fifteen-member management committee, chaired by the GAA President.

These developments were symbolic of the strengthening working relationship between the associations, a positive development that was seen on the pitch, too, when the LGFA All-Ireland Senior semi-finals were played in Croke Park for the first time in 2019.

Hoping to build on these milestones, the LGFA set out their key ambition going into the next decade: to be the sport of choice for females.[35]

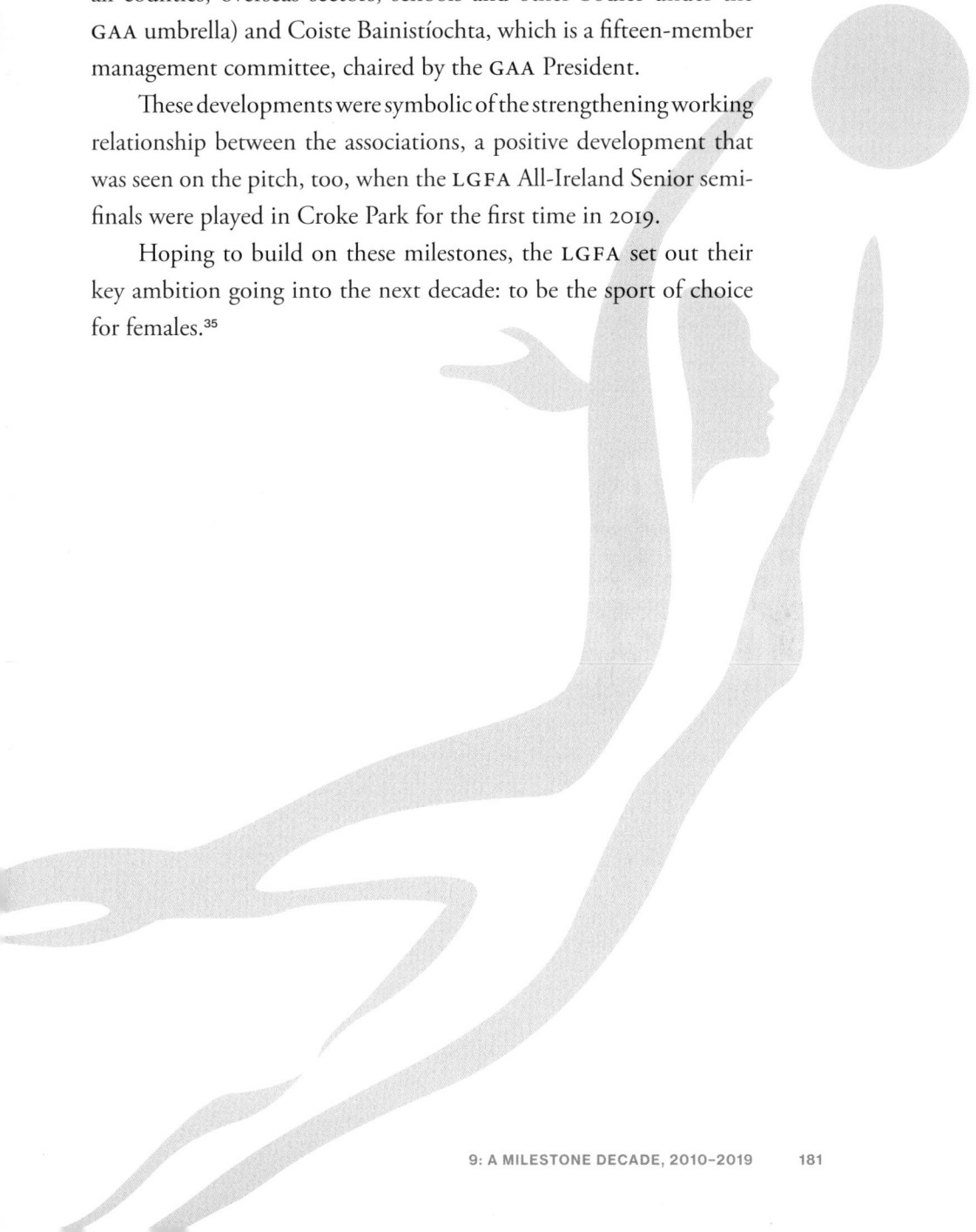

CHAPTER 10
AN ERA
FOR ALL,
2020–2024

At the 2020 LGFA Annual Congress, held in Galway on the first weekend in March, Helen O'Rourke finished her address to the delegates present by stating that there would be many challenges to face in the year ahead. The challenges ahead, according to O'Rourke, would mainly be in strengthening structures and ensuring an enjoyable playing experience for all, as well as improving the profile of the game and aiming to increase attendances at matches throughout the year.[1]

Days later, Taoiseach Leo Varadkar addressed the people of Ireland from Washington, announcing the first wave of measures to combat the spread of the Covid-19 virus. This included the closure of schools and limits on the number of people at gatherings.[2] People were encouraged to limit social interactions as much as possible, but it was hoped that after two weeks in place the restrictions would have halted the spread of the disease. In reality, the situation would get much more serious.

Immediately following the government's announcement on 12 March, the LGFA, the GAA and the Camogie Association suspended all activity for all ages and grades.[3] Before the end of March, the LGFA announced that, with just one round remaining in the National League fixtures, they had decided to cancel the competitions for 2020 due to the ongoing pandemic.[4] Other competitions, such as the higher education and post-primary competitions, the Under–14 tournament, the inter-provincials and Féile na nÓg were also cancelled.[5] By mid-April, the LGFA had confirmed that the provincial championships that had been due to take place in May and June would now not take place; furthermore, it was looking increasingly likely that championship action over the summer months would also be suspended.[6]

The pandemic truly was an extraordinary event. The risk of illness was serious, there was no precedent to follow, and the situation was continually evolving, which made it difficult for the LGFA to even put preliminary plans in place. This was conveyed by O'Rourke, who noted in an official statement that, 'while we must plan for the future, the health and safety of our members is our main priority at the present time.'[7]

The LGFA gauged members' views via a survey. It revealed that eighty-nine per cent felt that – in the event that restrictions were eased and sport could resume – priority should be given to club rather than county activities.[8] Aligning with this, club activity was the first to resume when restrictions were eased towards the end of June – albeit on a staggered basis and with various conditions in place to limit the potential for the spread of the virus.

In July, the LGFA were able to announce inter-county championships fixtures, scheduled for the remainder of the year. Starting on the weekend of 31 October/1 November, the championships would run right up to the Christmas period, setting the All-Ireland Senior and Intermediate finals for 20 December. The provincial competitions were scrapped in favour of a condensed championship, with counties guaranteed three matches in a group-stage before the competition filtered into the knock-out stages.[9]

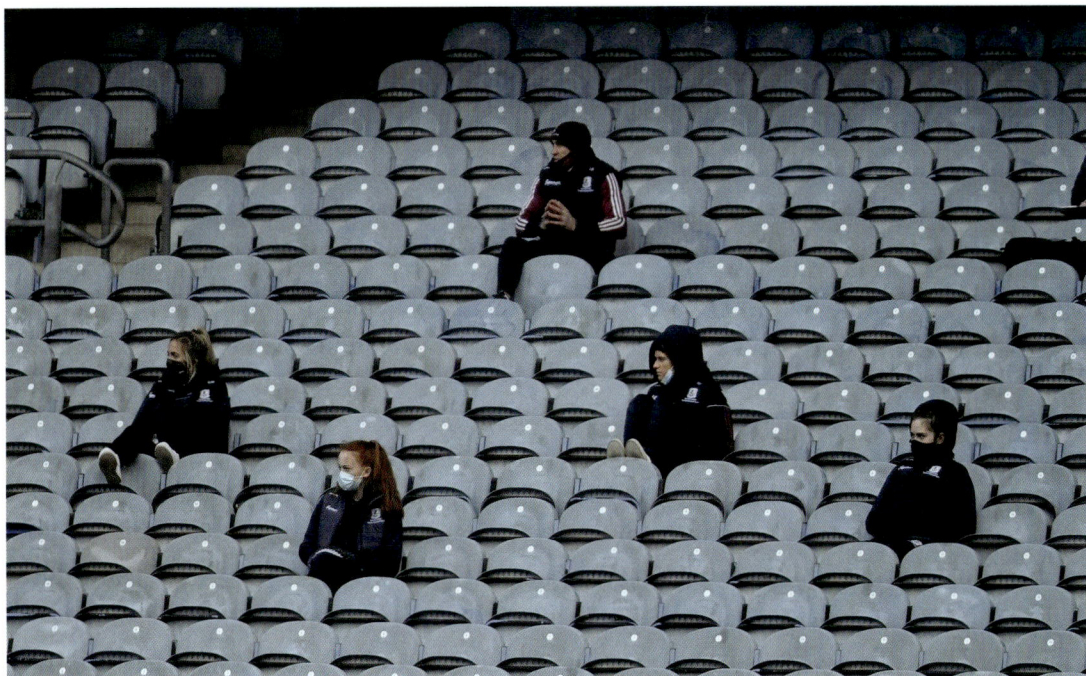

Just six teams competed at Junior level in 2020. Kilkenny did not compete in the championship for a second year running and overseas counties were not included due to the pandemic restrictions. This meant there were two groups of three teams, with the top two from each group competing in the semi-finals for a chance to reach the All-Ireland final. Wicklow and Limerick topped their groups to set up semi-finals against Antrim and Fermanagh respectively. Both games featured plenty of goals with Wicklow overcoming Antrim, 7–11 to 3–10, and Fermanagh beating Limerick, 4–10 to 4–3. Fermanagh's Eimear Smyth scored 1–5 in the All-Ireland final to steer the Erne County to their second Junior title in four years. Smyth also earned the accolade of Junior Player of the Year, thanks to her tally of 6–18 in the championship.

Clare, Meath, Roscommon and Westmeath were the four counties to make it out of the Intermediate groups. Meath easily dispatched Clare in the first semi-final, 4–13 to 0–4, while Westmeath and Roscommon played out a much tighter game that saw Westmeath

The whole world was turned upside down in spring 2020 when the Covid-19 pandemic broke out. All Gaelic games activity was postponed in line with government guidelines until it was safe to return to play. In the winter of 2020, the LGFA ran a condensed championship but teams had to be careful to follow health and safety guidelines as demonstrated by members of the Galway team who are sitting at a social distance from one another during the All-Ireland semi-final (Sportsfile).

emerge with a two-point victory, 2–9 to 0–13. Having lost the previous two Intermediate finals, Meath made sure that they did not squander their third chance and beat Westmeath, 2–17 to 4–5.

At Senior level, Armagh and Dublin faced each other in the first semi-final at Breffni Park in Cavan. The game was described by Cliona Foley as 'a game worthy of final status; end-to-end, full of dramatic scores and collisions and never-say-die defending from both sides'.[10] Dublin slotted a penalty in the third quarter that ultimately gave them the cushion they needed, as they pushed on to finish five points ahead of the Ulster side. So Dublin marched on to contest their seventh final in a row, chasing their fourth All-Ireland title in as many years.

The other semi-final, between Cork and Galway, was overshadowed by controversy. Originally fixed for the LIT Gaelic Grounds in Limerick, the LGFA was soon required to find an alternative venue. This was to facilitate the Limerick hurlers, who wanted to use the ground to train in ahead of their All-Ireland final. The LGFA had been made aware when they booked the venue that it would become unavailable should the Limerick hurlers qualify for the All-Ireland final. This transpired and other options such as Semple Stadium were initially explored, but the Tipperary County Board were concerned that availability of stewards would be an issue.[11]

Having to find an alternative venue to hold an All-Ireland semi-final, albeit in the most unusual of championship years in terms of timing and restrictions, highlighted the disadvantage of the LGFA not owning any of their own facilities.

Ultimately the fixture was moved to Parnell Park in Dublin. On the morning of the semi-final, however, Parnell Park was deemed unplayable due to a frozen pitch. The game, which was due to be thrown-in at 1.30 p.m., was moved to Croke Park, with an earlier throw-in of 1 p.m. (later changed to 1.10 pm) to ensure the game was over before the men's football semi-final between Mayo and Tipperary.

The change in venue and start time caused much disruption to both teams. The Galway team were in Kinnegad, Co. Westmeath, when they were informed at 11 a.m. of the rescheduling. They arrived at Croke Park at 12.30 p.m., meaning they had just seven minutes to warm up before the game began. At half-time, Galway trailed Cork by seven points and, in the end, Cork had ten points to spare over their opponents.

The debacle was reported on widely in the media and once again raised questions about the relationship between the LGFA and the GAA, and the general position or status afforded to women in sport in Ireland.

The final, held on the last Sunday before Christmas 2020, was the last act of a most unusual Gaelic games season. However, there was nothing unfamiliar about Dublin and Cork facing off in an All-Ireland final. This was the sixth time the two counties had met in the All-Ireland decider since 2009. In the past fifteen years no

Eimear Symth, Fermanagh forward and Junior Player of the Year for 2020, tries to evade a tackle from Wicklow's Lucy Dunne during that year's Junior All-Ireland final (Sportsfile).

other county had climbed the steps of the Hogan Stand to lift the Brendan Martin Cup.

The occasion was of course missing the usual colour and noise associated with All-Ireland final day, as the terraces of Croke Park stood empty, owing to the continuing Covid-19 restrictions. Cork led by a goal at the end of the first half, 1–3 to 0–3, but only managed two points in the second half to Dublin's 1–7, meaning Dublin were once again the All-Ireland champions. It was their fourth title in a row.

It turned out to be fortuitous that the All-Ireland finals went ahead pre-Christmas 2020, as there was another spike in Covid-19 cases over the Christmas period and into the beginning of the new year. The pandemic continued to impact the playing of sport in 2021 but with the experience of 2020 behind them, it was somewhat easier for the LGFA to plan. While some competitions were cancelled outright, such as the higher education championships, others were restructured, such as the inter-county league, where each county played three round robin games in groups determined by geography in order to limit the amount of travelling across the country.[12]

However, issues remained with organising other competitions. For example, by the end of April 2021, the LGFA had still not released inter-county championship fixtures because the current government guidelines only permitted training and the playing of National League games.[13] Fortunately, the government set out a plan for the phased easing of restrictions across May and June, which gave the LGFA's management committee the go-ahead to announce that the adult inter-county championship would begin in July. However, the difficult decision was also made to cancel the underage All-Ireland competitions for the year.[14]

In both the Junior and Intermediate championship, the runners-up of the 2020 season put the disappointment of the previous year behind them to claim the titles. Wicklow had a 2–17 to 1–9 win over Antrim to claim the West County Hotel Cup, their third title at the Junior grade. Westmeath, a decade on from the last time they won the Mary Quinn Memorial Cup, had an emphatic 4–19 to 0–6 win over Wexford.

Both counties had been firm favourites to win ahead of throw-in. There was a similar feeling that Dublin were on course to win their fifth All-Ireland title in a row at Senior level, particularly when their opponents in the final were Meath, who were playing Senior football for the first time since 2016.

It was a surprise to many that Meath had even made the Senior final. Facing eleven-time All-Ireland champions Cork in the semi-final, Meath had fallen seven points behind with three minutes left. At that point, it seemed a foregone conclusion that Dublin and Cork were fated to challenge each other once again. Particularly when you consider how, six years earlier, Cork handed out a forty-point thrashing to Meath in a Senior All-Ireland qualifier. The following year the county were regraded from Senior to Intermediate, from where their rebuilding had begun.

Imbued with the resilience from that rebuild, Meath refused to give up and scored 2–1 in the dying moments of the game to force it to extra-time. They went on to win by two points. Speaking after the remarkable comeback, Meath manager Eamonn Murray referenced the mental fortitude of the team: 'They have great belief in each other, that's one thing they have. And we always warned them that no matter what Cork throw at us, we stick to our plan, stick to our work rate. They all know their jobs very well and they have it down to perfection now.'[15]

Over 46,000 people packed into Croke Park for the 2022 All-Ireland finals. A semblance of normality was returning after a challenging few years.

The belief, the plan and the work rate would need to pay off again three weeks later when the Royals took on the Dubs in order to take home the Brendan Martin Cup and put a stop to their opponent's 'drive for five'.

The 2020 Intermediate Player of the Year, Vikki Wall, set the tone from the throw-in, bounding forward with pace and purpose towards the Dublin goal to win a free for Meath. The offence continued and built when Emma Duggan lobbed the Dublin goalkeeper in the seventh minute, all of which meant that at half-time the underdogs were ahead by five points, 1–8 to 0–6. Dublin staged something of a comeback in the second half, but, in the end, Meath had two points to spare over the reigning All-Ireland champions when the hooter sounded.

The win was seismic. It injected belief and hope into ladies' football, demonstrating that the dream of winning a Senior All-Ireland title was not just the destiny of Cork or Dublin who, between them, had won every All-Ireland title since 2004. Eamonn Sweeney of the *Irish Independent* surmised that 'it was the biggest upset in living memory, it was the bravest performance you'll ever see in Croke Park and it may have been the finest ladies football final of all time.'[16]

Dublin's Carla Rowe is surrounded by Orlagh Lally, Monica McGuirk, Shauna Ennis and Aoibhín Cleary of Meath during the 2021 All-Ireland final. Dublin were strong favourites to win a fifth title in a row but Meath achieved a shock win (Sportsfile).

Meath proved that their rise to the very top of ladies Gaelic football was no fluke when they secured the Division 1 National League title and retained the Brendan Martin Cup in 2022. This time they faced Kerry in the final, making it the first All-Ireland final since 2002 that didn't feature either Cork or Dublin. It was also the first time that Meath and Kerry met in the decider, having previously only faced each other in a decider in the Division 2 League final the year before. Although Meath started poorly, conceding 1–2 before registering their first score, once their counter-attacking system kicked in they easily overcame Kerry, 3–10 to 1–7.

The 2022 Junior title went north with Antrim, equalling Louth and Wicklow's tally of three Junior titles, while the Intermediate championship was won by Laois, who survived a late comeback from Wexford.

Following back-to-back All-Ireland Senior championship titles, Eamonn Murray stepped down as the Meath Ladies football manager at the end of the 2022 season. In his six years at the helm, Murray managed the team to five All-Ireland finals (two Senior, three Intermediate), three All-Ireland titles (two Senior and one Intermediate), and titles in Division 1, Division 2 and Division 3 of the National League.[17]

The incredible work done by Murray and his team was commended by Cora Staunton, who highlighted how Meath's back-to-back wins marked another step forward in the evolution of ladies Gaelic football and laid down a gauntlet to other counties: 'I thought Dublin [2017–20] brought the game to a new level – and they did – but Meath, with their physicality, power and strength, have matched that and upped it again. Dublin, Cork, Donegal, Mayo, Armagh and Galway now have to lift their game to that level if they want to knock them off their perch. They are the benchmark – and it's a truly brilliant one.'[18]

Over 46,000 people packed into Croke Park for the 2022 All-Ireland finals. The large crowd, though 10,000 off the record attendance pre-pandemic, pointed to a semblance of normality returning after a challenging few years.

There is no doubt that the pandemic put a huge strain on all aspects of society, including sporting associations such as the LGFA. Organisationally, the LGFA had to adapt the way they worked, the way they ran their competitions, and the way they interacted with and supported their community – players, coaches, supporters, volunteers and staff. Webinars replaced in-person training days, a club education programme was developed in cooperation with the GAA and the Camogie Association to support clubs in preparing for a safe return to activities, and with spectators barred or limited from attending matches in person, more games were streamed live on TV and online for supporters than ever before.

To support the running of the Gaelic games championships in a season where revenue was hard to generate, the government made €15m available to the three organising bodies.[19] The LGFA benefitted majorly from grant aid to offset the impact of Covid-19 in 2020. The accounts published for the year showed that the LGFA turned a profit of €2m despite gate receipts reducing by ninety-four per cent due to the requirement that championship games be held behind closed doors.[20]

In response to the Covid-19 pandemic, funding for players' travelling expenses was introduced by the LGFA for the first time, offering fifty cent per mile to cover games in the group stages of the All-Ireland series. Under the Covid-19 guidelines, players were to drive alone in their cars to training and matches, increasing the expenses on playing for your county. According to the WGPA, this was costing female Gaelic footballers €55 a week on average.[21]

North Asian Gaelic Games 2023

Linesight

An Áus

TAIPEI, TAIWAN
MAY 27, 2023

Ladies Gaelic football has been growing in popularity in Asia since the beginning of the twenty-first century, not just among Irish people living abroad but also among the Asian community in Asia, as seen in the make up of the Taiwan Celts at the North Asia Games in 2023 (Taiwan Celts).

The disparity in state funding for female sports was discussed by the Oireachtas committee on Media, Tourism, Arts, Culture, Sport and the Gaeltacht in 2021. Representations were made at the committee from the LGFA, the Camogie Association, the GPA and the Federation of Irish Sport; following on from that, a decision was made to write to the Department of Sport to request a review of the funding allocated to female sports.[22] The Department of Sport responded by committing to increase the funding available to female inter-county Gaelic players from €700,000 to €2.4 million that year so that it was in line with the funding received by their male counterparts.[23]

Another development during this period was the WGPA merging with the GPA in 2021 to form one representative body for Gaelic players. The decision to merge was passed almost unanimously with 100 per cent of GPA members and ninety-six per cent of WGPA members voting in favour of it.[24]

With the merger of the players' bodies, and the issue of the imbalance in funding raised in the Oireachtas, the push began for the three associations to cement plans for integration. The GPA put forward a motion to the GAA Annual Congress in 2022 to give priority to the amalgamation of the associations. This was passed with eighty-nine per cent support.[25] Galway put the same sentiment forward at the LGFA Congress that year with the motion passing by sixty-seven votes to eight. A similar motion was also passed by the Camogie Association.[26]

All of this meant that, before the end of the year, a steering group on integration had been established and Mary McAleese, former President of Ireland, was appointed as its chair.

Support for the integration of the three Gaelic games organisations had been advocated for by many people over the years, including the leadership of the associations themselves.

Dressed up for the action, members of the Armagh Harps Gaelic4Mothers&Others team watch the action on the pitch during the 2023 national blitz for the Gaelic4Mothers&Others competition. Like Gaelic4Girls and Gaelic4Teens, this initiative introduces new and returning players to ladies Gaelic football in a fun way (Sportsfile).

In June 2023 the GPA announced that county teams would be playing 'under protest' on the back of the 'State of Play' report which highlighted the inequalities that exist between male and female Gaelic players. Donegal players wear T-shirts with the protest's slogan, 'United for Equality', over their jerseys as they go through their pre-match routine (Sportsfile).

Concerted efforts had been made in the mid-2010s during Liam O'Neill's term as President of the GAA to amalgamate the three associations. However, this ultimately did not come to pass, with the LGFA in particular holding reservations about the process. Helen O'Rourke, in her annual report to Congress 2022, outlined that the LGFA was not against integration but felt concerned in 2014–15 that there had been a desire to rush the process.[27]

As pointed out by former Kerry player and senior lecturer at the School of Sport in Ulster University, Katie Liston, the integration of the Gaelic games governing bodies is tricky because it involves the merging of three associations rather than the typical two.[28] On top of that, Liston noted that 'the LGFA has no reason to be on bended knee when it comes to integration. Nor does the GAA need to rescue them, or the Camogie Association. The key issue is equality.'[29]

Indeed, the issue of equality took centre stage during the 2023 championship when the captains of the female inter-county football and camogie teams released a statement through the GPA to announce that they would be playing the rest of the season 'under protest'. Teams would still fulfil fixtures but would employ tactics such as delaying throw-in, covering the crests of national governing bodies, and refusing to engage with the media to raise awareness of their position.

The protest came on the back of a report released by the GPA that outlined the current 'State of Play', revealing a huge disparity between male and female Gaelic players in terms of expenses (the GPA's survey revealed that just 9.5 per cent of female inter-county players received travel expenses, with six per cent of those receiving less than twenty cent per mile from their county board, in comparison to male players who received seventy cent per mile) and accesses to facilities and resources (thirty-six per cent of female players did not have full access to a physio and seventy-nine per

Members of the Integration Steering Committee stand for a photo at a press event. They set 2027 as the deadline for the formation of One Association for the three Gaelic games bodies (Sportsfile).

Aimee Mackin of Armagh in full flight is tracked by Kerry's Ciara Murphy during the 2024 Division 1 National League final in Croke Park. Armagh claimed their first-ever Senior national title on this day (Sportsfile).

cent did not have regular access to a team doctor, in contrast to male players whose agreed charter between the GAA and the GPA guarantees medical and physio support).[30]

The aim of the protest was to ensure that a Players' Charter would be in place by the 2024 season, agreed by all three governing bodies and the GPA. The LGFA responded to the announcement by stating their surprise at the protest, as the issue of a charter was one of the areas being examined by the integration steering committee.[31]

A month later, the GPA suspended their protest, announcing that a resolution had been found and a framework established with the LGFA and the Camogie Association to deliver a standardised charter in 2024.[32]

Progress had also been made in the integration process with 2027 set as the target date for the establishment of One Association.

And, with it, a new era in Gaelic games.

CHAPTER 11
THE BEST IS YET TO COME

When the All-Ireland-winning Roscommon team of 1978 held their thirty-year reunion in 2008 a letter was read out by the team's goalkeeper, Olive Dufficy, who could not make it to the occasion. In it, she summed up the pivotal role played by her teammates and those involved in ladies' football in the 1970s in pushing the sport forward. She said:

> What a pioneering group you were!! When we consider that [ladies Gaelic football] is the fastest growing sport in Ireland today, your contribution at its inception is immeasurable. At a time when matches were played on Rugby grounds and the car boot was our changing room, you saw our potential. Roscommon and [ladies Gaelic football] should be, forever, thankful to you.[1]

Dufficy was right. The players, administrators, coaches, supporters and volunteers of the 1970s were trailblazers. They pushed against long-standing social attitudes that said that women and Gaelic football were not a match, and dared to show society that women could kick a football just as well as any man, if given the chance.

However, the trailblazing did not end in the 1970s. In every decade over the last fifty years, the LGFA and its membership have continued to make history and challenge the status quo. As a result, the sport has been transformed – and it has transformed the outlook of Irish sport, too. No longer is ladies Gaelic football a carnival sideshow; instead, it is at the heart of communities across Ireland and abroad. No longer does 'Gaelic footballer' or, indeed, any role associated with it, such as 'coach', 'manager', 'referee' or 'chairperson' automatically mean male.

When the LGFA was founded in 1974, just eight counties were affiliated to the association. Fifty years on, membership now stands at 185,007.

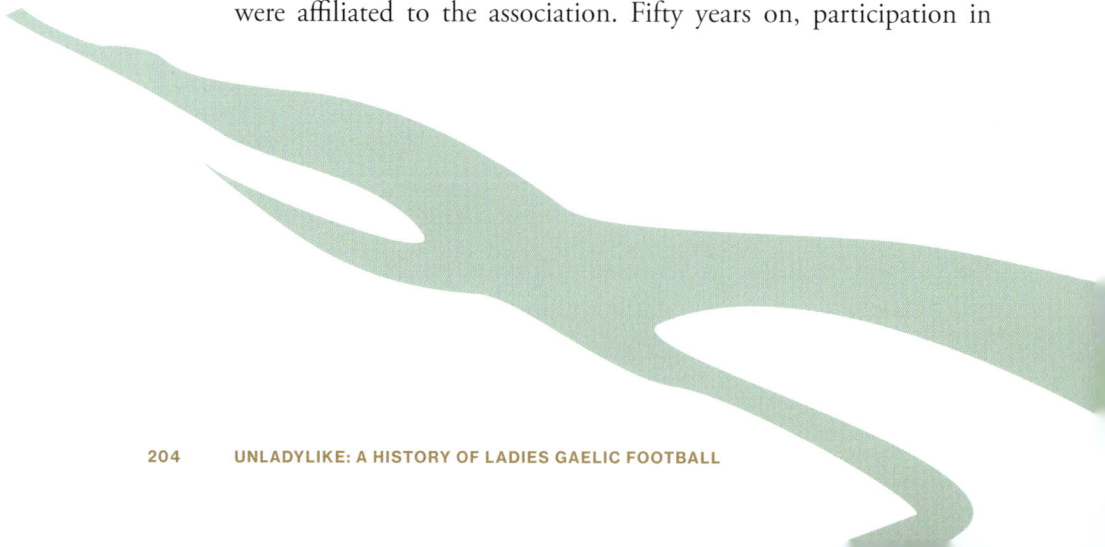

In a column in the *Sunday Independent* ahead of the 2022 All-Ireland finals, LGFA President Mícheál Naughton reflected on the year. This had been the first full season of activity since before the pandemic, which was in itself a cause for celebration. On top of that, the association had successfully renewed its relationships with TG4 and Lidl, as well as making progress on integration. The LGFA was in a healthy position. However, as always, the association had an eye on the future, with plans already in place for its next strategic plan in order to establish the long-term vision of the LGFA. Despite all the progress made in fifty years – or maybe because of this progress – the LGFA could not afford to 'stand still'.[2]

When the LGFA was founded in 1974 just eight counties were affiliated to the association. Fifty years on, participation in and support for ladies Gaelic football has grown remarkably. The membership of the LGFA stands at 192,698 and is made up of members not just in every county in Ireland but in Britain, Europe, North, South and Central America, the Middle East, Southeast Asia, Australia and New Zealand. From Gaelic4Girls to Gaelic4Mothers&Others, from club to county level, the LGFA provides women and girls with opportunities to play Gaelic football at all levels.

'We can be so critical and hard on ourselves,' Naughton said, 'but we've done so much in less than half a century and I'm firmly of the belief that the best is yet to come.'[3]

Given the staggering achievements of the past half century, this is a sentiment with which we can all agree.

ROLLS OF HONOUR

SENIOR COUNTY ALL-IRELAND CHAMPIONSHIP FINALS

Year	Winner	Runner-Up	Year	Winner	Runner-Up
1974	Tipperary	Offaly	1999	Mayo	Waterford
1975	Tipperary	Galway	2000	Mayo	Waterford
1976	Kerry	Offaly	2001	Laois	Mayo
1977	Cavan	Roscommon	2002	Mayo	Monaghan
1978	Roscommon	Tipperary	2003	Mayo	Dublin
1979*	Offaly	Tipperary	2004	Galway	Dublin
1980	Tipperary	Cavan	2005	Cork	Galway
1981	Offaly	Cavan	2006	Cork	Armagh
1982	Kerry	Offaly	2007	Cork	Mayo
1983	Kerry	Wexford	2008	Cork	Monaghan
1984	Kerry	Leitrim	2009	Cork	Dublin
1985	Kerry	Laois	2010	Dublin	Tyrone
1986	Kerry	Wexford	2011	Cork	Monaghan
1987	Kerry	Westmeath	2012	Cork	Kerry
1988	Kerry	Laois	2013	Cork	Monaghan
1989	Kerry	Wexford	2014	Cork	Dublin
1990	Kerry	Laois	2015	Cork	Dublin
1991	Waterford	Laois	2016	Cork	Dublin
1992	Waterford	Laois	2017	Dublin	Mayo
1993	Kerry	Laois	2018	Dublin	Cork
1994	Waterford	Monaghan	2019	Dublin	Galway
1995	Waterford	Monaghan	2020	Dublin	Cork
1996*	Monaghan	Laois	2021	Meath	Dublin
1997	Monaghan	Waterford	2022	Meath	Kerry
1998*	Waterford	Monaghan	2023	Dublin	Kerry

* replay

INTERMEDIATE COUNTY ALL-IRELAND CHAMPIONSHIP FINALS

Year	Winner	Runner-Up	Year	Winner	Runner-Up
1997	Kerry	Dublin	2011*	Westmeath	Cavan
1998	Cork	Laois	2012	Armagh	Waterford
1999	Louth	Wexford	2013	Cavan	Tipperary
2000	Laois	Cork	2014	Down	Fermanagh
2001	Not Played		2015	Waterford	Kildare
2002	Not Played		2016	Kildare	Clare
2003	Not Played		2017	Tipperary	Tyrone
2004	Not Played		2018	Tyrone	Meath
2005	Roscommon	Down	2019	Tipperary	Meath
2006	Not Played		2020	Meath	Westmeath
2007	Leitrim	Wexford	2021	Westmeath	Wexford
2008	Tipperary	Clare	2022	Laois	Wexford
2009	Clare	Fermanagh	2023	Kildare	Clare
2010	Donegal	Waterford			

JUNIOR COUNTY ALL-IRELAND CHAMPIONSHIP FINALS

Year	Winner	Runner-Up	Year	Winner	Runner-Up
1985	Galway	Cork	2005	Armagh	Sligo
1986	Waterford	Wexford	2006	Sligo	Leitrim
1987	Mayo	Wexford	2007	Kilkenny	London
1988	Leitrim	London	2008	London	Derry
1989*	Dublin	Clare	2009	Antrim	Limerick
1990	Wicklow	London	2010	Limerick	Louth
1991	Clare	London	2011*	Wicklow	New York
1992	Monaghan	London	2012	Antrim	Louth
1993	London	Donegal	2013	Offaly	Wexford
1994	Meath	Donegal	2014	Wexford	New York
1995	Cork	Tyrone	2015	Louth	Scotland
1996	Clare	Longford	2016	Longford	Antrim
1997	Longford	Tyrone	2017*	Fermanagh	Derry
1998	Louth	Roscommon	2018	Limerick	Louth
1999	Tyrone	New York	2019	Louth	Fermanagh
2000	Down	Galway	2020	Fermanagh	Wicklow
2001	Roscommon	Kildare	2021	Wicklow	Antrim
2002	Galway	Donegal	2022*	Antrim	Fermanagh
2003	Donegal	Kildare	2023	Down	Limerick
2004	Kildare	Sligo			

DIVISION 1 NATIONAL LEAGUE FINALS

Year	Winner	Runner-Up	Year	Winner	Runner-Up
1979	Tipperary	Galway	2002	Waterford	Mayo
1980	Kerry	Offaly	2003	Laois	Kerry
1981	Kerry	Tipperary	2004	Mayo	Cork
1982	Kerry	Tipperary	2005	Cork	Galway
1983*	Kerry	Leitrim	2006	Cork	Meath
1984	Kerry	Laois	2007	Mayo	Galway
1985	Kerry	Leitrim	2008	Cork	Kerry
1986	Wexford	Laois	2009	Cork	Mayo
1987	Kerry	Laois	2010	Cork	Galway
1988	Kerry	Waterford	2011	Cork	Laois
1989	Kerry	Waterford	2012	Monaghan	Cork
1990	Kerry	Waterford	2013	Cork	Mayo
1991*	Kerry	Waterford	2014	Cork	Dublin
1992	Waterford	Laois	2015*	Cork	Galway
1993	Laois	Cork	2016	Cork	Mayo
1994	Monaghan	Mayo	2017	Cork	Donegal
1995	Waterford	Mayo	2018	Dublin	Mayo
1996	Monaghan	Mayo	2019	Cork	Galway
1997*	Monaghan	Waterford	2021	Dublin	Cork
1998	Waterford	Clare	2022	Meath	Donegal
1999	Monaghan	Waterford	2023	Kerry	Galway
2000	Mayo	Tyrone	2024	Armagh	Kerry
2001	Clare	Monaghan			

DIVISION 2 NATIONAL LEAGUE FINALS

Year	Winner	Runner-Up	Year	Winner	Runner-Up
1981	Wexford	Laois	1998	Meath	Longford
1982	Leitrim	Laois	1999	Tyrone	Dublin
1983	Not Played		2000	Clare	Longford
1984	Not Played		2001	Laois	Kerry
1985	Not Played		2002	Galway	Donegal
1986	Waterford	Laois	2003	Cork	Roscommon
1987	Wexford	Dublin	2004	Kildare	Louth
1988	Cork	Dublin	2005	Armagh	Donegal
1989	Dublin	Galway	2006	Laois	Kildare
1990	Clare	Kerry	2007	Dublin	Wexford
1991	Clare	Mayo	2008	Clare	Donegal
1992	Cork	Monaghan	2009	Down	Tipperary
1993	Carlow	Roscommon	2010	Donegal	Kildare
1994**	Meath	Louth	2011	Dublin	Meath
1995	Sligo	Carlow	2012	Mayo	Galway
1996***	-	-	2013	Kerry	Galway
1997***	-	-	2014	Galway	Westmeath

*   replay
**   walkover conceded
***   Top Division 2 teams qualified for the Division 1 quarter-finals   **ROLLS OF HONOUR**

DIVISION 2 NATIONAL LEAGUE FINALS *continued*

Year	Winner	Runner-Up	Year	Winner	Runner-Up
2015	Armagh	Donegal	2020	Not Played	
2016	Donegal	Westmeath	2021	Meath	Kerry
2017*	Westmeath	Cavan	2022	Kerry	Armagh
2018	Tipperary	Cavan	2023	Armagh	Laois
2019	Waterford	Kerry	2024	Kildare	Tyrone

DIVISION 3 NATIONAL LEAGUE FINALS

Year	Winner	Runner-Up	Year	Winner	Runner-Up
1996	Tyrone	Leitrim	2010	Cavan	Waterford
1997	Longford	Roscommon	2011	Clare	Fermanagh
1998	Dublin	Louth	2012*	Westmeath	Leitrim
1999	Cork	Kildare	2013	Down	Armagh
2000	Leitrim	Galway	2014	Armagh	Waterford
2001	Roscommon	Cavan	2015	Sligo	Waterford
2002	Tipperary	Sligo	2016*	Waterford	Tipperary
2003	Galway B	Cork B	2017*	Tipperary	Wexford
2004	Wexford	Limerick	2018	Wexford	Meath
2005	Tipperary	Dublin B	2019	Meath	Sligo
2006	Clare	Leitrim	2021	Laois	Kildare
2007	Fermanagh	Westmeath	2022	Roscommon	Wexford
2008	Cavan	Limerick	2023	Kildare	Clare
2009	Roscommon	Wicklow	2024	Clare	Roscommon

DIVISION 4 NATIONAL LEAGUE FINALS

Year	Winner	Runner-Up	Year	Winner	Runner-Up
2004	Offaly	Wicklow	2014	Roscommon	Antrim
2005	Wicklow	Westmeath	2015	Offaly	Limerick
2006	Monaghan B	Galway B	2016	Limerick	Antrim
2007**	-	-	2017	Longford	Wicklow
2008**	-	-	2018	Wicklow	Louth
2009**	-	-	2019	Fermanagh	Antrim
2010	Leitrim	Limerick	2021	Louth	Leitrim
2011	Westmeath	Roscommon	2022	Offaly	Limerick
2012	Longford	Limerick	2023	Antrim	Leitrim
2013	Offaly	Roscommon	2024	Carlow	Limerick

*   replay
**   There were only three divisions of the national league in these years.

AISLING McGING MEMORIAL CUP (UNDER-21) CHAMPIONSHIP FINALS

Year	Winner	Runner-Up	Year	Winner	Runner-Up
2007	Cork	Dublin	2013	Cork	Galway
2008	Cork	Dublin	2014	Dublin	Meath
2009	Cork	Dublin	2015	Dublin	Cork
2010	Dublin	Cork	2016	Dublin	Galway
2011	Cork	Dublin	2017	Galway	Mayo
2012	Dublin	Kerry			

UNDER-18 ALL-IRELAND CHAMPIONSHIP 'A' FINALS

Year	Winner	Runner-Up	Year	Winner	Runner-Up
1980	Kerry	Cavan	2001	Waterford	Meath
1981	Kerry	Wexford	2002	Galway	Cork
1982	Wexford	Leitrim	2003	Cork	Mayo
1983	Wexford	Leitrim	2004	Cork	Laois
1984	Wexford	Cork	2005	Galway	Donegal
1985	Cork	Wexford	2006	Cork	Galway
1986	Wexford	Clare	2007	Cork	Dublin
1987	Mayo	Cork	2008	Dublin	Tyrone
1988	Cork	Wexford	2009	Donegal	Clare
1989	Clare	Laois	2010	Galway	Donegal
1990	Clare	Dublin	2011	Cork	Dublin
1991	Waterford	Roscommon	2012	Dublin	Tyrone
1992	Laois	Waterford	2013	Galway	Dublin
1993	Waterford	Wexford	2014	Galway	Cork
1994	Monaghan	Wexford	2015	Cork	Galway
1995	Kerry	Wexford	2016	Cork	Dublin
1996	Waterford	Mayo	2017	Cork	Galway
1997	Waterford	Mayo	2018	Galway	Cork
1998	Monaghan	Mayo	2019	Cork	Monaghan
1999	Monaghan	Mayo	2022	Cork	Galway
2000	Tyrone	Waterford	2023	Galway	Kildare

UNDER-16 ALL-IRELAND CHAMPIONSHIP 'A' FINALS

Year	Winner	Runner-Up	Year	Winner	Runner-Up
1976	Mayo	Kilkenny	1978	Tipperary	Roscommon
1977	Cavan	Roscommon	1979	Tipperary	Cavan

UNDER-16 ALL-IRELAND CHAMPIONSHIP
'A' FINALS *continued*

Year	Winner	Runner-Up	Year	Winner	Runner-Up
1980	Tipperary	Laois	2001	Meath	Galway
1981	Wexford	Tipperary	2002	Cork	Galway
1982	Wexford	Kerry	2003	Galway	Cavan
1983	Wexford	Tipperary	2004	Cork	Donegal
1984	Cork	Wexford	2005	Cork	Dublin
1985	Clare	Wexford	2006	Dublin	Cork
1986	Cork	Wexford	2007	Cork	Donegal
1987	Clare	Mayo	2008	Cork	Galway
1988	Laois	Kerry	2009	Meath	Donegal
1989	Dublin	Waterford	2010	Dublin	Kerry
1990	Clare	Offaly	2011	Kerry	Dublin
1991	Waterford	Roscommon	2012	Galway	Cork
1992	Waterford	Wexford	2013	Cork	Dublin
1993	Wicklow	Kerry	2014	Cork	Dublin
1994	Clare	Mayo	2015	Kerry	Galway
1995	Waterford	Monaghan	2016	Kerry	Dublin
1996	Waterford	Mayo	2017	Galway	Cork
1997	Monaghan	Kerry	2018	Galway	Kerry
1998	Waterford	Monaghan	2019	Galway	Meath
1999	Kerry	Meath	2022	Dublin	Cork
2000	Meath	Galway	2023*	Cavan	Cork

UNDER-14 ALL-IRELAND CHAMPIONSHIP
'A'/'PLATINUM' FINALS

Year	Winner	Runner-Up	Year	Winner	Runner-Up
1990	Wexford	Mayo	2007	Dublin	Galway
1991	Kerry	Clare	2008	Kerry	Galway
1992	Kerry	Meath	2009	Cork	Galway
1993	Kerry	Roscommon	2010	Galway	Dublin
1994	Mayo	Kerry	2011	Cork	Dublin
1995	Monaghan	Waterford	2012	Cork	Mayo
1996	Meath	Monaghan	2013	Cork	Kildare
1997	Monaghan	Kerry	2014	Kerry	Mayo
1998	Waterford	Meath	2015	Cavan	Cork
1999	Kerry	Meath	2016	Kildare	Kerry
2000	Cork	Mayo	2017	Galway	Kerry
2001	Cork	Monaghan	2018	Cavan	Dublin
2002	Cork	Galway	2019	Cork	Galway
2003	Cork	Mayo	2022	Kerry	Cork
2004	Dublin	Mayo	2023	Mayo	Cork
2005	Dublin	Donegal	2024	Galway	Cavan
2006	Cork	Dublin			

MICK TALBOT CUP (INTER-PROVINCIALS) FINALS

Year	Winner	Runner-Up	Year	Winner	Runner-Up
1976	Munster	Leinster	1998	Leinster	Connacht
1977	Munster	Connacht	1999	Ulster	Connacht
1978	Connacht	Leinster	2000	Connacht	Leinster
1979	Connacht	Leinster	2001	Not played due to foot and mouth	
1980	Munster	Leinster	2002	Ulster	Connacht
1981	Munster	Ulster	2003	Munster	Ulster
1982	Leinster	Munster	2004	Munster	Ulster
1983	Leinster	Munster	2005	Leinster	Munster
1984	Munster	Connacht	2006	Leinster	Ulster
1985	Munster	Leinster	2007	Munster	Ulster
1986	Munster	Leinster	2008	Ulster	Munster
1987	Munster	Leinster	2009	Munster	Leinster
1988	Munster	Leinster	2010	Ulster	Leinster
1989	Leinster	Connacht	2011	Munster	Ulster
1990	Leinster	Munster	2012	Ulster	Munster
1991	Munster	Leinster	2013	Ulster	Connacht
1992	Leinster	Munster	2014	Ulster	Connacht
1993	Munster	Leinster	2015	Ulster	Connacht
1994	Leinster	Munster	2016	Ulster	Connacht
1995	Munster	Leinster	2017	Ulster	Munster
1996	Munster	Combined Colleges	2018	Munster	Ulster
1997	Connacht	Combined Colleges	2019	Munster	Connacht

SENIOR CLUB ALL-IRELAND CHAMPIONSHIP FINALS

Year	Winner	Runner-Up
1977	Mullahoran (Cavan)	St Coman's (Roscommon)
1978	Newtownshandrum (Cork)	Mullahoran (Cavan)
1979	Newtownshandrum (Cork)	Mullahoran (Cavan)
1980	Castleisland (Kerry)	Rochfortbridge (Westmeath)
1981	Watergrasshill (Cork)	Galway Gaels (Galway)
1982	Galway Gaels (Galway)	Rochfortbridge (Westmeath)
1983	Castleisland (Kerry)	The Heath (Laois)
1984	Galway Gaels (Galway)	St Enda's (Cork)
1985	The Heath (Laois)	Ballymacarbry (Waterford)
1986	The Heath (Laois)	Castleisland (Kerry)
1987	Ballymacarbry (Waterford)	Hollymount (Mayo)
1988	Adamstown (Wexford)	Ballymacarbry (Waterford)
1989	Ballymacarbry (Waterford)	Rochfortbridge (Westmeath)
1990	Ballymacarbry (Waterford)	St Grellan's (Galway)
1991	Ballymacarbry (Waterford)	Rochfortbridge (Westmeath)

SENIOR CLUB ALL-IRELAND CHAMPIONSHIP FINALS *continued*

Year	Winner	Runner-Up
1992	Ballymacarbry (Waterford)	Rochfortbridge (Westmeath)
1993	Ballymacarbry (Waterford)	Crettyard (Laois)
1994	Ballymacarbry (Waterford)	Rochfortbridge (Westmeath)
1995	Ballymacarbry (Waterford)	Parnell's (London)
1996	Shelmaliers (Wexford)	St Eunan's (Donegal)
1997	Ballymacarbry (Waterford)	Shelmaliers (Wexford)
1998	Ballymacarbry (Waterford)	Portobello (Dublin)
1999*	Shelmaliers (Wexford)	Hollymount (Mayo)
2000	Monaghan Harps (Monaghan)	Timahoe (Laois)
2001	Donoughmore (Cork)	Ballyboden St Enda's (Dublin)
2002	Carnacon (Mayo)	Carrickmore (Tyrone)
2003	Donoughmore (Cork)	Seneschalstown (Meath)
2004	Ballyboden St Enda's (Dublin)	Donoughmore (Cork)
2005	Ballyboden St Enda's (Dublin)	Donaghmoyne (Monaghan)
2006	Donaghmoyne (Monaghan)	Carnacon (Mayo)
2007	Carnacon (Mayo)	Inch Rovers (Cork)
2008	Carnacon (Mayo)	Inch Rovers (Cork)
2009	Donaghmoyne (Monaghan)	Donoughmore (Cork)
2010	Inch Rovers (Cork)	Carnacon (Mayo)
2011	Carnacon (Mayo)	Na Fianna (Dublin)
2012	Donaghmoyne (Monaghan)	Carnacon (Mayo)
2013	Carnacon (Mayo)	Donaghmoyne (Monaghan)
2014	CLG An Tearmainn (Donegal)	Mourneabbey (Cork)
2015	Donaghmoyne (Monaghan)	Mourneabbey (Cork)
2016	Donaghymoyne (Monaghan)	Foxrock Cabinteely (Dublin)
2017	Carnacon (Mayo)	Mourneabbey (Cork)
2018	Mourneabbey (Cork)	Foxrock Cabinteely (Dublin)
2019	Mourneabbey (Cork)	Kilkerrin-Clonberne (Galway)
2021	Kilkerrin-Clonberne (Galway)	Mourneabbey (Cork)
2022	Kilkerrin-Clonberne (Galway)	Donaghmoyne (Monaghan)
2023	Kilkerrin-Clonberne (Galway)	Ballmacarbry (Waterford)

SENIOR CLUB ALL-IRELAND 7-A-SIDE CHAMPIONSHIP

Year	Winner	Runner-Up
1985	St Enda's (Cork)	Adamstown (Wexford)
1986	The Heath (Laois)	St Enda's (Cork)
1987	Ballymacarbry (Waterford)	St Enda's (Cork)
1988	Ballymacarbry (Waterford)	Adamstown (Wexford)
1989	Ballymacarbry (Waterford)	Crettyard (Laois)
1990	Ballymacarbry (Waterford)	Glanworth (Cork)

SENIOR CLUB ALL-IRELAND
7-A-SIDE CHAMPIONSHIP *continued*

Year	Winner	Runner-Up
1991	Beaufort (Kerry)	Coralstown (Westmeath)
1992	Beaufort (Kerry)	Abbeydorney (Kerry)
1993	Not played due to bad weather	
1994	Timahoe (Laois)	An Tochar (Wicklow)
1995	Parnells (London)	Timahoe (Laois)
1996	Ballymacarbry (Waterford)	Fergus Rovers (Clare)
1997	Fergus Rovers (Clare)	Parnells (London)
1998	Rochfortbridge (Westmeath)	Portobello (Dublin)
1999	Padraig Pearses (Roscommon)	Portobello (Dublin)
2000	Timahoe (Laois)	Crettyard (Laois)
2001	Cooraclare (Clare)	Corofin (Galway)
2002	Padraig Pearses (Roscommon)	Cooraclare (Clare)
2003	Corofin (Galway)	Ballymacarbry (Waterford)
2004	Carnacon (Mayo)	Shelmaliers (Wexford)
2005	Tyholland (Monaghan)	Shelmaliers (Wexford)
2006	Ballymacarbry (Waterford)	Shelmaliers (Wexford)
2007	Ballymacarbry (Waterford)	Corofin (Galway)
2008	Naomh Mearnóg/St Sylvester's (Dublin)	Clann Éireann (Armagh)
2009	Emyvale (Monaghan)	Donaghmoyne (Monaghan)
2010	Seneschalstown (Meath)	Emyvale (Monaghan)
2011	Ballymacarbry (Waterford)	The Banner (Clare)
2012	Donaghmoyne (Monaghan)	The Banner (Clare)
2013	Na Fianna (Dublin)	Confey (Kildare)
2014	Kilkerrin-Clonberne (Galway)	Parnells (London)
2015	Emyvale (Monaghan)	Kilkerrin-Clonberne (Galway)
2016	Kilkerrin-Clonberne (Galway)	Emyvale (Monaghan)
2017	The Banner (Clare)	Clann Éireann (Armagh)
2018	The Banner (Clare)	Emyvale (Monaghan)
2019	Emyvale (Monaghan)	The Banner (Clare)
2022	Kilkerrin-Clonberne (Galway)	Fethard (Tipperary)
2023	Kilkerrin-Clonberne (Galway)	Glencar-Manorhamilton (Leitrim)

O'CONNOR CUP

Year	Winner	Runner-Up	Year	Winner	Runner-Up
1987	Mary I	UCC	1995	UL	Garda College
1988	UCC	Mary I	1996	UL	UUJ
1989	Waterford RTC	Mary I	1997	UL	Garda College
1990	UCC	Mary I	1998	IT Tralee	IT Sligo
1991	Thomond College	Mary I	1999	IT Tralee	UCD
1992	Mary I	Thomond College	2000	IT Sligo	Waterford IT
1993	UL	Mary I	2001	UCD	IT Tralee
1994	UL	Waterford RTC	2002	UCD	UL

Year	Winner	Runner-Up	Year	Winner	Runner-Up
2003	UCD	UUJ	2013	QUB	DCU
2004	UL	NUI Maynooth	2014	UL	QUB
2005	UCD	NUI Galway	2015	UL	DCU
2006	UCD	IT Sligo	2016	UCD	UL
2007	UL	UUJ	2017	UL	UCC
2008	UUJ	IT Sligo	2018	DCU	UL
2009	DCU	UL	2019	UL	UCD
2010	DCU	UUJ	2022	UL	UCC
2011	DCU	UUJ	2023	DCU	UL
2012	UCC	UUJ	2024	DCU	UCC

SENIOR POST-PRIMARY SCHOOLS 'A' COMPETITION

Year	Winner	Runner Up
1985	Ballingeary Vocational School (Cork)	Adamstown Vocational School (Wexford)
1986	Mercy Covent Spanish Point (Clare)	Adamstown Vocational School (Wexford)
1987	Mercy Covent Spanish Point (Clare)	Adamstown Vocational School (Wexford)
1988	Presentation Convent (Laois)	Mercy Covent Spanish Point (Clare)
1989	Mercy Convent (Roscommon)	Tarbert Comprehensive (Kerry)
1990	Ramsgrange Community School (Wexford)	Tarbert Comprehensive (Kerry)
1991	Ballinrobe Community School (Mayo)	Salesian Convent Cahercon (Clare)
1992	Ballinrobe Community School (Mayo)	Cahercon Community School (Clare)
1993	Ballinrobe Community School (Mayo)	Bridgetown Community School (Wexford)
1994	Ballinrobe Community School (Mayo)	Coláiste Bríde Enniscorthy (Wexford)
1995	Ballinrobe Community School (Mayo)	Spanish Point (Clare)
1996	Spanish Point (Clare)	St Michael's Navan (Meath)
1997	Spanish Point (Clare)	Coláiste Muire Tourmakeady (Mayo)
1998	Intermediate School Killorglin (Kerry)	Eureka (Meath)
1999	John Bosco Cahersiveen (Kerry)	St Leo's (Carlow)
2000	St Louis (Monaghan)	Intermediate School Killorglin (Kerry)
2001	Coláiste na Sceilge (Kerry)	Coláiste Muire Tourmakeady (Mayo)
2002	Coláiste na Sceilge (Kerry)	St Michael's Loreto (Meath)
2003	Presentation College Tuam (Galway)	Coláiste na Sceilge (Kerry)
2004	St Louis (Monaghan)	Presentation College Tuam (Galway)
2005	St Louis (Monaghan)	Coláiste na Sceilge (Kerry)
2006	St Louis (Monaghan)	St Leo's (Carlow)
2007	St Leo's (Carlow)	Loreto Fermoy (Cork)
2008	St Mary's Mallow (Cork)	St Louis (Monaghan)
2009	Convent of Mercy (Roscommon)	Loreto Fermoy (Cork)
2010	St Leo's (Carlow)	Loreto Omagh (Tyrone)
2011	St Leo's (Carlow)	Coláiste na Sceilge (Kerry)
2012	Loreto Omagh (Tyrone)	Coláiste Íde agus Iosef Abbeyfeale (Limerick)
2013	Loreto Fermoy (Cork)	Presentation College Athenry (Galway)

SENIOR POST-PRIMARY SCHOOLS
'A' COMPETITION *continued*

Year	Winner	Runner-Up
2014	Coláiste Íosagáin (Dublin)	Coláiste Dún Iascaigh, Cahir (Tipperary)
2015	Glenamaddy Community School (Galway)	Coláiste Dún Iascaigh, Cahir (Tipperary)
2016	Scoil Mhuire, Carrick on Suir (Tipperary)	Coláiste Íosagáin (Dublin)
2017	John the Baptist Community School (Limerick)	St Ciaran's, Ballygawley (Tyrone)
2018	Loreto (Cavan)	Loreto, Clonmel (Tipperary)
2019	Scoil Chríost Rí, Portlaoise (Laois)	Loreto, Clonmel (Tipperary)
2022	St Mary's High School, Midleton (Cork)	Moate Community School (Westmeath)
2023	Loreto St Michael's, Navan (Meath)	Sacred Heart, Westport (Mayo)
2024	Our Lady's Castleblayney (Monaghan)	Sacred Heart, Westport (Mayo)

JUNIOR POST-PRIMARY SCHOOLS
'A' COMPETITION

Year	Winner	Runner-Up
1994	Ballinrobe Community School (Mayo)	St Joseph's College, Kilkee (Clare)
1995	Ballinrobe Community School (Mayo)	St Joseph's College, Kilkee (Clare)
1996	Intermediate School Killorglin (Kerry)	Heywood (Laois)
1997	Intermediate School Killorglin (Kerry)	St Louis Convent (Dublin)
1998	Intermediate School Killorglin (Kerry)	Coolmine (Dublin)
1999	Bridgetown (Wexford)	John Bosco Cahersiveen (Kerry)
2000	Coláiste na Sceilge (Kerry)	St Louis (Monaghan)
2001	Coláiste na Sceilge (Kerry)	St Michael's Loreto, Navan (Meath)
2002	Coláiste na Sceilge (Kerry)	St Louis (Monaghan)
2003	St Mary's Macroom (Cork)	Presentation College Tuam (Galway)
2004	St Mary's Edenderry (Offaly)	St Brigid's Killarney (Kerry)
2005	Intermediate School Killorglin (Kerry)	St Louis (Monaghan)
2006	St Louis (Monaghan)	St Joseph's Castleisland (Kerry)
2007	St Mary's Edenderry (Offaly)	Intermediate School Killorglin (Kerry)
2008	Loreto Omagh (Tyrone)	Dunmore (Galway)
2009	Loreto Omagh (Tyrone)	St Leo's (Carlow)
2010	St Patrick's Academy, Dungannon (Tyrone)	St Leo's (Carlow)
2011	Scoil Mhuire (Longford)	Glenamaddy Community School (Galway)
2012	Coláiste Dún Iascaigh, Cahir (Tipperary)	Loreto Omagh (Tyrone)
2013	Glenamaddy Community School (Galway)	St Paul's High School Bessbrook (Armagh)
2014	St Ciaran's, Ballygawley (Tyrone)	Coláiste Dún Iascaigh, Cahir (Tipperary)
2015	Coláiste Íosagáin (Dublin)	Loreto Omagh (Tyrone)
2016	Scoil Chríost Rí, Portlaoise (Laois)	St Ronan's, Lurgan (Armagh)
2017	John the Baptist (Limerick)	Loreto (Cavan)
2018	Loreto (Cavan)	Intermediate School Killorglin (Kerry)
2019	St Catherine's (Armagh)	Coláiste Bhaile Chláir (Galway)
2022	Loreto (Cavan)	Sacred Heart, Westport (Mayo)
2023	Loreto (Cavan)	St Mary's, Midleton (Cork)
2024	Loreto (Cavan)	FCJ Secondary School, Bunclody (Wexford)

ALL-STAR AWARDS

1980

1. Martina McGuire (Cavan)
2. Ann Maher (Tipperary)
3. Eileen O'Connor (Kerry)
4. Nuala Egan (Roscommon)
5. Bernadette Stankard (Galway)
6. Rose Dunican (Offaly)
7. Mary Troy (Laois)
8. Josie Stapleton (Tipperary)
9. Ann Molloy (Offaly)
10. Elizabeth O'Brien (Roscommon)
11. Eileen Lawlor (Kerry)
12. Mary Jo Curran (Kerry)
13. Lillian Gorey (Tipperary)
14. Agnes Gorman (Offaly)
15. Rose Curley (Meath)

1981

1. Martina McGuire (Cavan)
2. Ann Maher (Tipperary)
3. Eileen O'Connor (Kerry)
4. Bridget Sheridan (Cavan)
5. Bernadette Stankard (Galway)
6. Rose Dunican (Offaly)
7. Bernie Dunne (Offaly)
8. Mary Twomey (Kerry)
9. Jean Dunne (Offaly)
10. Bridget Reynolds (Offaly)
11. Elizabeth O'Brien (Roscommon)
12. Mary Jo Curran (Kerry)
13. Lillian Gorey (Tipperary)
14. Deirdre Quinn (Leitrim)
15. Patricia O'Brien (Cavan)

1982

1. Hilda O'Leary (Kerry)
2. Ann Molloy (Offaly)
3. Tracy Monahan (Leitrim)
4. Josie Briorty (Cavan)
5. Margaret Lawlor (Kerry)
6. Marion O'Shea (Tipperary)
7. Bernie Dunne (Offaly)
8. Mary Twomey (Kerry)
9. Jean Dunne (Offaly)
10. Claire Dolan (Galway)
11. Angela McCabe (Cavan)
12. Angie Hearne (Wexford)

13. Patricia O'Brien (Cavan)
14. Dell White (Kerry)
15. Bridget Reynolds (Offaly)

1983

1. Kathleen Kennedy (Dublin)
2. Agnes Gorman (Offaly)
3. Nora Foley (Kerry)
4. Tracy Monahan (Leitrim)
5. Claire Geraghty (Galway)
6. Rose Dunican (Offaly)
7. Jacinta Kehoe (Wexford)
8. Annette Walsh (Kerry)
9. Ann Cullen (Wexford)
10. Mary Dempsey (Galway)
11. Mary Jo Curran (Kerry)
12. Deirdre Quinn (Leitrim)
13. Bridget Reynolds (Offaly)
14. Mary Twomey (Kerry)
15. Eileen Lawlor (Kerry)

1984

1. Kathleen Kennedy (Dublin)
2. Bridget Leen (Kerry)
3. Christine Byrne (Wexford)
4. Connie Conway (Laois)
5. Marion Doherty (Kerry)
6. Jean Dunne (Offaly)
7. Edel Clarke (Westmeath)
8. Catherine Murphy (Wexford)
9. Mary Jo Curran (Kerry)
10. Theresa Rafferty (Galway)
11. Eileen Lawlor (Kerry)
12. Maeve Quinn (Leitrim)
13. Margaret Lawlor (Kerry)
14. Ann Whelan (Wexford)
15. Geraldine Wrynn (Leitrim)

1985

1. Kathleen Curran (Kerry)
2. Mary Rice (Wexford)
3. Connie Conway (Laois)
4. Joan Shannon (Cork)
5. Marion Doherty (Kerry)
6. Kathleen Murphy (Laois)
7. Edel Cullen (Wexford)
8. Maeve Quinn (Leitrim)
9. Lil O'Sullivan (Kerry)

10. Sheila Conroy (Laois)
11. Mary Jo Curran (Kerry)
12. Margaret Lawlor (Kerry)
13. Mary Conroy (Laois)
14. Dell White (Kerry)
15. Mairead O'Leary (Cork)

1986

1. Kathleen Curran (Kerry)
2. Mary Moore (Wexford)
3. Mary Thorpe (Wexford)
4. Nora Hallissey (Kerry)
5. Christine Harding (Wexford)
6. Anne White (Wexford)
7. Edel Clarke (Westmeath)
8. Mary Jo Curran (Kerry)
9. Catherine Murphy (Wexford)
10. Angie Hearne (Wexford)
11. Marie Crotty (Waterford)
12. Marina Barry (Kerry)
13. Jo Glennon (Westmeath)
14. Dell White (Kerry)
15. Catherine Conroy (Laois)

1987

1. Kathleen Curran (Kerry)
2. Mary Moore (Wexford)
3. Dell White (Kerry)
4. Connie Conway (Laois)
5. Ann Fitzpatrick (Waterford)
6. Jo Glennon (Westmeath)
7. Mary Lane (Kerry)
8. Annette Walsh (Kerry)
9. Rita Dowling (Laois)
10. Marina Barry (Kerry)
11. Mary Jo Curran (Kerry)
12. Edel Clarke (Westmeath)
13. Kathleen Moore (Wexford)
14. Marie Crotty (Waterford)
15. Siobhan Dunne (Wexford)

1988

1. Kathleen Curran (Kerry)
2. Mary Moore (Wexford)
3. Connie Conway (Laois)
4. Dolores Tyrell (Waterford)
5. Mary Quinn (Leitrim)
6. June Whyte (Waterford)
7. Phil Curran (Kerry)
8. Mary Jo Curran (Kerry)

9. Annette Walsh (Kerry)
10. Bridget Bradley (Wexford)
11. Mary Crotty (Waterford)
12. Eileen Lawlor (Kerry)
13. Sue Ramsbottom (Laois)
14. Bernie Ryan (Waterford)
15. Margaret Lawlor (Kerry)

1989

1. Theresa Furlong (Wexford)
2. Mary Moore (Wexford)
3. Phil Curran (Kerry)
4. Anne Dunford (Waterford)
5. Marion Doherty (Kerry)
6. Kathleen Moore (Wexford)
7. Mary Quinn (Leitrim)
8. Mary Jo Curran (Kerry)
9. Annette Walsh (Kerry)
10. Áine Wall (Waterford)
11. Bernie Ryan (Waterford)
12. Marina Barry (Kerry)
13. Sue Ramsbottom (Laois)
14. Angie Hearne (Wexford)
15. Siobhan Dunne (Wexford)

1990

1. Mary Keane (Clare)
2. Bridget Leen (Kerry)
3. Connie Conway (Laois)
4. Mary Mullery (Galway)
5. Marion Doherty (Kerry)
6. Ann Fitzpatrick (Waterford)
7. Mary Downey (Laois)
8. Amanda Donohue (Laois)
9. Mary Jo Curran (Kerry)
10. Áine Wall (Waterford)
11. Katie Liston (Kerry)
12. Marie Ryan (Waterford)
13. Margaret Lawlor (Kerry)
14. Sue Ramsbottom (Laois)
15. Eileen Lawlor (Kerry)

1991

1. Lulu Carroll (Laois)
2. Bridget Leen (Kerry)
3. Martina O'Ryan (Waterford)
4. Anne Dunford (Waterford)
5. Mary Gallagher (Westmeath)
6. Phil Curran (Kerry)
7. Anne Fitzpatrick (Waterford)

8. Marie Crotty (Waterford)
9. Julie Kavanagh (Dublin)
10. Marina Barry (Kerry)
11. Katie Liston (Kerry)
12. Michelle Donnelly (Clare)
13. Amanda Donohue (Laois)
14. Áine Wall (Waterford)
15. Margaret Brennan (Laois)

1992

1. Bernie Deegan (Laois)
2. Bridget Leen (Kerry)
3. Martina O'Ryan (Waterford)
4. June Whyte (Waterford)
5. Mary Gallagher (Westmeath)
6. Mary Casey (Laois)
7. Marie Gallagher (Clare)
8. Fionnuala Ruane (Kerry)
9. Bernie Ryan (Waterford)
10. Marina Barry (Kerry)
11. Geraldine O'Ryan (Waterford)
12. Edel Clarke (Westmeath)
13. Patricia Mimna (London)
14. Áine Wall (Waterford)
15. Pauline Mullen (Mayo)

1993

1. Bernie Deegan (Laois)
2. Margaret Buckley (Cork)
3. Bernie O'Neill (Mayo)
4. Katie Liston (Kerry)
5. Mary O'Gorman (Wexford)
6. Mary Casey (Laois)
7. Fionnuala Ruane (Kerry)
8. Denise Smith (Dublin)
9. Marie Fitzgerald (Kerry)
10. Patricia Mimna (London)
11. Mary Jo Curran (Kerry)
12. Sinead Cullinane (Clare)
13. Marina Barry (Kerry)
14. Sue Ramsbottom (Laois)
15. Áine Wall (Waterford)

1994

1. Kathleen Curran (Kerry)
2. Bridget Leen (Kerry)
3. Martina O'Ryan (Waterford)
4. Margaret Phelan (Laois)
5. Diane O'Hora (Mayo)
6. Noirin Walsh (Waterford)

7. Edel Clarke (Westmeath)
8. Jennifer Greenan (Monaghan)
9. Maeve Quinn (Leitrim)
10. Marie Gallagher (Clare)
11. Sue Ramsbottom (Laois)
12. Catriona Casey (Waterford)
13. Fiona Crotty (Waterford)
14. Áine Wall (Waterford)
15. Patricia Mimna (London)

1995

1. Anna Lisa Crotty (Waterford)
2. Regina Byrne (Waterford)
3. Bernie O'Neill (Mayo)
4. Cleona Walsh (Waterford)
5. Eileen Gill (Westmeath)
6. Fionnuala Ruane (Kerry)
7. Julianne Torpey (Waterford)
8. Jennifer Greenan (Monaghan)
9. Marie Fitzgerald (Kerry)
10. Fiona O'Driscoll (Cork)
11. Marie Crotty (Waterford)
12. Catriona Casey (Waterford)
13. Geraldine O'Ryan (Waterford)
14. Patricia Mullen (Mayo)
15. Geraldine O'Shea (Kerry)

1996

1. Anna Lisa Crotty (Waterford)
2. Mairead Kelly (Monaghan)
3. Noirin Walsh (Waterford)
4. Margaret Phelan (Laois)
5. Brenda McAnespie (Monaghan)
6. Jennifer Greenan (Monaghan)
7. Julianne Torpey (Waterford)
8. Christina Heffernan (Mayo)
9. Linda Farrelly (Monaghan)
10. Nicola Dunne (Wicklow)
11. Geraldine O'Shea (Kerry)
12. Anne Marie Curran (Westmeath)
13. Margaret Kerins (Monaghan)
14. Sue Ramsbottom (Laois)
15. Áine Wall (Waterford)

1997

1. Anna Lisa Crotty (Waterford)
2. Mairead Kelly (Monaghan)
3. Noirin Walsh (Waterford)
4. Eileen McElvaney (Monaghan)
5. Moira McMahon (Clare)

6. Brenda McAnespie (Monaghan)
7. Julianne Torpey (Waterford)
8. Jennifer Greenan (Monaghan)
9. Eithne Morrissey (Clare)
10. Christine O'Brien (Meath)
11. Angela Larkin (Monaghan)
12. Fiona Blessington (Longford)
13. Geraldine O'Ryan (Waterford)
14. Sue Ramsbottom (Laois)
15. Catriona Casey (Waterford)

1998

1. Patricia Bohan (Leitrim)
2. Eileen McElvaney (Monaghan)
3. Siobhan O'Ryan (Waterford)
4. Noirin Walsh (Waterford)
5. Anna Lisa Crotty (Waterford)
6. Anne Marie Dennehy (Meath)
7. Niamh Kindlon (Monaghan)
8. Christina Heffernan (Mayo)
9. Jennifer Greenan (Monaghan)
10. Margaret Kerins (Monaghan)
11. Edel Byrne (Monaghan)
12. Christine O'Brien (Meath)
13. Rebecca Hallihan (Waterford)
14. Áine Wall (Waterford)
15. Geraldine O'Ryan (Waterford)

1999

1. Denise Horan (Mayo)
2. Brenda McAnespie (Monaghan)
3. Siobhan O'Ryan (Waterford)
4. Marcella Heffernan (Mayo)
5. Anna Lisa Crotty (Waterford)
6. Mary Casey (Laois)
7. Assumpta Cullen (Wexford)
8. Christina Heffernan (Mayo)
9. Niamh McNelis (Meath)
10. Edel Byrne (Monaghan)
11. Fiona Blessington (Longford)
12. Catriona Casey (Waterford)
13. Christine O'Brien (Meath)
14. Eilish Gormley (Tryone)
15. Geraldine O'Ryan (Waterford)

2000

1. Denise Horan (Mayo)
2. Marcella Heffernan (Mayo)
3. Helena Lohan (Mayo)
4. Olivia Condon (Waterford)

5. Claire McGarvey (Tyrone)
6. Martina O'Ryan (Waterford)
7. Lynda Donnelly (Tyrone)
8. Anna Lisa Crotty (Waterford)
9. Christina Heffernan (Mayo)
10. Fiona Blessington (Longford)
11. Lynnette Hughes (Tyrone)
12. Mary O'Donnell (Waterford)
13. Diane O'Hora (Mayo)
14. Eilish Gormley (Tyrone)
15. Cora Staunton (Mayo)

2001

1. Denise Horan (Mayo)
2. Noelle Comyns (Clare)
3. Anna Connolly (Laois)
4. Margaret Phelan (Laois)
5. Marcella Heffernan (Mayo)
6. Jennifer Greenan (Monaghan)
7. Lorraine Muckian (Louth)
8. Christina Heffernan (Mayo)
9. Kathleen O'Reilly (Laois)
10. Louise Kelly (Dublin)
11. Majella Griffin (Clare)
12. Brianne Leahy (Kildare)
13. Sarah O'Connor (Kerry)
14. Eithne Morrissey (Clare)
15. Cora Staunton (Mayo)

2002

1. Suzanne Hughes (Dublin)
2. Donna Frost (Waterford)
3. Helena Lohan (Mayo)
4. Olivia Butler (Waterford)
5. Claire Egan (Mayo)
6. Jennifer Greenan (Monaghan)
7. Julianne Torpey (Waterford)
8. Christina Heffernan (Mayo)
9. Mary O'Donnell (Waterford)
10. Síle Ní Coitir (Dublin)
11. Niamh Kindlon (Monaghan)
12. Edel Byrne (Monaghan)
13. Orla Callen (Monaghan)
14. Geraldine O'Shea (Kerry)
15. Cora Staunton (Mayo)

2003

1. Andrea O'Donoghue (Kerry)
2. Nuala O'Se (Mayo)
3. Helena Lohan (Mayo)

4. Maria Kavanagh (Dublin)
5. Anna Lisa Crotty (Waterford)
6. Martina Farrell (Dublin)
7. Ever Flaherty (Galway)
8. Angie McNally (Dublin)
9. Mary O'Donnell (Waterford)
10. Lisa Cahill (Galway)
11. Christina Heffernan (Mayo)
12. Michelle McGing (Mayo)
13. Mary O'Rourke (Waterford)
14. Geraldine O'Shea (Kerry)
15. Kasey O'Driscoll (Kerry)

2004

1. Cliodhna O'Connor (Dublin)
2. Christine O'Reilly (Monaghan)
3. Ruth Stephens (Galway)
4. Helena Lohan (Mayo)
5. Rena Buckley (Cork)
6. Louise Keegan (Dublin)
7. Emer Flaherty (Galway)
8. Annette Clarke (Galway)
9. Claire Egan (Mayo)
10. Lisa Cahill (Galway)
11. Bernie Finley (Dublin)
12. Valerie Mulcahy (Cork)
13. Mary Nevin (Dublin)
14. Geraldine O'Shea (Kerry)
15. Cora Staunton (Mayo)

2005

1. Una Carroll (Galway)
2. Ruth Stephens (Galway)
3. Angela Walsh (Cork)
4. Leona Tector (Wexford)
5. Briege Corkery (Cork)
6. Aoibheann Daly (Galway)
7. Gemma Fay (Dublin)
8. Juliet Murphy (Cork)
9. Claire Egan (Mayo)
10. Geraldine Doherty (Meath)
11. Deirdre O'Reilly (Cork)
12. Lyndsay Davey (Dublin)
13. Valerie Mulcahy (Cork)
14. Niamh Fahy (Galway)
15. Lorna Joyce (Galway)

2006

1. Katrina Connolly (Sligo)
2. Caoimhe Marley (Armagh)

3. Angela Walsh (Cork)
4. Rena Buckley (Cork)
5. Aoibheann Daly (Galway)
6. Branagh O'Donnell (Armagh)
7. Patricia Fogarty (Laois)
8. Caroline O'Hanlon (Armagh)
9. Mary O'Donnell (Waterford)
10. Nollaig Cleary (Cork)
11. Grainne Nulty (Meath)
12. Sarah O'Connor (Kerry)
13. Tracey Lawlor (Laois)
14. Mary O'Connor (Cork)
15. Dymphna O'Brien (Limerick)

2007

1. Mary Rose Kelly (Wexford)
2. Rebecca Hallahan (Waterford)
3. Angela Walsh (Cork)
4. Rena Buckley (Cork)
5. Claire O'Hara (Mayo)
6. Brid Stack (Cork)
7. Briege Corkery (Cork)
8. Juliet Murphy (Cork)
9. Brianne Leahy (Kildare)
10. Sarah McLoughlin (Leitrim)
11. Cora Staunton (Mayo)
12. Tracey Lawlor (Laois)
13. Valerie Mulcahy (Cork)
14. Gemma Begley (Tyrone)
15. Deirdre O'Reilly (Cork)

2008

1. Elaine Harte (Cork)
2. Linda Barrett (Cork)
3. Angela Walsh (Cork)
4. Sharon Courtney (Monaghan)
5. Briege Corkery (Cork)
6. Brid Stack (Cork)
7. Neamh Woods (Tyrone)
8. Juliet Murphy (Cork)
9. Amanda Casey (Monaghan)
10. Nollaig Cleary (Cork)
11. Niamh Kindlon (Monaghan)
12. Michaela Downey (Down)
13. Edel Byrne (Monaghan)
14. Cora Staunton (Mayo)
15. Edel Hanley (Tipperary)

2009

1. Cliodhna O'Connor (Dublin)
2. Noelle Tierney (Mayo)
3. Angela Walsh (Cork)
4. Geraldine O'Flynn (Cork)
5. Briege Corkery (Cork)
6. Martha Carter (Mayo)
7. Siobhan McGrath (Dublin)
8. Juliet Murphy (Cork)
9. Norita Kelly (Cork)
10. Nollaig Cleary (Cork)
11. Edel Byrne (Monaghan)
12. Noelle Earley (Kildare)
13. Ciara McAnespie (Monaghan)
14. Sinead Aherne (Dublin)
15. Cora Staunton (Mayo)

2010

1. Edel Murphy (Kerry)
2. Rachel Ruddy (Dublin)
3. Lorraine Muckian (Laois)
4. Sinead McLoughlin (Tyrone)
5. Siobhan McGrath (Dublin)
6. Brid Stack (Cork)
7. Gemma Fay (Dublin)
8. Denise Masterson (Dublin)
9. Tracey Lawlor (Laois)
10. Cathy Donnelly (Tyrone)
11. Gemma Begley (Tyrone)
12. Amy McGuinness (Dublin)
13. Yvonne McMonagle (Donegal)
14. Sinead Aherne (Dublin)
15. Joline Donnelly (Tyrone)

2011

1. Irene Munnelly (Meath)
2. Gráinne McNally (Monaghan)
3. Sharon Courtney (Monaghan)
4. Deirdre O'Reilly (Cork)
5. Briege Corkery (Cork)
6. Brid Stack (Cork)
7. Geraldine O'Flynn (Cork)
8. Juliet Murphy (Cork)
9. Tracey Lawlor (Laois)
10. Therese McNally (Monaghan)
11. Elaine Kelly (Dublin)
12. Mary Kirwan (Laois)
13. Ciara McAnespie (Monaghan)
14. Rhona Ní Bhuachalla (Cork)
15. Sinead Aherne (Dublin)

2012

1. Elaine Harte (Cork)
2. Cáit Lynch (Kerry)
3. Brid Stack (Cork)
4. Christina Reilly (Monaghan)
5. Briege Corkery (Cork)
6. Rena Buckley (Cork)
7. Geraldine O'Flynn (Cork)
8. Sinead Goldrick (Dublin)
9. Caroline O'Hanlon (Armagh)
10. Sarah Houlihan (Kerry)
11. Cora Staunton (Mayo)
12. Ciara O'Sullivan (Cork)
13. Cathriona McConnell (Monaghan)
14. Valerie Mulcahy (Cork)
15. Louise Ní Mhuircheartaigh (Kerry)

2013

1. Yvonne Byrne (Mayo)
2. Gráinne McNally (Monaghan)
3. Sharon Courtney (Monaghan)
4. Deirdre O'Reilly (Cork)
5. Briege Corkery (Cork)
6. Sinead Goldrick (Dublin)
7. Geraldine O'Flynn (Cork)
8. Annette Clarke (Galway)
9. Juliet Murphy (Cork)
10. Sarah Houlihan (Kerry)
11. Caoimhe Mohan (Monaghan)
12. Cora Courtney (Monaghan)
13. Valerie Mulcahy (Cork)
14. Cora Staunton (Mayo)
15. Louise Ní Mhuircheartaigh (Kerry)

2014

1. Ciamh Dollard (Laois)
2. Mairead Tennyson (Armagh)
3. Angela Walsh (Cork)
4. Brid Stack (Cork)
5. Vera Foley (Cork)
6. Sinead Goldrick (Dublin)
7. Geraldine O'Flynn (Cork)
8. Briege Corkery (Cork)
9. Caroline O'Hanlon (Armagh)
10. Noelle Healy (Dublin)
11. Ciara O'Sullivan (Cork)
11. Cora Courtney (Monaghan)
13. Lyndsey Davey (Dublin)
14. Sinead Aherne (Dublin)
15. Aileen Pyers (Monaghan)

2015

1. Linda Martin (Monaghan)
2. Marie Ambrose (Cork)
3. Aislinn Desmond (Kerry)
4. Geraldine O'Flynn (Cork)
5. Vera Foley (Cork)
6. Sinead Finnegan (Dublin)
7. Sinead Goldrick (Dublin)
8. Briege Corkery (Cork)
9. Rena Buckley (Cork)
10. Cora Courtney (Monaghan)
11. Cora Staunton (Mayo)
12. Carla Rowe (Dublin)
13. Valeria Mulcahy (Cork)
14. Lyndsey Davey (Dublin)
15. Aimee Mackin (Armagh)

2016

1. Mary Hulgraine (Kildare)
2. Marie Ambrose (Cork)
3. Brid Stack (Cork)
4. Leah Caffrey (Dublin)
5. Sinead Goldrick (Dublin)
6. Deirdre O'Reilly (Cork)
7. Gráinne McNally (Monaghan)
8. Fiona McHale (Mayo)
9. Briege Corkery (Cork)
10. Noelle Healy (Dublin)
11. Ciara O'Sullivan (Cork)
12. Carla Rowe (Dublin)
13. Ciara McAnespie (Monaghan)
14. Sinead Aherne (Dublin)
15. Orla Finn (Cork)

2017

1. Ciara Trant (Dublin)
2. Emma Spillane (Cork)
3. Sarah Tierney (Mayo)
4. Rachel Ruddy (Dublin)
5. Caroline Kelly (Kerry)
6. Ciara Hegarty (Donegal)
7. Leah Caffrey (Dublin)
8. Lorraine Scanlon (Kerry)
9. Aileen Gilroy (Mayo)
10. Aimee Mackin (Armagh)
11. Niamh Hegarty (Donegal)
12. Nicole Owens (Dublin)
13. Sinead Aherne (Dublin)
14. Cora Staunton (Mayo)
15. Noelle Healy (Dublin)

2018

1. Ciara Trant (Dublin)
2. Treasa Doherty (Donegal)
3. Róisín Phelan (Cork)
4. Sinéad Burke (Galway)
5. Sinead Goldrick (Dublin)
6. Siobhan McGrath (Dublin)
7. Emma Spillane (Cork)
8. Neamh Woods (Tyrone)
9. Lauren McGee (Dublin)
10. Ciara O'Sullivan (Cork)
11. Noelle Healy (Dublin)
12. Lyndsey Davey (Dublin)
13. Sinead Aherne (Dublin)
14. Doireann O'Sullivan (Cork)
15. Sarah Houlihan (Kerry)

2019

1. Monica McGuirk (Meath)
2. Sinéad Burke (Galway)
3. Niamh Collins (Dublin)
4. Melissa Duggan (Cork)
5. Nicola Ward (Galway)
6. Sinead Goldrick (Dublin)
7. Olwen Carey (Dublin)
8. Louise Ward (Galway)
9. Siobhan McGrath (Dublin)
10. Carla Rowe (Dublin)
11. Niamh McEvoy (Dublin)
12. Lyndsey Davey (Dublin)
13. Tracey Leonard (Galway)
14. Rachel Kearns (Mayo)
15. Orla Finn (Cork)

2020

This Covid-affected year saw three 'Teams of the Championship' chosen, rather than the traditional All-Stars:

Junior

1. Shauna Murphy (Fermanagh)
2. Emily Mulhall (Wicklow)
3. Sarah Jane Winders (Wicklow)
4. Rebekah Daly (Limerick)
5. Alanna Conroy (Wicklow)
6. Saoirse Tennyson (Antrim)
7. Sarah McCarville (Fermanagh)
8. Aoife Gorman (Wicklow)
9. Róisín O'Reilly (Fermanagh)
10. Áine Cunningham (Limerick)

11. Laura Hogan (Wicklow)
12. Aisling Maguire (Fermanagh)
13. Meadhbh Deeney (Wicklow)
14. Marie Kealy (Wicklow)

Intermediate
1. Monica McGuirk (Meath)
2. Rachel Dillon (Westmeath)
3. Lucy Power (Westmeath)
4. Emma Troy (Meath)
5. Róisín Considine (Clare)
6. Fiona Claffey (Westmeath)
7. Megan Thynne (Meath)
8. Jennifer Higgins (Roscommon)
9. Máire O'Shaughnessy (Meath)
10. Emma Duggan (Meath)
11. Vikki Wall (Meath)
12. Anna Jones (Westmeath)
13. Stacey Grimes (Meath)
14. Niamh O'Dea (Clare)
15. Róisín Byrne (Kildare)

Senior
1. Martina O'Brien (Cork)
2. Martha Byrne (Dublin)
3. Clodagh McCambridge (Armagh)
4. Eimear Meaney (Cork)
5. Melissa Duggan (Cork)
6. Blaitin Mackin (Armagh)
7. Sinead Goldrick (Dublin)
8. Jennifer Dunne (Dublin)
9. Louise Ward (Galway)
10. Carla Rowe (Dublin)
11. Lyndsey Davey (Dublin)
12. Aimee Mackin (Armagh)
13. Áine O'Sullivan (Cork)
14. Aishling Moloney (Tipperary)
15. Noelle Healy (Dublin)

2021
1. Monica McGuirk (Meath)
2. Emma Troy (Meath)
3. Mary Kate Lynch (Meath)
4. Leah Caffrey (Dublin)
5. Erika O'Shea (Cork)
6. Aoibhín Cleary (Meath)
7. Orlagh Nolan (Dublin)
8. Hannah Looney (Cork)
9. Máire O'Shaughnessy (Meath)
10. Hannah Tyrrell (Dublin)
11. Rachel Kearns (Mayo)

12. Niamh O'Sullivan (Meath)
13. Vikki Wall (Meath)
14. Emma Duggan (Meath)
15. Geraldine McLoughlin (Donegal)

2022
1. Monica McGuirk (Meath)
2. Shauna Ennis (Meath)
3. Kayleigh Cronin (Kerry)
4. Danielle Caldwell (Mayo)
5. Aishling O'Connell (Kerry)
6. Emma Troy (Meath)
7. Aoibhín Cleary (Meath)
8. Cáit Lynch (Kerry)
9. Niamh McLaughlin (Donegal)
10. Niamh Carmody (Kerry)
11. Emma Duggan (Meath)
12. Shauna Howley (Mayo)
13. Aimee Mackin (Armagh)
14. Stacey Grimes (Meath)
15. Louise Ní Mhuircheartaigh (Kerry)

2023
1. Abby Shiels (Dublin)
2. Eilís Lynch (Kerry)
3. Leah Caffrey (Dublin)
4. Danielle Caldwell (Mayo)
5. Lauren Magee (Dublin)
6. Martha Byrne (Dublin)
7. Cáit Lynch (Kerry)
8. Jennifer Dunne (Dublin)
9. Lorraine Scanlon (Kerry)
10. Niamh Carmody (Kerry)
11. Orlagh Nolan (Dublin)
12. Ciara O'Sullivan (Cork)
13. Hannah Tyrrell (Dublin)
14. Carla Rowe (Dublin)
15. Louise Ní Mhuircheartaigh (Kerry)

MOST ALL-STAR AWARDS

11 = Mary Jo Curran (Kerry), Cora Staunton (Mayo)

10 = Briege Corkery (Cork)

8 = Áine Wall (Waterford)

7 = Brid Stack (Cork), Christina Heffernan (Mayo), Kathleen Curran [née Kennedy (Kerry/Dublin), Anna Lisa Crotty (Waterford), Jennifer Greenan (Monaghan), Sinead Aherne (Dublin), Sinead Goldrick (Dublin),

6 = Geraldine O'Flynn (Cork), Angela Walsh (Cork), Marina Barry (Kerry), Sue Ramsbottom (Laois), Juliet Murphy (Cork)

5 = Edel Clarke (Westmeath), Eileen Lawlor (Kerry), Margaret Lawlor (Kerry), Bridget Leen (Kerry), Connie Conway (Laois), Geraldine O'Ryan (Waterford), Rena Buckley (Cork), Valerie Mulcahy (Cork), Geraldine O'Shea (Kerry), Ciara O'Sullivan (Cork), Patricia Mimna (née O'Brien) (Cavan and London)

LGFA PRESIDENTS

Year	President	County
1974–77	Jim Kennedy	Tipperary
1977–79	Tom Kenny	Offaly
1979–82	Tom Dowd	Cavan
1982–85	Mick Fitzgerald	Kerry
1985–88	Pat Quill	Wexford
1988–91	Mary Wheatley	Laois
1991–94	Peter Rice	Wexford
1994–97	Helen O'Rourke	Dublin
1997–2000	Noel Murray	Waterford
2000–03	Walter Thompson	Dublin
2003–06	Geraldine Giles	Westmeath
2006–09	Geraldine Giles	Westmeath
2009–12	Pat Quill	Wexford
2012–15	Pat Quill	Wexford
2015–21	Marie Hickey	Laois
2021–25	Mícheál Naughton	Donegal
2025–	Trina Murray	Westmeath

COUNTY BOARDS ESTABLISHMENT

Year	County	Year	County
1971	Tipperary (–1990)	1986	Carlow
	Waterford		London
1974	Galway	1988	Wicklow
	Offaly	1991	Donegal
	Kerry		Limerick (re-established)
	Roscommon (–1981)		Monaghan
1975	Mayo		Tyrone
1976	Armagh (–1980)		Meath (re-established)
	Cavan (–1984)	1992	Armagh (re-established)
	Cork		Sligo
	Laois		Kildare (re-established)**
	Louth (–1977)		New York
	Meath (–1978)	1993	Fermanagh
1978	Leitrim		Tipperary (re-established)
1979	Wexford		Louth (re-established)
1980	Longford	1994	Down
1982	Limerick (–1985)	1995	Antrim
1983	Clare		Cavan (re-established)
1985	Roscommon (re-established)		Derry
	Dublin*	2003	Kilkenny (re-established)***

* Efforts were made to set up a county board in Dublin around 1981 and it appears that Dublin, backboned by the Rathcoole club, did compete in some LGFA competitions prior to the founding of the county board in 1985.

** Kildare established a county board in the 1970s but the exact year is unclear, as is for how long it was running.

*** Kilkenny did affiliate with the LGFA in the 1970s for a period but the exact year the board was set up and how long it operated for is unclear.

SOURCES

PRIMARY SOURCES

GAA Library and Archives

GAA Central Council Minutes

Camogie Association Central Council Minutes

LGFA Collection

Newspapers, magazines and periodicals

Anglo-Celt

Belfast Telegraph

Clare Champion

Connacht Sentinel

Connacht Tribune

Connaught Telegraph

Corkman

Donegal News

Drogheda Independent

Echo

Evening Echo

Evening Herald

Evening Press

Freeman's Journal

Irish Farmers Journal

Irish Independent

Irish Press

Kilkenny People

Longford Leader

Leinster Express

Leitrim Observer

Mayo News

Meath Chronicle

Munster Express

Nationalist and Leinster Times

Nenagh Guardian

Northern Standard

Offaly Independent

Roscommon Herald

Southern Star

Sunday Independent

The Irish Examiner
   (The Cork Examiner, pre-1996/
      The Examiner, 1996–2000)

The Irish Times

The Kerryman

The Nationalist

The Sligo Champion

Tipperary Star

Tuam Herald

Ulster Herald

Waterford News and Star

Western People

Westmeath Independent

Official Publications

Bunreacht na hÉireann, Constitution of Ireland, 1937

Commission on the Status of Women, report to the Minister for Finance, 1972

Dáil Éireann Debates

'Increased Funding for Female Inter-County Players,' Gaelic Players Association, accessed 28 March 2024, https://www.gaelicplayers.com/increased-funding-for-female-inter-county-players/

LGFA and GPA Publications

'Record tv audience for TG4 Ladies Football Final 2003', *LGFA*, 7 October 2003: https://ladiesgaelic.ie/record-tv-audience-for-tg4-ladies-football-final-2003/

Mary McAleese, 'Speech by President of Ireland Mary McAleese at the Ladies Gaelic Football Association All-Star Banquet', *LGFA*, 17 November 2003: https://ladiesgaelic.ie/speech-by-president-of-ireland-mary-mcaleese-at-the-ladies-gaelic-association-all-star-banquet/

'Lidl behind "Ladyball" Concept to Promote Partnership with LGFA', *LGFA*, 15 January 2016: https://ladiesgaelic.ie/lidl-and-lgfa-behind-ladyball-concept/

'Lidl and The Ladies Gaelic Football Association Announce Landmark €1.5m Partnership,' *LGFA*, 21 January 2016: https://ladiesgaelic.ie/lidl-and-the-ladies-gaelic-football-association-announce-landmark-e1-5m-partnership/

'LGFA Strategic Roadmap 2017–2022', *LGFA*, April 2018: https://ladiesgaelic.ie/wp-content/uploads/2018/04/LGFA-Strategic-Roadmap_April-2018.pdf

'Congress 2020 National Reports', *LGFA*, March 2020, p. 46: https://ladiesgaelic.ie/wp-content/uploads/2021/09/Congress-2020-National-Reports.pdf

'Covid-19 response: Joint Media Release from the GAA, An Cumann Camógaíochta and the LGFA,' *LGFA*, 12 March 2020: https://ladiesgaelic.ie/joint-media-release-from-the-gaa-an-cumann-camogaiochta-and-the-lgfa/

'Covid-19 – Ladies Gaelic Football Association Competitions and Development Update,' *LGFA*, 24 March 2020: https://ladiesgaelic.ie/covid-19-ladies-gaelic-football-association-competitions-and-development-update/

'Covid19: Ladies Gaelic Football Association Statement,' *LGFA*, 8 May 2020, https://ladiesgaelic.ie/covid19-ladies-gaelic-football-association-statement/

'2021 TG4 All-Ireland Ladies Football Championships to commence in July', *LGFA*, 4 May 2021: https://ladiesgaelic.ie/2021-tg4-all-ireland-ladies-football-championships-to-commence-in-july/

'LGFA Congress National Report 2022', *LGFA*: https://ladiesgaelic.ie/the-lgfa/about-us/national-congress/

'State of Play: Equality Snapshot for Female Intercounty Gaelic Games', *GPA*, 19 April 2023: https://www.gaelicplayers.com/document/state-of-play-equality-report/

'LGFA Statement – 19/6/23', *LGFA*, 19 June 2023: https://ladiesgaelic.ie/lgfa-statement-19-6-23/

'Pathway for Success, 2011–2016', *LGFA*, accessed 20 March 2024, p. 5: https://ladiesgaelic.ie/wp-content/uploads/2011/02/LGFA-strategicPlan_small.pdf

Private Papers of Marie McAleer

Account written by Francis Quill and Pat Chapman, 'Where did it all begin? The initial history of An Cumann Peil Gael na mBan up to 1974,' 2006

Account written by Michael Naughton, 'Ladies Gaelic Football: The Early Years', date unknown

'Charter, Constitution & Rules of Ladies Gaelic Football Association,' document included with a note from the Hon. Secretary of the LGFA, Margaret Colleran, 26 February 1975

Letter written by Michael Naughton, Secretary of the Roscommon Ladies County Board to Secretary of the LGFA, 24 August 1976

Letter written by Marie Holland, Hon. Sec. of the LGFA to all county board secretaries, 1 January 1977

Letter from Sister Mary Leonie, Reverend Mother, to Michael Naughton, 14 October 1977

Letter written by Michael Naughton to Mother Superior, Augustinian Order, St George's Retreat, Sussex, confirming the date of the final, 20 November 1977

Letter from Olive Dufficy, 2008

Press Release from All-Ireland Ladies Football Central Council, September 1976

Roscommon Ladies County Board Minute Books, 1974 – 1980

Tom Rowley, 'Ladies Football and Press Relations,' date unknown

Private Papers of Pam O'Mahony

Minute Book of New South Wales GAA, 1991

Murphy, Kerry, Kerry Murphy's Memories: The Diaries of an Irish Immigrant, (Walla Walla Press, 1998), p. 226

'Australia', GAA World Games 2023 Programme, p. 51. Private Papers of Pam O'Mahony

Private Papers of Fina Golden

LGFA Congress 2000 Minutes

LGFA Congress 2002, Financial Report for 2001

LGFA Congress 2003, Financial Report for 2002

Letter written by Paul Swift, Secretary of the Monaghan LGFA County Board to the LGFA County Secretaries, 21 June 2001

Letter to Walter Thompson, Helen O'Rourke, and all county secretaries signed by various representatives and delegates, 16 July 2001

Letter written by Helen O'Rourke to County Secretaries, 2001

Summary Report on Increased Participation Meetings written by Pat Quill, 7 December 2001

Letter written by Helen O'Rourke to County Secretaries, 2001

Letter written by Helen O'Rourke to County Secretaries, 2001

Ladies Gaelic Football Association Presentation to Council, Strategic Plan 2003, pp. 4–6

'Ladies Integration Pilot Scheme Launched', Press Release issued by the GAA, the Camogie Association and the LGFA, 25 February 2003

Letter to county boards written by Helen O'Rourke, 2004

Letter to county boards written by Helen O'Rourke, 25 July 2005

GAA Oral History Project Interviews

Geraldine Giles
Helen O'Rourke
Hugh Devenney and Mícheál Naughton
Karen Plunkett
Marie McAleer
Mary O'Connor
Mick Fitzgerald
Members of the Antrim Ladies Football Team
Nollaig Cleary

Órla Brennan
Pat Chapman
Rose McEnaney
Rosie O'Reilly
Ted Maloney, Martin Seery, Dermot Walsh
The Quinn Sisters
RTÉ Archives
'Football Not Just For Men', RTÉ Archives, 1985
The Late Late Show, RTÉ, 3 October 1987

SECONDARY SOURCES

Books & Articles

Cronin, Mike, Duncan, Mark, and Rouse, Paul, *The GAA: A People's History*. Cork: Collins, 2009

Dunning, Eric, Maguire, Joseph A., and Pearton, Robert E., *The Sports Process*. Champaign, IL: Human Kinetics Publishers, 1993

Ferriter, Diarmaid, *Ambiguous Republic: Ireland in the 1970s*. London: Profile Books, 2012

Griffin, Pádraig, *The Politics of Irish Athletics 1850–1990*. Leitrim: Marathon Publications, 1990

Judge, Yvonne, *Chasing Gold: Sportswomen of Ireland*. Dublin: Wolfhound, 1995

Maguire, Joseph, *Sport Worlds: A Sociological Perspective*. Leeds: Human Kinetics, 2002

McAnallen, Dónal, Hassan, David, and Hegarty, Roddy (eds), *The Evolution of the GAA: Ulaidh, Éire agus Eile*, Belfast: Stair Uladh, 2009

Moran, Mary, *A Game of Our Own: Camogie's Story*. Dublin: Camogie Association, 2011

Nic Congáil, Ríona, '"Looking on for Centuries from the Sideline": Gaelic Feminism and the Rise of Camogie', *Éire-Ireland*, Vol. 48, No. 1&2 (2013)

North American County Board Gaelic Athletic Association, 'Our Story Reviewed 1884–1993', accessed 16 April 2024

O'Brien, Denis, *The Rise of Gaelic Sports in Europe*. Great Britain: Amazon, 2021

O'Donovan, Diarmuid, 'Íde Bean Uí Shé, Cork Camogie's Feminist Influencer', *Studies in Arts and Humanities 7*, No. 1 (2021)

White, Mary, *Relentless: The Inside Story of the Cork Ladies Footballers*. Cork: Mercier Press, 2019

Williams, Jean, *A Game for Rough Girls? A History of Women's Football in Britain*. London: Routledge, 2003

Videos

'Introducing The #Ladyball!,' The Ladyball YouTube Channel, 13 January 2018: https://www.youtube.com/watch?v=5bWbIZl0G5s&t=30s

NOTES

INTRODUCTION

1 T. F. O'Sullivan, *Story of the GAA* (1916), p. 13. Cited in Mike Cronin, Mark Duncan and Paul Rouse, *The GAA: A People's History* (Cork: Collins, 2009), p. 32. Emphasis added.

2 Regina Fitzpatrick, Paul Rouse and Dónal McAnallen, 'The Freedom of the Field: Camogie before 1950', in *The Evolution of the GAA: Ulaidh, Éire agus Eile*, (eds) Dónal McAnallen, David Hassan and Roddy Hegarty (Belfast: Stair Uladh, 2009), pp. 304–305.

CHAPTER 1

1 'Keep women out of Croke Park!' *Sunday Independent*, 27 August 1967, p. 14.

2 Ibid.

3 Constitution of Ireland, enacted 1 July 1937: https://www.irishstatutebook.ie/eli/cons/en/html#part13.

4 Joseph Maguire, *Sport Worlds: A Sociological Perspective* (Leeds: Human Kinetics, 2002), p. 203.

5 'Ladies Gaelic Football Match', *Evening Herald,* 17 September 1920, p. 3.

6 'Ladies' Football Match In Dublin', *Freeman's Journal*, 22 September 1920, p. 6.

7 'Grand One-Day Carnival', *Evening Herald*, 13 September 1924, p. 3.

8 Sheila Fletcher, *Women First: The Female Tradition in English Physical Education 1880–1980*. Cited in Jean Williams, *A Game for Rough Girls? A History of Women's Football in Britain* (London: Routledge, 2003), p. 29.

9 Jennifer Hargreaves, 'The Victorian cult of the family and the early years of female sport', in *The Sports Process,* (eds) Eric Dunning, Joseph A. Maguire and Robert E. Pearton (Champaign, IL: Human Kinetics, 1993), p. 58.

10 'Women Athletes', *The Irish Times*, 4 May 1928, p. 6.

11 Cronin, Duncan and Rouse (2009), p. 323.

12 Pádraig Griffin, *The Politics of Irish Athletics 1850-1990* (Leitrim: Marathon Publications, 1990), p. 254.

13 Ibid., pp. 254–255.

14 Yvonne Judge, *Chasing Gold: Sportswomen of Ireland* (Dublin: Wolfhound, 1995), p. 10. Maeve

Kyle was the first woman to represent Ireland in an athletics event at the Olympic Games. She ran in the 100m and 200m races at the 1956 Melbourne Games and subsequently represented Ireland again at the Olympic Games in Rome (1960) and Tokyo (1964).

15 Griffin (1990), pp. 254–255.

16 Ibid., p. 255.

17 'Mixed Athletics', *Irish Press*, 24 February 1934, p. 6.

18 Griffin (1990), p. 255.

19 Judge (1995), p. 13.

20 Ibid., p. 11.

21 McAnallen, Hassan and Hegarty (2009), pp. 125–130.

22 Ríona Nic Congáil, 'Looking on for Centuries from the Sideline: Gaelic Feminism and the Rise of Camogie', *Éire-Ireland* 48, no. 1&2, p. 175–178.

23 Cronin, Duncan and Rouse (2009), p. 328.

24 Mary Moran, *A Game of Our Own: Camogie's Story*, (Dublin: Camogie Association, 2011), p. 36.

25 Commission on the status of women, report to Minister for Finance (Dublin, 1972).

26 Diarmaid Ferriter, *Ambiguous Republic: Ireland in the 1970s* (London: Profile Books, 2012), p. 665.

27 'Should G.A.A. bar women?', *Sunday Independent,* 3 September 1967, p. 14.

28 Dunning, Maguire and Pearton (1993), p. 62.

CHAPTER 2

1 Marie McAleer, interviewed by Arlene Crampsie for the GAA Oral History Project, 22 November 2010. https://www.gaa.ie/the-gaa/oral-history/marie-mcaleer/.

2 *Evening Herald*, 4 October 1945, p. 4.

3 *The Nationalist*, 20 August 1949, p. 5.

4 'Kilsheelan Fete', ibid., 27 August 1949, p. 5.

5 *Nationalist and Leinster Times*, 30 June 1945, p. 5.

6 *The Nationalist*, 7 June 1947, p. 7.

7 'Ladies Football', *Offaly Independent*, 16 September 1967, p. 5.

8 'Ladies' Football Competition', ibid., 23 September 1967, p. 7.

9 Ibid., p. 10.

10 'A Look At The Sports Scene in Offaly', *Leinster Express*, 14 October 1967, p. 2.

11 Ibid., 20 January 1968, p. 9.

12 Ibid., 20 April 1968, p. 2.

13 Ibid.

14 'Ladies night At Kill', *Irish Press,* 2 September 1970, p. 20.

15 'Comeragh Chimes', *Munster Express*, 4 August 1967, p. 18.

16 'Showerings in Ladies' Football Final', *The Nationalist*, 11 October 1969, p. 2.

17 *Southern Star,* 17 July 1965, p. 8.

18 Ibid.

19 P. J. Hennelly, 'Camogie: Mayo Regraded', *Connaught Telegraph*, 23 February 1967, p. 11.

20 'Now a Ladies' Football Team?', *Mayo News*, 18 February 1967, p. 1; 'The Ladies Want to Join In', *Western People*, 18 February 1967, p. 1.

21 Diarmuid O'Donovan, 'Íde Bean Uí Shé, Cork Camogie's Feminist Influencer', *Studies in Arts and Humanities* 7, no. 1 (2021), pp. 91–92.

22 'Ladies Football', *Meath Chronicle*, 23 March 1968, p. 11.

23 Ibid.

24 Ibid.

25 'Carrigaline Notes', *Southern Star*, 9 July 1960, p. 2.

26 *Evening Echo*, 19 July 1960, p. 8.

27 'A Look At The Sports Scene in Offaly', *Leinster Express,* 11 May 1968, p. 3.

28 'Ladies Football League', *Waterford News and Star*, 24 July 1970, p. 6.

29 'Girls Football', *Drogheda Independent*, 7 June 1968, p. 4.

30 *The Nationalist*, 20 November 1971, p. 5; 'Co. Tipperary Ladies' Football Notes', *The Nationalist*, 29 January 1972, p. 21.

31 'Ladies Football Notes', ibid., 9 October 1971, p. 17.

32 Ibid., 13 November 1971, p.19.

33 Jim Kennedy, 'Give Ladies' Football Recognition', *Evening Echo*, 30 November 1971. p. 10.

34 Seamus O Cinneide, 'Ladies, Stand Up and Be Counted', ibid., 29 February 1972, p. 12.

35 'Ladies Football Notes', *The Nationalist*, 30 September 1972, p. 18.

36 Account written by Francis Quill and Pat Chapman, 'Where did it all begin? The initial history of An Cumann Peil Gael na mBan up to 1974', 2006. Private papers of Marie McAleer.

37 Mick Fitzgerald, interviewed by Arlene Crampsie for the GAA Oral History Project, 11 April 2011. https://www.gaa.ie/the-gaa/oral-history/mick-fitzgerald/.

38 Seán Ó Dunagáin, 'Offaly ladies team', *Westmeath Independent*, 1 June 1973, p. 11.

39 'Offaly v. Kerry in July', *Evening Herald*, 24 July 1973, p. 18.

40 Ibid.

41 'Who said Offaly and Kerry would not meet in final?', *Offaly Independent*, 27 July 1973, p. 12.

42 'Girls getting their kicks', *Evening Press*, 30 July 1973, p. 3.

43 Ibid.

44 'Killrossanty News/Views', *Waterford News and Star*, 3 August 1973, p. 22.

45 'Bonmahon', ibid., 14 September 1973, p. 22.

46 'Girls getting their kicks', *Evening Press*, 30 July 1973, p. 3.

CHAPTER 3

1 'Ladies Football', *Tipperary Star*, 6 July 1974, p. 14.

2 'Ladies Football', *The Nationalist*, 6 July 1974, p. 19. In April 1974 the Tipperary Ladies' Board had reported in their notes that a trip to New York might happen in October of that same year, as noted in the following newspapers: 'Co. Tipp Ladies' GF Notes,' *The Nationalist*, 6 April 1974, p. 19; 'Co Tipp. Ladies Football', *Tipperary Star*, 27 April 1974, p. 14. However, in the notes of 6 July 1974, it was stated that the trip was now in doubt.

3 Ibid.

4 Roscommon Ladies County Board Minute Book, 9 July 1974. Private papers of Marie McAleer.

5 Account written by Francis Quill and Pat Chapman, 'Where did it all begin? The initial history of An Cumann Peil Gael na mBan up to 1974,' 2006. Private papers of Marie McAleer. This type of free is commonly known as a '45' today, as it is taken from the 45-metre line (i.e. 50 yards).

6 *Evening Herald*, 3 August 1974, p. 15.

7 'Galway Ladies Surprise Offaly', *Connacht Tribune*, 8 August 1974, p. 17.

8 'Lively Afternoon', *Westmeath Independent*, 16 August 1974, p. 15.

9 'Ladies Football', *Tipperary Star*, 17 August 1974, p. 16.

10 'Kerry ladies clash', *The Kerryman*, 16 August 1974, p. 13.

11 'Cork girls beaten', *The Corkman,* 30 August 1974, p. 22.

12 'Ladies Football Notes', *The Nationalist*, 31 August 1974, p. 17.

13 Ibid., 7 September 1974, p. 16.

14 'Tipp ladies too good for Kerry', *The Cork Examiner*, 16 September 1974, p. 8.

15 'Ladies' Football', *Offaly Independent*, 4 October 1974, p. 7.

16 'All Ireland final for Durrow', *Kilkenny People*, 11 October 1974, p. 20; 'Ladies Football', *Tipperary Star,* 5 October 1974, p. 5.

17 Liam Kelly, 'Make Way For That Other All-Ireland Final', *Irish Press*, 11 October 1974, p. 11.

18 Ibid.

19 'Ladies' Football Notes', *The Nationalist*, 28 September 1974, p. 16.

20 Ibid., 12 October 1974, p. 17.

21 'Ladies Football Notes', ibid., 12 October 1974, p. 16.

22 'Ladies Football', *Tipperary Star,* 5 October 1974, p. 5.

23 Liam Kelly, 'Make Way For That Other All-Ireland Final', *Irish Press*, 11 October 1974, p. 11.

24 Dan Coen, 'All-Ireland "first" for the Women', ibid., 14 October 1974, p. 1.

25 Ibid.; 'Offaly fail to Tipperary', *Westmeath Independent*, 18 October 1974, p. 12.

26 Ibid.

27 'Tipp. Lady Footballers Congratulated', *Tipperary Star*, 9 November 1974, p. 11.

28 'Ladies Football Notes,' ibid., 23 November 1974, p. 14.

CHAPTER 4

1 'Ladies football', *Irish Farmers Journal*, 26 April 1975, p. 37.

2 Ibid.

3 'Mitchel's ladies team', *Connaught Telegraph*, 3 April 1975, p. 8. Prendergast and Loftus both played for the Mayo men's Gaelic football team (1965–72 and 1949–53 respectively). In his post-playing career Loftus refereed the 1965 and 1958 men's All-Ireland football finals and he acted as President of the GAA from 1985 to 1988.

4 'A Female County Board?', ibid., 8 May 1975, p. 1.

5 *Connacht Tribune,* 16 January 1976, p. 10.

6 Ibid.

7 *Nationalist and Leinster Times*, 9 January 1976, p. 9.

8 'Like Mother, Like Daughter', *Connaught Telegraph*, 7 April 1976, p. 1.

9 'Ladies' Gaelic Football', *Meath Chronicle*, 20 March 1976, p. 16.

10 'Cork ladies beaten by Kerry', *The Corkman*, 16 July 1976, p. 9.

11 'Great year for ladies football', *The Cork Examiner*, 2 February 1977, p. 36.

12 'Ladies Football', *Westmeath Examiner*, 14 August 1976, p. 10.

13 'Cavan dispose of Meath', *Anglo-Celt*, 26 November 1976, p. 13.

14 'An Offaly week-end hosting in London', *Westmeath Independent*, 20 June 1975, p. 8.

15 Ibid.

16 Ibid.

17 'Ladies Football in New York', *Anglo-Celt,* 10 June 1977, p. 19.

18 '"Women's Lib" in Galway Football', *Western People*, 8 February 1975, p. 11.

19 Ibid.

20 'Charter, Constitution & Rules of Ladies Gaelic Football Association,' document included with a note from the Hon. Secretary of the LGFA, Margaret Colleran, 26 February 1975. Private papers of Marie McAleer.

21 'Call For New Rules For Ladies' Football,' *Western People*, 12 February 1977, p. 11.

22 Letter written by Michael Naughton, Secretary of the Roscommon Ladies County Board to Secretary of the LGFA, 24 August 1976. Private papers of Marie McAleer.

23 Letter written by Marie Holland, Hon. Sec. of the LGFA, to all county board secretaries, 1 January 1977. Private papers of Marie McAleer.

24 Ibid.

25 'All-Ireland Ladies Football Congress at Cavan', *Anglo-Celt*, 25 March 1977, p. 21.

26 'Versatile Mary Geaney', *The Kerryman,* 5 July 1974, p. 16; 'Kerry's sportswoman supreme'*, The Kerryman,* 14 February 1975, p. 10.

27 Atlas, 'Tipperary has one All-Ireland in 1975', *Tipperary Star*, 27 September 1975, p. 18.

28 'Mayo Girls Are Ireland's U-16 Football Queens', *Mayo News*, 24 April 1976, p. 16.

29 Divot, 'Hurling semi-final was a let down', *The Nationalist*, 31 July 1976, p. 16. [Note: Divot was a pen-name for Bill O'Donnell: columnists-have-cast-a-critical-eye-on-tipperary-gaa-through-the-decades.html].

30 'Easy win for Tipperary', *The Nationalist*, 12 July 1975, p. 21.

31 'Galway Ladies Win Title Race Opener', *Connacht Sentinel*, 15 July 1975, p. 8.

32 'Women's sports', *Irish Farmers Journal*, 28 June 1975, p. 40.

33 'She-Men', *Meath Chronicle*, 10 April 1976, p. 6.

34 'Lady Footballers Seek Full Recognition', *Tipperary Star,* 7 February 1976, p. 20.

35 Tom Rowley, 'Ladies football and Press Relations', date unknown. Private papers of Marie McAleer.

36 Mick Fitzgerald, interviewed by Arlene Crampsie, 11 April 2011 for the GAA Oral History Project, https://www.gaa.ie/the-gaa/oral-history/mick-fitzgerald.

37 Tom Rowley, 'Ladies Football and Press Relations', date unknown. Private papers of Marie McAleer.

38 'Why was ladies' final postponed?' *Westmeath Independent*, 28 October 1977, p. 13.

39 'Somebody doesn't like us girls', *Offaly Independent*, 2 December 1977, p. 20.

40 'Ladies' football: Congress Adjourned', *Westmeath Independent*, 3 March 1978, p. 12.

41 Account written by Michael Naughton, 'Ladies Gaelic Football: The Early Years', date unknown. Private papers of Marie McAleer.

42 Letter written by Michael Naughton to Mother Superior, Augustinian Order, St George's Retreat, Sussex, confirming the date of the final, 20 November 1977. Private papers of Marie McAleer.

43 Letter from Sister Mary Leonie, Reverend Mother to Michael Naughton, 14 October 1977. Private papers of Marie McAleer.

44 Account written by Michael Naughton, 'Ladies Gaelic Football: The Early Years', date unknown. Private papers of Marie McAleer.

45 'Big match prayers for Sister Pauline', *Irish Press*, 26 November 1977, p. 1.

46 Cois Laoi, 'Cork Retain Interest in Nat. League',' *Southern Star*, 3 December 1977, p. 19.

47 'Ladies are no joke', ibid., 7 January 1978, p. 8.

48 '"Blackout" on women's final condemned', *Irish Press*, 26 September 1978, p. 4.

49 'Lack Of Publicity Is Noted', *Irish Independent*, 14 April 1980, p. 11.

50 Geraldine Brennan, 'Nice Turn of Foot', *Evening Herald*, 21 August 1980, p. 12.

51 Ibid.

52 'Galway Ladies Furious', *Connacht Tribune*, 12 October 1979, p. 10.

53 'All-Ireland for Tipperary Ladies', *Tipperary Star*, 27 September 1980, p. 22.

54 Geraldine Grennan, 'Nice Turn of Foot', *Evening Herald*, 21 August 1980, p. 12.

55 'Ladies Football All-Stars XV', *Irish Independent*, 19 November 1980, p. 14.

56 'Proposal To Start Competition For Women', *Donegal News*, 27 January 1979, p. 10.

57 Roscommon Ladies County Board Minute Book, 27 October 1976. Private papers of Marie McAleer.

58 Ibid.

59 'Ladies Football in National Schools', *Anglo-Celt*, 10 March 1978, p. 20.

60 'Digital Move to Top In Inter-Firms', *Connacht Sentinel*, 22 June 1976, p. 10.

61 'Ladies Football', *Connacht Sentinel*, 28 June 1977, p. 9.

62 'Cork Side An Utter Disgrace Board Told', *Evening Echo*, 30 July 1979, p. 12.

63 Ibid.

64 'Dissatisfaction with Ladies Football Board', *Anglo-Celt*, 8 February 1980, p. 17.

65 *Irish Press*, 22 April 1974.

66 Roscommon Ladies County Board Minute Book, Secretary's Report for the Year 1979, 24 February 1980. Private papers of Marie McAleer.

67 'Readers' Views', *Offaly Independent*, 19 October 1979, p. 16.

68 Ibid.

69 'Girls – The G.A.A. wants you', ibid., 2 February 1980, p. 13.

70 Ibid.

CHAPTER 5

1 Marie McAleer, interviewed by Arlene Crampsie, 22 November 2010 for the GAA Oral History Project, https://www.gaa.ie/the-gaa/oral-history/marie-mcaleer.

2 'Ladies Football Notes', *The Nationalist*, 31 August 1974, p. 17; ibid., 7 September 1974, p. 16.

3 *Irish Press*, 17 December 1974, p. 16.

4 'No official support for Ladies Football', *Tuam Herald*, 4 January 1975, p. 12.

5 'Girls prefer football to camogie!', ibid., 22 November 1975, p. 1.

6 Ibid.

7 'Looking After The Ladies', *Western People*, 27 December 1975, p. 3.

8 Ibid.

9 'All Ireland Ladies Football Convention', *Tipperary Star*, 31 January 1976, p. 14.

10 'Lady Footballers Seek Full Recognition,' ibid., 7 February 1976, p. 20.

11 GAA Central Council Minute Books 1976, GAA/CC/01, GAA Library and Archive.

12 Ibid.

13 Tom Rowley, 'Doctor's warning for those high-kicking women footballers', *Irish Independent*, 19 May 1977, p. 3.

14 Ibid.

15 Geraldine Grennan, 'Nice Turn of Foot', *Evening Herald*, 21 August 1980, p. 12.

16 'All-Ireland U/16 Ladies' Football for Mayo', *Tipperary Star*, 24 April 1976, p. 14.

17 'Kildare girls take football seriously', *Nationalist and Leinster Times*, 21 May 1976, p. 10.

18 GAA Central Council Minute Books 1976, GAA/CC/01, GAA Library and Archive.

19 Camogie Central Council Minute Books 1976, CAM/CC/01, GAA Library and Archive.

20 'Ladies' Gaelic Football', *Meath Chronicle*, 21 August 1976, p. 7.

21 Ibid.

22 Ibid.

23 Press Release from All-Ireland Ladies Football Central Council, September 1976. Private papers of Marie McAleer.

24 'Ladies Football', *Evening Echo*, 3 March 1977, p. 12.

25 'Tipp motions at G.A.A. Congress', *Nenagh Guardian*, 6 April 1977, p. 6.

26 'Lack Of Publicity Is Noted', *Irish Independent*, 14 April 1980, p. 11.

27 'Several Rules Changes Likely From Annual Congress', *Munster Express*, 28 March 1980, p. 13; 'Cavan Adjourned G.A.A. Convention', *Anglo-Celt*, 2 February 1981, p. 13.

28 GAA Central Council Minute Books 1982, GAA/CC/01, GAA Library and Archive.

29 Mick Fitzgerald, interviewed by Arlene Crampsie, 11 April 2011 for the GAA Oral History Project, https://www.gaa.ie/the-gaa/oral-history/mick-fitzgerald.

30 'Breakthrough for Ladies Football', *The Cork Examiner*, 28 September 1976, p. 11.

CHAPTER 6

1 Paul Donaghy, 'Connie, the first lady of football', *Nationalist and Leinster Times*, 4 September 1987, p. 10.

2 Michael Fitzgerald, 'Kerry ladies lead fair sex in football', *The Kerryman*, 18 May 1984, p. 18.

3 Sinéad Kissane, 'There were two sides to Kingdom's Golden story', *Irish Independent*, 2 July 2022, pp. 8–9.

4 'Ladies' football', *The Kerryman*, 15 May 1987, p. 12.

5 Pam McKay, 'More deadly than the males!. *Evening Herald*, 15 October 1987, p. 22.

6 'Bit of history at headquarters!', *Irish Independent,* 9 October 1986, p. 11.

7 'Mixed luck', *Nationalist and Leinster Times,* 22 May 1987, p. 26.

8 'Emergency Ladies Co. Board Meeting', *Leitrim Observer*, 7 March 1987, p. 16.

9 'Tough Test Against Kerry', ibid., 18 April 1987, p. 14.

10 'One Short - But So Easy For Kerry', *The Kerryman,* 24 April 1987, p. 21.

11 The Quinn sisters, interviewed by Arlene Crampsie, 17 February 2010, for the GAA Oral History Project, https://www.gaa.ie/the-gaa/oral-history/the-quinn-sisters.

12 'With the Ladies', *Longford Leader,* 13 March 1987, p. 23.

13 Ibid.

14 Ibid.

15 'Ear to the Ground', *Clare Champion,* 18 December 1987, p. 20.

16 Paul Donaghy, 'Connie, the first lady of football', *Nationalist and Leinster Times,* 4 September 1987, p. 10.

17 Roscommon Folder, LGFA Archival Collection, GAA Library and Archive.

18 'Sally O'Brien stars in Galway R.T.C. win', *Tuam Herald,* 8 November 1975, p. 11.

19 'Fourth Title For Galway Students', *Connacht Tribune*, 16 April 1976, p. 14.

20 Higher Education Folder, LGFA Archival Collection, GAA Library and Archive.

21 Ibid.

22 Ibid.

23 Ibid.

24 Ibid.

25 Ibid.

26 'Ladies Football Congress in Cavan', *Anglo-Celt*, 11 February 1983, p. 18.

27 Ibid.

28 Ibid.

29 'Busy Time for Administrators', *Offaly Independent*, 10 February 1984, p. 11.

30 'Irish Sports Bodies Share £1/4m,' *Irish Independent*, 25 February 1977, p. 14; 'Olympic Council gets £40,000,' *The Cork Examiner*, 24 March 1978, p. 12.

31 Dáil Éireann debate, 'Written Answers – Expenditure on Sport', 7 February 1985.

32 '13th ladies football congress', *The Cork Examiner,* 28 March 1987, p. 19.

33 Pam McKay, 'More deadly than the males!' *Evening Herald*, 15 October 1987, p. 22.

34 'Women on Women', *Leitrim Observer*, 23 February 1985, p. 1; 'Promoting ladies' football', *The Kerryman*, 1 March 1985, p. 8; 'Ladies football on television', *The Kerryman*', 15 March 1985, p. 13; 'Football Not Just For Men', RTÉ Archives, 1985: https://www.rte.ie/archives/exhibitions/1666-women-and-society/388941-women-in-the-gaa/.

35 'Ladies football on television', *The Kerryman*, 15 March 1985, p. 13.

36 'Football Not Just For Men', RTÉ Archives, 1985: https://www.rte.ie/archives/exhibitions/1666-women-and-society/388941-women-in-the-gaa/. Segment from *The Women's Programme* broadcast in March 1985.

37 Geraldine Giles, interviewed by Regina Fitzpatrick, 11 June 2011, for the GAA Oral History Project, https://www.gaa.ie/the-gaa/oral-history/geraldine-giles.

38 *The Late Late Show*, RTÉ, 3 October 1987.

39 GAA Central Council Minute Books 1986, GAA/CC/01, GAA Library and Archive.

40 'New Camogie President', *Evening Echo,* 29 March 1985, p. 11.

41 'Ladies football is alive and well', *The Kerryman,* 31 May 1985, p. 46.

42 Pam McKay, 'More deadly than the males!' *Evening Herald*, 15 October 1987, p. 22.

43 'Three in-a-row ladies angry over match venue', *The Kerryman,* 14 September 1984, p. 1.

44 'Kerry girls pull off the three-in-a-row', ibid., 14 September 1984, p. 12.

45 LGFA All-Ireland finals were held in Durrow, Co. Laois (1974), Athy, Co. Kildare (1975), Littleton, Co. Tipperary (1976), Hyde Park, Co. Roscommon (1977), Ballinasloe, Co. Galway (1978 and 1981), Portarlington, Co. Laois (1979), Edenderry, Co. Offaly (1980), Nenagh, Co. Tipperary (1982), Kilsheelan, Co. Tipperary (1983), Timahoe, Co. Laois (1984), and Páirc Uí Chaoimh, Co. Cork (1985).

46 'Bit of history at headquarters!', *Irish Independent,* 9 October 1986, p. 11.

47 Eamon Horan, 'Sportschat', *The Kerryman*, 14 November 1986, p. 15.

CHAPTER 7

1 'More Ladies' G.A.A. Publicity – Rice', *Northern Standard,* 11 March 1993, p. 29.

2 Cliona Foley, 'Ladies in a classic thriller', *Irish Independent,* 7 October 1996, p. 5.

3 Frank Roche, 'Timely move by the GAA!', *Evening Herald*, 3 September 1998, p. 35.

4 Brendan Larkin, 'Ladies undertake a timely move for the All-Ireland final,' *The Examiner,* 4 September 1998, p. 16.

5 Cliona Foley, 'Great time thanks to the clock!', *Irish Independent*, 5 October 1998, p. 1.

6 'More Ladies' G.A.A. Publicity – Rice', *Northern Standard,* 11 March 1993, p. 29.

7 Ibid.

8 Sean Kilfeather, 'Women's football given huge boost', *The Irish Times,* 20 May 1998, p. 21.

9 Paul McCabe, 'Defence holds the key', *Northern Standard,* 22 October 1998, p. 32.

10 Jim O'Sullivan, 'Ladies football in fast lane', *Irish Examiner,* 5 November 2002, p. 21.

11 Cliona Foley, 'Girls spice up the GAA', *Evening Herald,* 31 October 1997, p. 78.

12 Helen O'Rourke, interviewed by Regina Fitzpatrick, 16 July 2013, for the GAA Oral History Project, https://www.gaa.ie/the-gaa/oral-history/helen-bourke.

13 Ibid.

14 Ibid.

15 Ibid.

16 Cliona Foley, 'Girls spice up the GAA', *Evening Herald,* 31 October 1997, p. 78.

17 Ibid.

18 'Ladies need support to keep playing', *The Examiner,* 6 March 2000, p. 20.

19 'Donegal Lose', *Northern Standard,* 14 October 1993, p. 26.

20 Lancashire LGFA Archival Collection, GAA Library and Archive.

21 Ibid.

22 Ibid.

23 'More Ladies' G.A.A. Publicity – Rice', *Northern Standard,* 11 March 1993, p. 29; North American County Board Gaelic Athletic Association, 'Our Story Reviewed 188 –1993': https://usgaa.org/wp-content/uploads/2019/04/NACB-Our-Story-Reviewed-1884-1993-Full-File.pdf, accessed April 16, 2024, 150 – 152.

24 North American Board, LGFA Archival Collection, GAA Library and Archive.

25 Rosie O'Reilly, interviewed by Seán Kearns, 2 September 2009, for the GAA Oral History Project, https://www.gaa.ie/the-gaa/oral-history/rosie-reilly.

26 'Tipperary ladies with New York All-Stars', *Tipperary Star,* 17 September 1994, p. 25.

27 Ibid.

28 'All-Stars Get Tough Welcome From Home Side', *Roscommon Herald*, 23 September 1994, p. 16; 'New Yorkers deny Leitrim's Ladies', *Leitrim Observer*, 21 September 1994, p. 18.

29 'New Yorkers deny Leitrim's Ladies', *Leitrim Observer*, 21 September 1994, p. 18; 'New York impress in defeat of Dublin champs', *Evening Herald*, 21 September 1994, p. 56.

30 'Tyrone girls lift All-Ireland crown at third attempt', *Ulster Herald*, 7 October 1999, p. 23.

31 Rosie O'Reilly, interviewed by Seán Kearns, 2 September 2009, for the GAA Oral History Project, https://www.gaa.ie/the-gaa/oral-history/rosie-reilly.

32 Kerry Murphy, *Kerry Murphy's Memories: The Diaries of an Irish Immigrant* (Walla Walla Press, 1998), p. 226. From the private collection of Pam O'Mahony.

33 Ibid.

34 Minute Book of New South Wales GAA, meeting on 13 May 1991. Private Papers of Pam O'Mahony.

35 Minute Book of New South Wales GAA, meeting on 23 September 1991. Private Papers of Pam O'Mahony.

36 'Australia', GAA World Games 2023 Programme, p. 51. Private Papers of Pam O'Mahony.

CHAPTER 8

1 Fr Liam Kelleher, 'President-elect, Westmeath's Geraldine Giles, welcomes increased profile', *The Corkman,* 13 March 2003, p. 4.

2 Mary White, 'Conference to address important issues', *Evening Echo*, 18 February 2006, p. 51.

3 'Adamstown suggested as home for Ladies' GAA', *The Echo*, 15 March 2001, p. 11.

4 Helen O'Rourke, interviewed by Regina Fitzpatrick, 16 July 2013, for the GAA Oral History Project, https://www.gaa.ie/the-gaa/oral-history/helen-bourke.

5 Denise Horan, 'Ladies final to return to Croke Park', *Western People*, 8 August 2001, p. 36.

6 Ibid.

7 'Record tv audience for TG4 Ladies Football Final 2003', *LadiesGaelic.ie*, 7 October 2003, https://ladiesgaelic.ie/record-tv-audience-for-tg4-ladies-football-final-2003/.

8 Malachy Clerkin, 'The story behind the amazing growth of women's Gaelic football', *The Irish Times*, 6 March 2021: the-story-behind-the-amazing-growth-of-women-s-gaelic-football-1.4501155.

9 Jim O'Sullivan, 'Ladies football in fast lane', *Irish Examiner*, 5 November 2002, p. 21.

10 'Suzuki Ireland agree new three year sponsorship deal', *Northern Standard*, 2 February 2006, p. 50.

11 'Ladies Gaelic Football Major Sponsorship Deal', *Anglo-Celt*, 19 October 2006, p. 22.

12 LGFA Congress 2000 Minutes. Private papers of Fina Golden.

13 Ibid.

14 LGFA Congress 2002 Financial Report for 2001. Private papers of Fina Golden.

15 XE currency exchange, rate given as 1 IEP = 1.26974 EUR, accessed March 19, 2024, https://www.xe.com/currencyconverter/convert/?Amount=454355.26&From=IEP&To=EUR.

16 LGFA Congress 2002, Financial Report. Private papers of Fina Golden.

17 LGFA Congress 2003, Financial Report for 2002. Private papers of Fina Golden.

18 Ibid.

19 Letter written by Paul Swift, Secretary of the Monaghan LGFA County Board to the LGFA County Secretaries, 21 June 2001. Private papers of Fina Golden.

20 Letter to Walter Thompson, Helen O'Rourke, and all county secretaries signed by various representatives and delegates, 16 July 2001. Private papers of Fina Golden.

21 Vincent Hogan, 'GAA Helen of Troy launches a thousand football careers', *Irish Independent,* 29 September 2001, p. 25.

22 Letter written by Helen O'Rourke to County Secretaries, 2001. Private papers of Fina Golden.

23 Summary Report on Increased Participation Meetings written by Pat Quill, 7 December 2001. Quill and Helen O'Rourke sat on a committee set up by then President of the GAA, Joe McDonagh, and chaired by Barney Winstone as a follow-up to motions to GAA Congress from the LGFA and the Camogie Association for affiliation to the GAA and McDonagh's desire to see greater cooperation between the Gaelic Games bodies. Private papers of Fina Golden.

24 Letter written by Helen O'Rourke to County Secretaries, 2001. Private papers of Fina Golden.

25 Cliona Foley, 'Laois hoodoo ends in Mayo late mistake', *Irish Independent*, 1 October 2001, p. 5.

26 Cliona Foley, 'Mayo glee as Staunton lands a bizarre winner', ibid., 2 October 2000, p. 5.

27 Letter to county boards written by Helen O'Rourke, 2004. Private papers of Fina Golden.

28 Letter to county boards written by Helen O'Rourke, 25 July 2005. Private papers of Fina Golden.

29 'Womens' GAA is a fast, clean, skilled game - it's fun to play and to watch', *Irish Independent City Life*, 6 August 2002, p. 2.

30 Geraldine Giles, interviewed by Regina Fitzpatrick, 11 June 2011, for the GAA Oral History Project, https://www.gaa.ie/the-gaa/oral-history/geraldine-giles.

31 Ladies Gaelic Football Association Presentation to Council, Strategic Plan 2003, pp. 4–6. Private papers of Fina Golden.

32 'Ladies Gaelic Football Association', *Leinster Express,* 3 April 2004, p. 56.

33 Brendan O'Brien, 'Ladies football plan unveiled', *Irish Examiner*, 7 March 2006, p. 24.

34 Aiden Henry, 'Ladies €22,000 fine is as laughable as it is farcical', *Connaught Telegraph,* 5 November 2003, p. 12.

35 Padraig Burns, 'A turbulent week in Mayo ladies football', *Western People*, 21 April 2004, p. 31.

36 Cliona Foley, 'Mayo ladies told they shall not be going to the ball', *Irish Independent*, 16 April 2004, p. 18.

37 Padraig Burns, 'A turbulent week in Mayo ladies football', *Western People*, 21 April 2004, p. 31.

38 Geraldine Giles, interviewed by Regina Fitzpatrick, 11 June 2011, for the GAA Oral History Project, https://www.gaa.ie/the-gaa/oral-history/geraldine-giles.

39 'Taoiseach launches Suzuki Ladies National Football League', *Munster Express*, 8 November 2002, p. 5.

40 Carmel Marzouk, 'Ladies call for fair play at annual congress with a vote to introduce red and yellow cards,' *Irish Examiner*, 22 May 2001, p. 12.

41 Colm O'Connor, 'Sin bin system to be introduced in ladies football,' ibid., 8 March 2004, p. 24.

42 Mary White, *Relentless: The Inside Story of the Cork Ladies Footballers* (Cork: Mercier Press, 2019), p. 309.

43 The Quinn sisters, interviewed by Arlene Crampsie, 17 February 2010, for the GAA Oral History Project, https://www.gaa.ie/the-gaa/oral-history/the-quinn-sisters.

44 Mary McAleese, 'Speech by President of Ireland Mary McAleese at the Ladies Gaelic Football Association All-Star Banquet', *LadiesGaelic.ie*, 17 November 2003, https://ladiesgaelic.ie/speech-by-president-of-ireland-mary-mcaleese-at-the-ladies-gaelic-association-all-star-banquet/.

45 'Jenny will represent Monaghan in New York', *Northern Standard*, 12 February 2004, p. 40.

46 'Beades makes All-Star cut', *Roscommon Herald*, 18 February 2004, p. 46.

47 Paddy Hickey, 'Historic trip for Ladies All-Stars', *Irish Independent*, 11 February 2004, p. 45.

48 Mary White, 'Ladies football is truly international', *Evening Echo*, 28 October 2006, p. 47.

49 Ibid.

50 Ibid.

51 Ibid.

52 Denis O'Brien, *The Rise of Gaelic Sports in Europe* (Great Britain: Amazon, 2021), p. 124.

53 Jim Cook, 'Around the world of Sport', *Irish Examiner*, 18 March 2005, p. 27.

54 Ibid.

55 'Ladies name their Rules squad', *Irish Independent*, 7 September 2006, p. 25.

56 Mary White, 'Ladies football is truly international', *Evening Echo*, 28 October 2006, p. 47.

57 In International Rules the scoring system is given as follows: goals (worth six points), an over (kicked over the crossbar and between the larger set of upright posts, worth three points), and a behind (kicked between the large and small posts on either side of the goal, worth one point).

58 Christy O'Connor, '"It was the most bizarre thing ever. We just went back to zero and still hammered them"', *Irish Examiner*, 30 October 2021, p. 14.

59 'National Forum on women in Gaelic games', *The Sligo Champion*, 2 February 2000, p. 16.

60 Ibid.

61 Vincent Hogan, 'GAA Helen of Troy launches a thousand football careers', *Irish Independent*, 29 September 2001, p. 25.

62 National Forum on women in Gaelic games', *The Sligo Champion*, 2 February 2000, p. 16.'

63 'Ladies Integration Pilot Scheme Launched', Press Release issued by the GAA, the Camogie Association and the LGFA, 25 February 2003. Private papers of Fina Golden.

64 Fr Liam Kelleher, 'President-elect, Westmeath's Geraldine Giles, welcomes increased profile', *The Corkman*, 13 March 2003, p. 4.

65 Brendan O'Brien, 'Amalgamation will benefit everyone, says Kelly,' *Irish Examiner*, 27 April 2005, p. 26.

66 'Ladies aim to double up with Dubs and Tyrone at Croke Park', *Irish Independent*, 17 August 2005, p. 1.

67 'Kelly's dressing down', *Belfast Telegraph*, 3 September 2005, p. 57.

68 Colm Keys and Helen Bruce, '"I don't view female fans as 'prize heifers' says under-fire GAA chief"', *Irish Independent,* 1 September 2005, p. 3.

69 Ibid.

70 Geraldine Giles, interviewed by Regina Fitzpatrick, 11 June 2011, for the GAA Oral History Project, https://www.gaa.ie/the-gaa/oral-history/geraldine-giles.

CHAPTER 9

1 'Pathway for Success, 2011–2016', *LadiesGaelic.ie*, accessed 20 March 2024, p. 5, https://ladiesgaelic.ie/wp-content/uploads/2011/02/LGFA-strategicPlan_small.pdf.

2 Ibid.

3 Ibid.

4 Donnchadh Boyle, 'Croke Park to host ladies finals replays', *Irish Independent*, 29 September 2011, p. 7.

5 Terry Reilly, 'New York ladies to get €10,000 helping hand for final reply', *Irish Examiner*, 7 October 2011, p. 29.

6 'The Game at a Glance', *Irish Independent*, 10 October 2011, p. 17.

7 Brendan O'Brien, 'Quill: Tyrone violence a one-off', *Irish Examiner*, 6 July 2011, p. 24.

8 Ibid.

9 Cliona Foley, 'Fitzgerald seeks merger for good of the game', ibid., 10 July 2019, p. 8.

10 'Murphy return statement of intent from Rebelettes – Quill', *Irish Independent*, 9 August 2013, p. 64.

11 Mary White, 'Cork comeback sets up Kerry tie', *Evening Echo*, 26 August 2013, p. 45.

12 Cliona Foley, 'Flynn snatches victory in Cork's 10-point revival', *Irish Independent*, 29 September 2014, p. 10.

13 Hawk-Eye is a computer system which tracks the trajectory of the ball and it is used in Gaelic games at select venues to confirm if a point has been scored. It was first introduced in 2013.

14 Stephen Lennon, 'Fahy steps down as Galway ladies football boss after appeal gets short shrift', *Connacht Tribune*, 22 September 2006, p. 4a.

15 Ibid.

16 Jackie Cahill, 'LGFA approves use of video evidence to check scores', *Irish Examiner*, 6 March 2017, p. 7.

17 John Fogarty, 'Ryan gets blessing of Ladies Board', *Irish Examiner*, 21 December 2015, p. 10.

18 'Introducing The #Ladyball!', The Ladyball Youtube Channel, 13 January 2018, https://www.youtube.com/watch?v=5bWbIZl0G5s&t=30s.

19 'Lidl behind "Ladyball" Concept to Promote Partnership with LGFA', *LadiesGaelic.ie*, 15 January 2016, https://ladiesgaelic.ie/lidl-and-lgfa-behind-ladyball-concept/.

20 'Lidl and The Ladies Gaelic Football Association Announce Landmark €1.5m Partnership', ibid., 21 January 2016, https://ladiesgaelic.ie/lidl-and-the-ladies-gaelic-football-association-announce-landmark-e1-5m-partnership/.

21 Colm O'Connor, 'LGFA promise full inquiry into Mayo withdrawal', *Irish Examiner*, 12 June 2010, p. 30.

22 Aiden Henry, 'Clubs to appeal county board decision', *Connaught Telegraph*, 15 June 2010, p. 2.

23 Aiden Henry, 'Mayo Ladies County Board decision overturned as Senior team reinstated in championship', ibid., 13 July 2010, p. 2.

24 'Mayo Ladies Football Review Committee Report: the full text', *Mayo News,* 21 December 2010, p. 3.

25 Ibid.

26 Daniel Carey, 'Ladies boss offers "blank canvas"', *Mayo News,* 18 January 2011, p. 4.

27 Jackie Cahill, 'Crisis talks fail to ease unrest of Tipp ladies', *Irish Independent*, 23 April 2014, p. 63.

28 Jackie Cahill, 'LGFA set to mediate in Tipp dispute', *Irish Examiner*, 9 May 2014, p. 29.

29 Eoghan Cormican, 'Twists and turns in the row that tore a team apart', ibid., 20 September 2018, p. 10.

30 Donnchadh Boyle, 'Mayo row has gone too far – it's time to sit down and talk', *Irish Independent*, 19 September 2018, pp. 54–55.

31 Eoghan Cormican, 'Carnacon to appeal four-week bans on players', *Irish Examiner*, 20 September 2018, p. 10.

32 Donnchadh Boyle, 'Carnacon eight await news of fate', *Irish Independent*, 10 October 2018, p. 1.

33 John Connolly, 'Where to now for Ladies game?', *Leitrim Observer*, 9 May 2018, p. 70.

34 Cliona Foley, 'We need to stand alone and speak out – WGPA', *Irish Independent*, 21 January 2015, p. 65.

35 LGFA Strategic Roadmap 2017–2022, *LadiesGaelic.ie*, April 2018, https://ladiesgaelic.ie/wp-content/uploads/2018/04/LGFA-Strategic-Roadmap_April-2018.pdf.

CHAPTER 10

1 Congress 2020 National Reports, *LadiesGaelic.ie*, March 2020, p. 46, https://ladiesgaelic.ie/wp-content/uploads/2021/09/Congress-2020-National-Reports.pdf.

2 Pat Leahy, Paul Cullen, Suzanne Lynch, and Fiach Kelly, 'Coronavirus: Schools, colleges and childcare facilitites in Ireland to shut', *The Irish Times,* 12 March 2020: https://www.irishtimes.com/news/health/coronavirus-schools-colleges-and-childcare-facilities-in-ireland-to-shut-1.4200977.

3 'Covid-19 response: Joint Media Release from the GAA, An Cumann Camógaíochta and the LGFA', *LadiesGaelic.ie*, 12 March 2020, https://ladiesgaelic.ie/joint-media-release-from-the-gaa-an-cumann-camogaiochta-and-the-lgfa/.

4 John Fogarty, 'GAA set to pull plug on league after sports ban extended until April 19', *Irish Examiner,* 25 March 2020, p. 14.

5 'Covid-19 – Ladies Gaelic Football Association Competitions and Development Update', *LadiesGaelic.ie*, 24 March 2020, https://ladiesgaelic.ie/covid-19-ladies-gaelic-football-association-competitions-and-development-update/.

6 Eoghan Cormican, 'Ladies football campaigns set to be delayed', *Irish Examiner*, 17 April 2020, p. 21.

7 'Covid19: Ladies Gaelic Football Association Statement,' *LadiesGaelic.ie*, 8 May 2020, https://ladiesgaelic.ie/covid19-ladies-gaelic-football-association-statement/.

8 John Fogarty, 'GAA considering easing access to club grounds prior to July 20', *Irish Examiner*, 16 May 2020, p. 20.

9 Stephen Barry, 'Ladies football final set for December 20', ibid., 22 July 2020, p. 16.

10 Cliona Foley, 'Dublin dig deep to hold off Armagh to stay in hunt for four in a row', ibid., 30 November 2020, p. 14.

11 Eoghan Cormican, 'Fitzgerald fumes over Parnell Park venue call', ibid., 2 December 2020, p. 17.

12 Eoghan Cormican, 'Harty Cup decision to be made in coming weeks, Munster GAA officials say', ibid., 22 January 2021, p. 2; Eoghan Cormican, 'Fitzgerald staying put as Cork ladies football boss', ibid., 27 January 2021, p. 18.

13 Eoghan Cormican, 'Ladies GAA in limbo amid Government indecision', ibid., 29 April 2021, p. 15.

14 '2021 TG4 All-Ireland Ladies Football Championships to commence in July', *LadiesGaelic.ie*, 4 May 2021, https://ladiesgaelic.ie/2021-tg4-all-ireland-ladies-football-championships-to-commence-in-july/; Michael Verney, 'LGFA "shooting themselves in foot" with underage cull', *Irish Independent*, 11 May 2021, p. 48.

15 Donnchadh Boyle, 'Duggan leads stunning Royal revival', *Irish Independent*, 16 August 2021, pp. 12–13.

16 Eamonn Sweeney, 'A true Royal fairytale with many stars and no egos', ibid., 6 September 2021, p. 2.

17 Eoghan Cormican, 'Murray has few Royal regrets but feels Hogan Stand snub was avoidable', *Irish Examiner*, 31 August 2022, p. 10.

18 Cora Staunton, 'Champions' lethal formula has raised bar for everyone', *Irish Independent*, 1 August 2022, p. 7.

19 Eoghan Cormican, 'Government allocates €15m fund to run championships', *Irish Examiner,* 26 September 2020, p. 11.

20 Eoghan Cormican, 'LGFA records €2m surplus despite gate receipts collapsing by 94%', ibid., 3 March 2021, p. 18.

21 Cliona Foley, 'Ladies' footballers get travel expenses for first time to tackle mounting costs', *Irish Independent*, 29 October 2020, p. 48.

22 Eoghan Cormican, 'Oireachtais committee blasts "scandalous" gender funding gap', *Irish Examiner,* 28 April 2021, p. 14.

23 'Increased Funding for Female Inter-County Players', Gaelic Players Association, accessed 28 March 2024, https://www.gaelicplayers.com/increased-funding-for-female-inter-county-players/.

24 Colm Keys, 'GPA and WGPA vote to combine associations', *Irish Independent*, 15 December 2020, p. 41.

25 Colm Keys, 'GAA takes another big step towards full integration', *Sunday Independent*, 27 February 2022, p. 10.

26 Eoghan Cormican, 'Retaining their rulebook amongst LGFA's must-have in integration', *Irish Examiner*, 9 March 2022, p. 6.

27 LGFA Congress National Report 2022, *LadiesGaelic.ie*, https://ladiesgaelic.ie/the-lgfa/about-us/national-congress/.

28 Katie Liston, 'Ambition really is the name of the integration game', *Sunday Independent*, 11 June 2023, pp. 10–11.

29 Katie Liston, 'Legacy of inertia should no longer cloud progress', ibid., 13 August 2023, p. 10.

30 Sinéad Kissane, 'Pressure on LGFA and Camogie Association to finally level playing field for women', *Irish Independent*, 20 June 2023, pp. 46–47; 'State of Play: Equality Snapshot for Female Intercounty Gaelic Games,' *GaelicPlayers.com*, 19 April 2023, https://www.gaelicplayers.com/document/state-of-play-equality-report/.

31 'LGFA Statement – 19/6/23', *LadiesGaelic.ie*, 19 June 2023, https://ladiesgaelic.ie/lgfa-statement-19-6-23/.

32 Gordon Manning, 'Female intercounty players suspend equality protest after framework for player charter agreed', *The Irish Times*, 19 July 2023, online: https://www.irishtimes.com/sport/gaelic-games/2023/07/19/female-intercounty-players-suspend-equality-protest-after-framework-for-player-charter-agreed/.

CHAPTER 11

1 Letter from Olive Dufficy, 2008. Private papers of Marie McAleer.

2 Mícheál Naughton, 'Best is yet to come as games continue to grow and thrive', *Sunday Independent,* 31 July 2022, p. 4.

3 Ibid.

ACKNOWLEDGEMENTS

Since the age of 11, when I first lined out for St Mary's Under–12 girls' Gaelic football team (the first time the club fielded a team at this grade for girls), this sport has been a huge part of my life. It has been an outlet for me – to play sport, to have lots of fun, and to make lasting friendships. Such has its influence been on my life that it has driven my interest in this research. For all these reasons I want to thank the LGFA. Thank you to everyone who has played some role in the LGFA – from the pioneers of the 1970s to the community of players, coaches, administrators and volunteers who lead the LGFA today from club level all the way up to national level. The influence the LGFA has had on the lives of girls and women extends far beyond the football field and your work is not unnoticed. Thank you to the LGFA for supporting my research, in particular Helen O'Rourke, Lyn Savage, Jackie Cahill and the whole staff and management committee.

To everyone who has contributed material and information to this book, I am so grateful for your input. There are too many people to mention everyone by name – and inevitably I will forget someone – so to everyone who I spoke to, whether by phone or email or in person over the last two years, thank you for your help. I hope we will speak again as I continue working on my PhD research.

The Irish Newspaper Archive has been of great importance to me in carrying out this research. A word of appreciation to those who gave coverage to ladies Gaelic football in its early years and to those who continue to push the game's profile.

Thank you to Paul Rouse, Patrick O'Donoghue, Phyllis Price, Adam Staunton, Fina Golden, Sportsfile, and the various PhD students, historians, and academics who have given me feedback, help and guidance at different stages in the researching and writing of this book. Huge thank you to Aoife K. Walsh, Noel O'Regan, Niall McCormack, and all the team at New Island Books for your work on this book – your energy for and interest in this book has been heartening and has made this whole experience so enjoyable.

Thank you to my family and friends for all your support and encouragement. To my parents, Eileen and T. J., my brother Dylan, and sister Evanne, thank you for reading drafts, sending links, keeping newspaper cuttings and being a sounding-board whenever I needed one. To my friends: thank you for your enthusiasm for and interest in my work, and all the laughs and chats. It has meant so much to me while I've been doing this research.

I have been so lucky to share a football pitch with incredible teammates while representing St Mary's (Sligo), Ursuline College, Sligo underage teams, UCD Cs, Connacht Ladies (Boston) and

Portobello (Dublin). The enjoyment I have gotten out of playing Gaelic football has been because of your camaraderie and commitment. Thank you to all the coaches and volunteers who have steered us along the way, too. Special mention to my 'football friends' – Shauna, Honor, Aisling, M. J., Darielle, and Anna.

Finally, my research into the history of the LGFA started six years ago when I was a master's student at UCD. It would not have been possible for me to put together that master's thesis (and it's likely that I would not have been able to write this book or take on a PhD) if it had not been for Marie McAleer. Marie generously gave up some time to meet me and share with me the various scrapbooks and notebooks she had diligently kept from the beginning of her involvement in the LGFA. This kickstarted my research. I was in awe of Marie's passion for and dedication to ladies Gaelic football over forty-plus years and I would like to dedicate this book to her memory.

INDEX

All County Boards are LGFA unless otherwise specified

20x20 campaign 174–5

A

Adamstown-Cloughbawn, Co. Wexford 104–5
advertising 174
Ahern, Bertie 139, 140, 142
AIB 142
Aisling McGing Cup 153, 211
All-Ireland Championship 32–3, 34–5, 48, 54, 68–9, 86, 151
All-Ireland Club Championship (Dolores Tyrrell Cup) 47, 65, 93, 122, 141, 151, 153, 177
All-Ireland Under-14 Championship 184, 212
All-Ireland Under-16 Championship 47, 49, 58, 64, 70, 93, 211–12
All-Ireland Under-18 Championship 48, 93–4, 211
All-Ireland finals 27–8, 68, 97, 139–40, 207–8
    1974: 37–43
    1975: 56
    1976: 56, 61
    1977: 63–4, 70
    1978: 56, 65
    1979: 56, 68, 72
    1980: 56
    1982–90: 95–6
    1984: 112
    1987: 109
    1991: 118
    1993: 118, 127
    1996, 1998: 121–2
    1997, 1998: 123
    2000s: 145, 147
    2001: 148
    2003: 144–5
    2005–9: 165
    2010: 165–6
    2012: 168
    2013: 168–9
    2014, 2015: 169
    2016: 171
    2017, 2018: 171, 179
    2019: 179
    2020: 187–8
    2021: 190
    2022: 191–2
All-Star Awards 69, 95–6, 114, 119–21, 128–9, 147–8, 153, 156, 159, 168–9, 218–26
All-Star Tour 153–6
Annalees, New York 51
Antrim, Co. 117, 152, 185, 189, 191
Ardfinnan, Tipperary 43
Armagh, Co. 48–9, 167, 169–70, 186
Armagh County Board 71, 117
Armagh Harps 195
Athlone 102
Athy festival 16
Auckland 131–2
Australia 131–3, 157
Australian Football League (AFL) 157–8
Australasian Championships 131–2
Azzurri 148–9

B

Ballycumber, Co. Offaly 19
Ballyduff, Co. Waterford 22
Ballymacarbry, Co. Waterford 119–20, 153
Bandon, Co. Cork 18
Bank of Ireland 124, 139, 158
Banteer, Co. Cork 26, 34, 56
Barlow's Ltd, Clonmel 40
Barrett, John E. 110–11
Barry, Marina 95
Beijing 157
Bonner, S.C. 6
Bowler (née Doherty), Marion 95
Breffni Park, Co. Cavan 65, 157, 186
Brendan Martin Cup 37, 40, 43, 68, 95, 97, 119–20, 147–8, 150–1, 168, 188, 190–1 *see also* All-Ireland finals
Brosnan, Bridie 26
Brussels, 157
Bryant, Lucy 50
Buckley, Rena 152
Buggy, Paddy 90
Bunreacht na hÉireann 2
Bunyan, Johnny 119
Burns, Jarlath 157
Byrne, Gay 109

C

Cagney, Fr 51

Callaghan, Bernie 70

camogie 7–10

Camogie Association x, 7, 10, 18–21, 75–6, 82, 85–8, 158, 179, 183, 194–5, 200 *see also* LGFA (relations with the Camogie Association)

Carlow, Co. 97

Carlow RTC 102

Carnacon, Co. Mayo 152, 176–8

Carney, Jim 125

carnivals, matches at 4, 12, 15–19, 22, 29, 32–4, 56, 71, 80, 85, 204

Carrigaline, Co. Cork 22

Carysfort College 102

Casey, Angela 147

Castlebar Mitchels, Co. Mayo 48, 176

Cavan, Co. 48–9, 56, 62–5, 70, 97

Cavan County Board 70, 88, 117

Cavan Ladies New York 129

Celtic Tiger 133

Central Coast, Sydney 131–2

CIÉ 70

Clann na Gael, New South Wales 132

Clare, Co. 97, 99, 167, 185

Clarke, Peter 176

Cleary, Aoibhín 191

Clonakilty, Co. Cork 18

Clondalkin, Co. Dublin 15

club finals 65, 90, 178, 213–15

coaching 101, 138

Codd, Jackie 108

Coen, Dan 41

Cogley, Fred 68

'Cois Laoi' 64

Coiste Camogie Vigilance Committee 18

Colgan, Lynda 54–5, 84

colleges *see* third-level competitions

Commission on the Status of Women (1972) 10

Community Games 65, 70

Connacht 59, 65, 97, 102, 146, 156, 176–7

Connacht Council (GAA) 76–7, 148

Connaughton, Terry 129

Constitution of Ireland (1937) 2

Conway, Connie 99–101

Coogan, Aoife 161

Cooney, Anne 28

Cooraclare, Co. Clare 5

Corbett, Jimmy 176

Cork, Co. 23, 26, 34, 49, 59, 80–1, 151, 165–74, 186–90

Cork County Board 49, 70

Corkery, Briege 152

Corofin Carnival, Galway 33–4

Costello, Pat 175

countdown clock 122–3, 125

Covid-19 183–5, 188–9, 192–3

Croke Park 35–6, 75, 106, 113–14, 118, 143–5, 159, 171–4, 181, 186–8, 192

Crossmaglen, Co. Armagh 71

Culloville, Co. Armagh 71

Cumann Peil Gael na mBan *see* LGFA

Curran (née Kennedy), Kathleen 95

Curran, Mary Jo 96, 148

Curran, Phil 108

Currid, Caroline 155

D

D'Arcy, Ruth 85

Dardis (née Lawlor), Eileen 119

Department of Sport 194

Derry, Co. 26, 117

Digital 70

Dingle Peninsula, Co. Kerry 27

'Divot' (Bill O'Donnell) 58–9

Doherty (Bowler), Marion 95

Dolores Tyrrell Cup 122, 152–3 *see also* All-Ireland Club Championship

Donegal, Co. 117, 166

Donegal County Board (GAA) 69

Donoughmore, Co. Cork 151–2

Donovan, John 40, 44

Dowd, Tom 55, 88, 108–9

Down, Co. 117, 167

Dubai 157

Dublin, Co. 97, 145, 166, 168–9, 171–3, 186–92

Dublin County Board 169

Dublin County Board (GAA) 3–4

Dufficy, Olive 203

Duffy, Paraic 162

Duggan, Emma 190

Duggan, Margaret 50

Duggan, Sally 76

Dulane, Co. Meath 22
Dunne, Kieran 108
Dunne, Lucy 187
Durrow, Co. Laois 37

E

Egan, Attracta 50
emigration 101, 130
Ennis, Shauna 191
Erin's Rovers, Chicago 129

F

Fahy, P.J. 170
Fairview Park, Dublin 27
Farrell, A. 50
Farrell, Sean 'Whooper' 63
Farrelly, Alice 60
Feighery, Joe 32
Féile na nÓg 184
Fermanagh, Co. 117, 185
festivals, matches at 12, 15–16, 18, 22, 26
Fitzgerald, Mick 61, 76, 90, 94–5, 106–7
Fitzgerald Stadium, Killarney 34, 90
Fitzpatrick, Ultan 55
Flanagan, Margaret 32
Foley, Cliona 125, 186
Fox, Garrett 60
Foy, Maura 50
Fr Griffins, Galway 75
France 157

G

GAA (Gaelic Athletic Association) 1–2, 12, 73, 75, 158, 179, 183, 194–5 see also LGFA (relations with the GAA)
    Annual Congress (1980) 88
    Annual Convention (1977) 88
    Ard Comhairle 181
    Australia 131
    Coiste Bainistíochta 181
    foundation ix, 2
    US 129
    women's participation in 1–2
Gaelic Football and Hurling Association of Australasia 131
Gaelic games bodies, proposed integration 195–7
Gaelic Park, New York 130, 153
Gaelic4Girls 146, 157, 179, 205

Gaelic4Mothers&Others 146, 195, 205
Gaelic4Teens 146
Gaeltarra Éireann 70
Gallagher, Mary 149
Galway, Co. 33–4, 56, 59, 68, 150, 170–1, 186–7
Galway hospital 70
Galway County Board 54
Galway RTC 102
Garry, Fr Michael 5
Garry, Tom 5
Geaney, Mary 26, 56
Gibbons, Pauline 63–7
Giles, Geraldine 137–9, 146–7, 150, 160–2
Gillespie, Fr Gerry 48, 77–82
Goodwin, Ruth 154
Gorey, Lilian 41, 44, 69
Gorman, Agnes 43
Gorman, Liz 76
Gormley, Eilish 130
GPA (Gaelic Players Association) 179, 194–7, 200
Grennan, Geraldine 84
Grennan, Jennifer 121

H

Haberlin, Áine 175
Hackett, Phyllis 36, 38–9, 50–1, 62–3, 72
Hargreaves, Jennifer 12
HawkEye 169
Hayes Hotel, Thurles ix, 31–2, 40
Heffernan, Christina 121
Hogan, Vincent 158
Holland, Marie see McAleer, Marie
Hong Kong 157
Howard, Liz 158
Hutchins, Meg 159
Hyde Park, Roscommon 63, 90, 113
Hynes, Catherine 50
Hynes, Marian 50

I

Inch Rovers, Co. Cork 152
Industrial Revolution 2
Integration Task Force 160
inter-county competitions 23, 25, 28–9, 47, 55, 70, 117, 119, 138, 147, 150, 152, 162, 184
    championship 31, 93, 189
    league 47–8, 93, 189

inter-county players 156, 159–60, 178–9, 194, 196–7

inter-firms competition 70

intermediate competitions 117, 151–3, 166, 176, 184–6, 189–92, 208

International Rules 157–8

inter-provincial competitions 47, 55, 93, 153, 184, 213

Irish Cancer Society 84

Irish Countrywomen's Association (ICA) 18

Irish Rugby Football Union (IRFU) 2

Irish Sports Council 146

J

junior competitions 49, 97–8, 100–1, 114, 117–20, 124, 127–8, 130, 141, 151–2, 166–7, 185, 187, 189, 191, 208, 217

K

Keane, Josie 41

Kearney, Anne 76

Kearney, Frank 76

Keenan, Donal 82–5

Kells, Co. Meath 22

Kelly, Erin 179

Kelly, Josie 34

Kelly, Sean 160–1

Kennedy, Jim 23, 32, 35–6, 40

Kennedy (Curran), Kathleen 95

Kenny, Tom 36, 49, 55, 76, 87

Kerr (née Maher), Ann 129

Kerry, Co. 23, 26–8, 31, 34, 36, 56–7, 61, 63, 94–8, 108–11, 113–14, 118, 166, 168, 171, 176, 191

Kerry Association, Dublin 27

Kerry County Board (GAA) 90

Kildare, Co. 48

Kildare County Board 117

Kilkenny, Co. 49, 58, 133, 152, 167

Kilkerrin-Clonberne, Co. Kerry 177

Kilrossanty, Co. Waterford 22

Kilsheelan Sportsfield Fund 16

Kilsheelan Super Fete (1949) 16

Kissane, Sinéad 96

Knockmore, Co. Mayo 176

L

'Ladyball' 171–4

Lally, Orlagh 191

Lancashire 101, 128

Lancashire County Board 128

Lane, Aoife 178–9

Lane, Mary 108

Laois, Co. 34, 36, 44, 48–9, 97, 118, 120–1, 147, 166, 168, 191

Late Late Show 109

Lawlor (Dardis), Eileen 95, 119

Lawlor, Margaret 95, 107, 112, 114, 119

Leahy, Brianne 159

Leahy, John 177

Leahy, Peter 177

Leddy, Kathleen 51

Leen, Bridget 95

Leinster 68, 97, 102, 146

Leitrim, Co. 48, 98, 101, 129, 153, 178

Leitrim, Co. Clare 5

Leitrim County Board (GAA) 88

Leitrim County Board 98, 178

Leixlip 15

Leyden, Terry 65

LGFA (Ladies Gaelic Football Association)

    Annual Congress: (1977) 55, 63; (1980) 68; (1983) 103–6; (1984) 106; (2001) 142; (2020) 183; (2022) 195–6

    Annual Convention (1976) 60, 64, 82

    Central Council 170, 176

    charter 54, 79–81

    County Boards 227

    foundation ix, 31–2, 204

    funding: 71–2, 106, 109, 139, 142–3, 162, 179–80; government 193–4

    integration steering committee 195, 200

    international reach 50–2, 101, 128–9, 131–3, 153, 157, 205

    membership 69, 73, 106, 117, 126, 132–3, 138, 146, 165, 179, 205

    National Appeal Committee 177

    objectives 86, 107

    official guide of 108

    presidents 226

    recognition 73, 75, 82, 85–90

    relations with the Camogie Association 82, 85–7, 109, 143, 162, 179, 192, 195

    relations with the GAA 75, 82, 85–90, 109–12, 158–62, 179, 192, 195

    response to Covid-19 183–5, 188–9, 192–3

    review 146

    sponsorship 40, 107, 124, 133, 138–42, 165, 174, 204

    staff 125–7, 133, 145–6

    structure 107

Lidl 174, 179, 204

Limerick, Co. 97, 185

Limerick County Board, 117

Linehan, Tim 56

Liston, Katie 196

Littleton, Co. Tipperary 56

Loftus, Mick 48

Loftus, P.J. 150

Lombard, Mai 56

London 50, 97, 120, 127–8, 133

London County Board 101

Long, Denis 26

Longford, Co. 97, 99

Louth, Co. 48–9, 166, 191

Louth County Board 117

Lucan Pipe Band 15

Luxembourg 157

Lyons, Tommy 77

M

McAleer (née Holland), Marie 15, 32, 76, 82

McAleese, Mary 156, 195

McAnespie, Brenda 123

McBride's, Chicago 129

McDermott, Karen 175

McGee, Jimmy 60

McGing, Aisling 153

McGonigle, Gregory 169

McGuirk, Monica 191

McHugh, Nono 34

McLoughlin, Maureen 72

McQuaid, Archbishop John Charles 7

Mackin, Aimee 198

Macra na Feirme 18

Magnier, Dr 6

Maher (Kerr), Ann 129

Maloney, Karen 155

Mannion, Niamh 155

Martin, Brendan 28, 32, 36–7, 76

Mary Immaculate College 102

Mary Leonie, Sister 67

Mary Quinn Memorial Cup 153, 189

Maye, Fiona 154

Mayo, Co. 23, 48, 58–9, 120, 134–5, 145, 147, 156, 169, 171
    jerseys row 148–50
    player/manager conflict 175–7

Mayo County Board (GAA) 19, 77

Mayo County Board 48, 54, 149–50, 175–7

Meath, Co. 17, 21, 48–9, 185–6, 189–92

Meath County Board 117

Meath GAA County Board 49

media 31, 58–61, 63–8, 106, 108 see also RTÉ;
    television; TG4

medical myths 3–5, 55, 84–5, 88

Michael Cusack's, New South Wales 131–2

Mick Talbot Cup 153, 213

Midlands County League 17, 22

Mimna (née O'Brien), Patricia 128

Molloy, Willie 51

Monaghan, Co. 117, 120–2, 124, 127, 167–8

Monaghan County Board 120

Moore, P.C. 6–7

Moylett, Josephine 49

Mulcahy, Valerie 152, 168

Mullahoran, Co. Cavan 65

Mulvihill, Liam 162

Munster 56, 71, 90, 94, 97, 102–3, 118, 146, 151, 167–8

Munster Council 102–3

Murphy, Ciara 199

Murphy, Con 84–5

Murphy, Juliet 152, 168–9

Murphy, Fr Michael 176

Murray, Carmel 19

Murray, Eamonn 190, 192

N

National Athletics and Cycling Association of Ireland
    (NACAI) 6–7

National Forum on Women in Gaelic Games (2000)
    158–9

National League 68, 93–4, 98, 117–20, 124, 140, 142, 147,
    150–1, 165, 169, 184, 189, 191–2, 209–10

National Track and Field Championship 6

Naughton, Liam 65–8

Naughton, Michael 54–5, 63, 67, 71–2, 84

Naughton, Mícheál 204–5

Netherlands 157

Nevin, Mary 32

New South Wales 131–2

New York 51, 127, 129–31, 133, 153, 156, 166–7

New York County Board 156–7, 167

New Zealand 131, 133

newspapers see media

Ní Bhuacalla, Rhona 169
North America 128–9
North American Championships 129
North Asia Games 194
Northern Ireland 71
Northern Telecom 70

O

O'Beirne, Valerie 155
O'Brien (Mimna), Patricia 128
Ó Chaoimh, Padraig 21
O'Connell, Joanne 154
O'Connor, Mary 151
O'Connor Cup 103, 180, 215–16
O'Connor Park, Tullamore 28
O'Donnell, Bill ('Divot') 58–9
Ó Dunagáin, Seán 26
Offaly, Co. 17, 25–8, 31, 33–7, 41–3, 47, 50–1, 56–7, 61–4, 68, 121
Offaly Association, Dublin 27–8
Offaly Association, London 50–2
Offaly GAA County Board 28
O'Flynn, Geraldine 152, 169
Ó Gallachóir, Pól 140–1
O'Gorman, Niall 140, 142
O'Keefe, Padraig 6
O'Keefe, Saoirse 179
Olympic Games 7
One Club Model 179–80
O'Neill, Liam 196
O'Neill, Pat 49
O'Neill's 126, 148
Ontario 128–9
O'Reilly, Rosie 129–31
O'Rourke, Helen 125–6, 138–9, 143–6, 149–50, 158–9, 161, 175, 183, 196
O'Ryan, Geraldine 121, 123
O'Ryan, Martina 121, 123
O'Shea, Lorraine 175
O'Shea, Marian 88
Ó Síocháin, Seán 35–40, 82, 85
O'Sullivan, Ciara 169
O'Sullivan, Siobhan 154

P

Páirc Uí Chaoimh, Cork 113
Parnell Park, Dublin 157, 186
Pat the Baker 141
Pendergast, Alice 62
Phoenix Park, Dublin 27
Pike-Killrossanty 18
Pius XI, Pope 6
Players' Charter 200
Portobello, Dublin 129–30
Post Office 70
post-primary competitions 126–7, 141, 184, 216–17
Power O'Shea, Mary 41, 44
Power Charity Home 16
Prendergast, Ray 48
Prenty, John 149–50
protective equipment 82–4
Purcell, Sean 75–6

Q

Quigley, Pat 68
Quill, Pat 108, 167, 175
Quinn, Mary 98, 153
Quinnsworth 70

R

radio *see* media, RTÉ
Ramsbottom, Sue 121
referees 121–2
regional training centres 102
Rice, Peter 108, 123–4
Ríomhaire Teo 70
Roman Catholic Church 6–7
Roscommon, Co. 34, 56, 62–4, 72, 97, 129, 185, 203
Roscommon County Board 63, 69, 71, 97
Rowe, Carla 169, 191
Rowley, Tom 60
RTÉ 60, 65–8, 106, 108–9, 123–5
rules of play 21–3, 32–3, 54–5, 79–81, 83, 150, 170
    bodily contact 55
Ryan, Biddy 76
Ryan, Eamonn 152, 169–71
Ryan (Ryan-Savage), Kitty 37, 43, 68
Ryan, Michael 125

S

St Coman's, Co. Roscommon 65
St James's Park, Dublin 3
St Mary's College, Marino 102
San Francisco Ladies 129
Scally, Eimear 169
Scotland 166
Scott, Seamus 65–8
secondary schools *see* post-primary competitions
Seoul Gaels 193
Sexton, Rosemary 50
Shamrocks 22
Shanahan, Dermot 84
Sheridan, Aishling 175
Singapore 157
Singapore Gaelic Lions 193
Slattery, Anne 76
Slattery, Willie 119
Sligo, Co. 117, 152, 154–5, 167
Smyth, Eimear 185, 187
Spain 157
Stack, Bríd 152
State of Play report 196–7
Staunton, Cora 141, 147–8, 178, 192
Suzuki 140, 142
Sweeney, Eamonn 190
Swift, Paul 143
Sydney 132

T

Taiwan Celts 194
Talbot, Mick 36, 153
Taniane, Jason 176
television 123–5, 137, 192 *see also* media; RTÉ; TG4
TG4 139–43, 157, 162, 204
third-level competitions 102–3
Thomond College 180
Thompson, Walter 138, 142
Tierney, Sarah 177
Timahoe, Co. Laois 112–13
Tipperary, Co. 17, 23, 26, 34, 36–7, 40–4, 47–8, 55–6, 58–9, 64, 68, 167, 177
Tipperary County Board (GAA) 88, 186
Tipperary County Board 40, 84, 117
Tralee, Co. Kerry 27
Troubles, the 71
Tyrone, Co. 117, 130, 166

U

UCD GAA Club 26
Uí Phuirséil, Úna 85
Ulster 71, 97, 133
underage competitions 69–70, 93, 151, 211–12
University College Galway (UCG) 70
University of Limerick 180
University of Ulster Jordanstown 103
USA 156

V

Varadkar, Leo 183
VHI 141
video technology 170

W

Wall, Áine 120
Wall, Vikki 190
Walsh, Angela 152
Waterford, Co. 17, 23, 26, 28, 34, 59, 118–22, 147
West Cork Festival (1965) 18
West Cork Ladies Football Board 64
West County Hotel Cup 166
Westmeath, Co. 17, 48–9, 109, 185–6
Wexford, Co. 23, 48, 97, 108, 189
Wheatley, Mary 108
White, Dell 95
White, Mary 152, 168
Wicklow, Co. 97, 167, 185, 189, 191
WGPA (Women's Gaelic Players Association) 178–9, 193
    merges with GPA 194–5
women's sport
    criticisms of 6–7, 59–60, 64, 73, 88–9, 101, 109
    growth of 12, 18
    restrictions on 1–10
women's tournaments 17
    Offaly (1967) 16–17
Woods, Siobhan 169
Wren, Charlie 50–1

Y

Young Ireland's, New South Wales 131–2

Photo by Fnatic Headshots

HAYLEY KILGALLON is a PhD student at the School of History in University College Dublin. She holds a BA in History and Spanish and a MA in Public History at UCD and has won a number of awards and scholarships for her research. Her research area is the history of women's sport in Ireland with a particular focus on ladies' Gaelic football and she has contributed on this subject for RTÉ, TG4, BBC Gaeilge and numerous journals. Hayley is currently a tutor at the School of History in UCD and has been a Programme Manager at Social Entrepreneurs Ireland. She has also been a judge for the Young Social Innovators Ireland Awards. Hayley has played Gaelic football at club level in Sligo, Boston and Dublin.